Playful Learning and Teaching

Playful Learning and Teaching

Integrating Play into Preschool and Primary Programs

Judith E. Kieff
University of New Orleans

Renée M. Casbergue
University of New Orleans

Allyn and Bacon

Boston ■ London ■ Toronto ■ Sydney ■ Tokyo ■ Singapore

Series Editor: *Norris Harrell*
Editorial Assistant: *Bridget Keane*
Marketing Manager: *Brad Parkins*
Director of Education Programs: *Ellen Mann Dolberg*
Production Editor: *Christopher H. Rawlings*
Editorial-Production Service: *Omegatype Typography, Inc*
Composition and Prepress Buyer: *Linda Cox*
Manufacturing Buyer: *Suzanne Lareau*
Cover Administrator: *Jennifer Hart*
Electronic Composition: *Omegatype Typography, Inc.*

Many of the designations used by manufacturers and sellers to distinguish their products are
claimed as trademarks. Where those designations appear in this book, and Allyn and Bacon was
aware of a trademark claim, the designations have been printed in initial or all caps.

Library of Congress Cataloging-in Publication Data

Kieff, Judith E.
   Playful learning and teaching : integrating play into preschool
and primary programs / Judith E. Kieff, Renée M. Casbergue.
      p.   cm.
   Includes bibliographical references (p.   ) and index.
   ISBN 0-205-28547-3 (alk. paper)
      1. Play.   2. Early childhood education—Curricula.   3. Learning.
   I. Casbergue, Renee Michelet.   II. Title.
LB1139.35.P55K45   2000
372.19–dc21
                                                                98-53533
                                                                CIP

Printed in the United States of America

10 9 8 7 6 5 4 3 2 1   04 03 02 01 00 99

In loving memory of Hollis E. Kieff
For Clayton, Daniel, and Emily

CONTENTS

PREFACE

Placing play at the center of the curriculum for young children has historically been a major focus of early childhood education. No research exists that diminishes the importance of play to the learning and development of young children. However, current information regarding the development of the brain, multiple intelligence, learning styles, and the role of culture in play and learning creates a need to develop strategies that recognize and celebrate children's unique playing and learning styles. *Playful Learning and Teaching: Integrating Play into Preschool and Primary Programs* describes the relationship between play and learning in children from birth through age eight and outlines strategies for embedding opportunities for play into curricula and for creating a classroom culture that promotes playful learning.

This book is based on the philosophy that children construct knowledge while actively engaged in the process of understanding their world. One important context for this engagement is play. We define play as open-ended, self-chosen, enjoyable actions and activities that unite and integrate cognitive, language, social, emotional, and motor aspects of learning within rich, culturally sensitive, child-centered, and supportive contexts. Playful learning refers to the process of learning through play and the spirit that encompasses this process. Playful teaching refers to strategies that create the environment and support the process of learning through play and the spirit that encompasses these actions. We use the terms *playful learning* and *playful teaching* to draw attention to the reciprocal nature of play and learning in the lives of children and the adults who teach and care for them.

We develop the concept that teachers have three major roles regarding play. The first role is to plan for and create multiple opportunities for children to learn through play. The second role involves interacting with children as they play, scaffolding learning and promoting cognitive and social competence, creative expression, and the development of dispositions that promote healthy lifestyles. The third role is to develop a system for ongoing assessment that uses the rich context created through playful learning.

Embedded within each role are actions of advocacy. Teachers will need to advocate for children and children's right to learn through play. They must work diligently with families and administrators to explain and display the powerful relationship between children's play and their learning and development. One feature that distinguishes this book from others is its focus on advocacy as an essential role of early childhood educators. Each chapter contains activities that develop advocacy skills and help teachers demonstrate to parents and administrators the importance of play in the lives of children.

In this text, we present multiple perspectives on the role of play in learning and development. Included among these are multicultural considerations for playful learning. We also offer specific strategies for including children with special needs in the play experiences of any classroom. The perspectives of professional organizations that steer curricula development, including the National Association for the Education of Young Children, the International Reading Association, National Council of Teachers of Mathematics, and the National Research Council, are also discussed.

We ask readers to begin their study of each chapter by spending about ten minutes responding to a writing prompt designed to help them recall how a particular aspect of play affected their lives. This writing and reflecting process provides an entry point into the material covered in the chapter. At the conclusion of each chapter, readers review their initial writing and reflect on how their understanding of the value of play and of the pragmatic aspects of creating a culture of playfulness has changed.

This journaling process represents a constructivist perspective on teaching and learning. This perspective is also demonstrated by the text's spiraling structure. Early chapters introduce major concepts that are revisited and then expanded in later chapters. In this way, each chapter creates a scaffold for the chapters that follow. This constructive learning theme extends to the Instructor's Manual, which provides the instructor with summaries of each chapter and also ideas for activities that will create a playful learning environment that gives adults the opportunity to reconstruct their understanding of the role of play in learning and development.

Each chapter is framed by Stories from the Field. These stories reflect the issues concerning the use of play as a teaching strategy as expressed by early childhood educators in the United States. We use these stories as a springboard to further the discussion of the real issues teachers face and as examples of creative solutions teachers develop to deal with their unique situations. Some voices are actual accounts expressed by individual educators; others represent a composite of ideas and experiences drawn from interactions with teachers we have worked with over the years.

The text is organized into three sections. Part One, Connecting Theories of Play, Learning, and Development, reviews current perspectives on the powerful connection between children's learning and their play. Chapters 1 and 2 provide the philosophical and theoretical basis for considering play as a vital element of the classroom environment. Part Two, Connecting Play Theory and Practice in Preschool Programs and Primary Classrooms, delineates strategic approaches useful to embedding play into curricula, routines, and transitions common to preschool programs and primary classrooms. Chapter 3 describes strategies for developing an integrated, thematic curriculum embedded with opportunities for children to pursue projects. Chapter 4 describes the process of developing and maintaining a learning center system that promotes optimal learning opportunities for all children. Chapter 5 describes the role of pretense in learning and development, as well as strategies for using pretense and dramatic play. Chapter 6 deals with ongoing assessment and describes strategies teachers can use to document learning within the context of play.

Part Three, Connecting Play and Content in Preschool Programs and Primary Classrooms, offers suggestions for fostering learning through playful engagement with concepts and ideas. Chapter 7 discusses the relationship between play and the development of dispositions for healthy living. Chapter 8 relates to the development of creative expression. Chapter 9 explains the relationship between play and literacy development, and Chapter 10 reviews the relationship between play and cognitive competence.

Acknowledgments

The authors would first like to thank the many teachers we have worked with over the years who have shared their experiences and concerns regarding the use of play as a teaching strategy. Their dilemmas and creative solutions form the foundation for this text.

We very much appreciate and are grateful for the support and guidance provided by JoAnn Brewer, Salem State College, and Karyn Wellhousen, University of New Orleans.

They read the early drafts of this text and discussed with us the possibilities and responsibilities inherent in undertaking a project such as this. Our gratitude also extends to Pat Austin, University of New Orleans, for guidance and editorial assistance with the Instructor's Manual.

The reviewers of this text—Kathleen Dailey, Edinboro University of Pennsylvania; Deborah Diffily, Texas Wesleyan University; Sue Grossman, Eastern Michigan University; Chung-Soon Kim, San Jose State University; and Mary Patton, Texas Christian University—supplied cogent comments and advice that guided the final formulation and organization of this text. We are grateful for their time, insight, professionalism, and commitment to the process of review. We also thank our editor, Frances Helland, who initiated this project and supported our efforts throughout the process.

Playful Learning and Teaching

Connecting Theories of Play, Learning, and Development

CHAPTER

1 Defining Play from Many Perspectives

Prereading Guide

First Impressions.   Describe in your journal how you played when you were a child by considering these questions. What are your earliest memories of play? Approximately how old were you? As a young child, what materials did you enjoy playing with most? Who, if anyone, did you enjoy playing with most? What do you think you gained from your play?

Stories from the Field

Participants attending "Get-Acquainted Night" at a public elementary school in a southwestern community were asked to define play and describe their beliefs concerning the role of play in an early childhood classroom. The group in attendance represented a diverse population in terms of race, ethnicity, age, and educational background. Participants included students' families, the principal, and teachers of preschool, kindergarten, and first through third grades. Here is a sample of their responses (Kieff, 1994).

What is play?

"Play is a child's work."

"Play is the way children express themselves."

"Play is fun."

"Play is the way children learn about their world."

"Play is the way children learn motor skills."

"Play is the most important thing children do."

"It's running off all that energy."

"Play is how children learn to get along."

" After school, and on weekends, that's when children can play."

"Play is painting and building with blocks."

"Messing around and having fun with other children, that's play."

Describe the role play should have in early childhood classrooms.

"Play supports academic learning by giving children a chance to practice what they have learned."

"In school, children should be engaged in serious learning tasks that prepare them to achieve. Play is a socialization activity that is best left to recess or physical education periods."

"Play should be confined to recess and lunchtime breaks."

"Play is the basis for the curriculum in the classroom."

"I know children need to play, but I don't understand why they play at school. It seems like they are just wasting time."

"Play should be a reward for work well done."

Multiple Perspectives Regarding Play

How many ways are there to define play and describe its importance to the learning and development of young children? As illustrated in this small sample, the range of definitions for play is extensive, and the values assigned to the role of play in educational settings represent a broad spectrum of opinions. Because there is no single or comprehensive definition of play, there is often confusion concerning the use of play in educational settings. Is play the way young children learn? Or is it a way to release energy so that learning can occur? Should it be the basis for curriculum in early childhood programs? Or should it be confined to recess or excluded completely? Indeed, do we need to define divergent positions regarding the use of play in programs for young children, or can we work toward a compromise that supports all those concerned about children and childhood development? These are important questions to consider as we begin to develop our understanding of the role of play in the lives of children and develop strategies for its use in early childhood programs.

Why is it so difficult to find agreement about play among adults, even among a small group of adults such as those described earlier, who confirm a shared interest in the well-being of children by attending a Get-Acquainted Night? The answer, like play itself, is both complex and dynamic. The meaning and value of play are embedded in one's knowledge about play, past experiences with play, and cultural values regarding play. This meaning changes and evolves as one encounters play in new circumstances and contexts. Therefore, to better understand what play is, how it affects learning and development, and its role in early childhood education, we first need to examine the historical, theoretical, and cultural perspectives that underlie each individual's personal definition of and belief about play.

Classical Perspectives of Play

Theories that explain the role of play often conflict with each other. Until about 1920, classical theories influenced beliefs about play. These theories emphasized a biological basis for children's play. Although these theories are not strongly supported by modern psychologists, they may still be affecting the way we think about play (Hughes, 1999). Some of the classical perspectives of play are surplus energy, recapitulation, practice for adulthood, and renewal of energy; a summary of each follows.

Surplus Energy. According to the surplus energy perspective, first proposed by Herbert Spencer in 1873 (in Hughes, 1999), humans are naturally equipped with energy needed for survival. If this energy is not used for the purpose of survival, it must be discharged in some way. Therefore, the purpose of play is to allow children to use up this excess energy. Letting children go out to recess to run off steam is an example of a modern extension of this belief. Some children do seem more relaxed after play and may be better able to concentrate on specific learning tasks. However, other children may play to the point of exhaustion or may even build up more energy during recess and therefore find it more difficult to concentrate when they return to the classroom.

Recapitulation. The theory of recapitulation was first proposed by G. Stanley Hall, a leading figure in early American psychology (in Hughes, 1999). Recapitulation is the idea that humans follow, from birth to adulthood, an innate sequence of development that mirrors the development of the entire human species. Play is the retracing of the developmental progress of our ancestors, and children progress through play in stages similar to the stages of human evolution. Furthermore, through play, the undesirable traits of humanity can be eliminated. In other words, children's play prepares them for more sophisticated activities necessary in the modern world. A modern extension of this theory is the tendency for adults to assign, arbitrarily, ages after which certain play behaviors are no longer acceptable. For example, some believe that it is inappropriate for preadolescents to continue to play with dolls or action figures.

Practice for Adulthood. According to the practice for adulthood theory, children play to practice and perfect their instincts for survival and tasks they will need to perform as adults (Groos, 1901). This theory might explain why children like to play with building materials, trucks, dolls, dishes, and other housekeeping toys. They may be practicing for adulthood. A modern extension of this theory is evident when parents and teachers choose representational toys and models such as toy lawn mowers, vacuum cleaners, and doctor's kits for young children.

Renewal of Energy. The renewal of energy theory was proposed by G. T. W. Patrick (1916) and states that work puts unnecessary strain on the brain and fine muscle coordination. When this happens, a person is prone to accidents. Play is therefore a way to release tension and fatigue and restore energy needed to maintain competence. The use of motor activities to offset fatigue and restore competency is a modern application of this theory. Children become fatigued during the process of concentrating on academic tasks. Recess or playtime is used to restore their energy so they can return to the "work" of learning. Therefore, this theory directly opposes Spencer's surplus energy theory. A modern extension of this theory is the idea that summer vacation is needed to reenergize students (and teachers) for the upcoming academic year. Another extension of this theory can be seen in the alternation of intense work and free play in daily classroom schedules.

Modern Perspectives of Play

Teachers have several learning theories available to inform their decisions about classroom practice. Some of these theoretical perspectives outline a specific role or function of play in learning and development. Others inform the practical application of play in the classroom. Because the nature of children's play is so complex, no single theory completely explains the value of play to children's growth and development. Viewed together, these theories offer insight into the multiple purposes and values of play in the lives of both children and adults.

Psychoanalytical Perspective of Play.   The psychoanalytical theory of play is based on the work of Freud and has been revised and extended over the years by others. Freud (1958) viewed the role of play as an emotional release for children as they grew. Erikson (1963) believed that play helped children develop self-esteem and gain mastery of their thoughts, bodies, objects, and social behavior. According to this perspective, children use play as a way to react to their world and to learn to deal with the difficult situations they encounter as they mature. Through play, children gain power over the situations that frighten, confuse, or upset them. For example, while playing, a child might take the role of his teacher, parent, or social worker and act out, through play, perceptions of the adult's power. Over time, children begin to act out their fantasies about significant adults in their lives. Sometimes, in play, terrible things happen to the adults portrayed in their play. At other times, the portrayed adults begin to exhibit the behaviors children wish for. Therefore, through play, children are able to take charge of the events that frighten them and are able to reduce feelings of anxiety and helplessness (Levy, 1978).

Cognitive-Developmental Perspective of Play.   Piaget (1952) proposed that children individually create their own knowledge about the world through interactions with people, objects, and materials. As they become more aware, they practice using what they know. A child's play therefore mirrors the child's emerging abilities, and through observing play, adults gain insight into the developmental abilities of children (Brunner, 1966; Piaget, 1962; Sutton-Smith, 1986). Through play, children test new ideas and behaviors. Piaget discusses two important by-products of play. One is pleasure or joy and the other is adaptation or learning. Therefore, learning, from the cognitive-developmental perspective, is the act of adapting behavior to fit new understanding, and play is one vehicle through which the child both constructs and displays this understanding.

Sociocultural Perspective of Play.   According to the sociocultural view, children's first encounter with knowledge is through social interaction with parents, teachers, siblings, and peers. Therefore, understanding is influenced, in fact, shaped, by cultural values and beliefs. As children play, they incorporate the cultural values implicit in their culture. When children encounter supportive interactions with peers or adults, they discover culturally appropriate ways to express ideas and solve problems. Vygotsky (1978) saw play as "a leading factor in development" (p. 101), having its most significant impact during the early childhood years. Through play, children stretch beyond their own understanding and develop new skills and abilities that support further development and learning.

Behaviorist Perspective of Play.   Behavioral theory, sometimes known as traditional learning theory, examines behaviors that can be seen and measured. Because the concept of play is elusive, it is not addressed directly within the behaviorist framework. Behavioral theory, however, does impact views of work and play and might influence adults' decisions regarding children's play. A leading behavioral theorist, B. F. Skinner (1953, 1957, 1974), believed that a child's behavior is learned and can be shaped by adults or environmental influences through operant conditioning. When a child feels rewarded for a particular behavior, that behavior will be repeated. Therefore, we can infer that one role of play within the behaviorist framework would be to serve as a reward for desired behavior. Indeed, we often hear adults telling children that they will be allowed to play when they have finished their work.

One branch of behavioral theory is social learning theory. Bandura (1977) believed that children learn social behavior not only through direct experience but also through observation. A child may imitate a particular behavior she has seen based on anticipated rewards. For example, if one child watches another child play with blocks, and the child playing with blocks gets positive attention from a teacher, then the first child may imitate the block play in order to get the same positive attention from the teacher. In this way, play acts as a resource for imitation and the learning that results from it.

Ecological Perspective of Play.   Ecology is the study of the interrelationships between humans and their environment. The perspective of this theoretical framework is that the context, or environment surrounding individual interactions and experiences, determines the degree to which individuals can develop their abilities and realize their potential. Cultural-ecological frameworks of behavior and development (Bronfenbrenner, 1979; Jibson, 1991; Ogbu, 1981; Tobin, Wu, & Davidson, 1989) stress the importance of three interacting layers of environmental influence on play: (1) physical and social aspects of children's immediate settings; (2) historical influences that affect the way adults (and children) conceptualize play; and (3) cultural and ideological beliefs relative to the meaning of play for subgroups of children (Roopnarine, Johnson, & Hooper, 1994). Therefore, the potential of play to support the learning and development of any one child is determined by the context in which that child plays.

Contexts for play, as well as for any other interactions, are extremely complex and are influenced by many variables. Ecological researchers focus on understanding what influences the way children play and how play influences the way children learn. They study the different contexts in which children play (e.g., at home, in schools, in centers, and on public playgrounds) and the different systems that influence play (e.g., culture of the family, philosophy of the school or center, culture of the community, and political climate) and determine how the interactions between contexts and systems affect the growth and development of children. Some questions concerning play that would promote study by ecological theorists include: Do the systems that children live within provide them with opportunities to develop play skills? How do play settings and environment affect children's play behaviors? How do materials and activities affect a child's attention, interactions, and conversations?

Cultural Perspectives of Play

Perceptions concerning the definition and role of play are greatly affected by one's cultural background. Roopnarine et. al (1994) note that "Children's play, then, is an outcome of being a participant within a particular culture or subcultural milieu" (p. 4). Current uncertainty on the part of educators concerning the developmental significance and educational value of play is an appropriate response to the concerns being expressed by parents and teachers from diverse ethnic groups (Phillips, 1996). Voices from these groups question the importance of play to early development and cognitive growth. Renatta Cooper (in Lakin, 1996) describes one African American view of play.

> Ours is a culture that does not view play as something that should take place in school. Play is amusing, and an appropriate part of childhood, but it isn't viewed as a critical part of the learning process. Do black children learn through play differently from children of the dominant culture? Probably, given a cultural context in which different things are valued." (p. 39)

Cooper goes on to state that issues concerning play as the focal point of early childhood programs and curriculum extend beyond the African American community. These concerns are shared by many Latinos and Asian Americans. It is important to note that Cooper, an early childhood teacher-educator, has chosen neither to abandon the belief that play supports learning and development and is an important component of early education nor to embrace a playless "back-to-basics" philosophy. Instead she believes that, "It will probably take a blend of both philosophies to achieve the best possible educational outcome for black children" (p. 40). Therefore, practice based solely on traditional knowledge of child development can no longer be assumed to be universal (Delpit, 1988; Rogoff, 1990; Rogoff, Mistry, Goncu, & Mosier, 1993). The cultural beliefs, values, and experiences of parents and children must be integrated into the strategies that define any one classroom.

It is not only vital that educators understand adults' perceptions regarding the role of play in learning and development, but they must also understand how culture affects the actual play of the child. When children play, they represent the world as they know it. Therefore, a child's play simultaneously reflects, influences, and is influenced by the cultural context of his or her life.

Meier (1996) suggests that children's understanding of their world, which they reconstruct through play, cannot be fully understood by adults through simple observations. Only when adults have an understanding of the sociocultural contexts in which play occurs can they understand both the qualities of play and what it reveals about a child's knowledge, skills, and his or her family's values and actions. For example, a child who has learned, through family experiences, not to express emotion outwardly and to keep his clothes clean (because the cost of cleaning and maintaining clothes is significant to the family budget, or because appearance is a subliminal statement of the family's child-rearing skills) will approach sensory play materials such as paint, sand, and water in a controlled or even cautious fashion. On the other hand, a child who has learned, through experiences with her family, to express emotion and feelings through sensory play materials will approach the same materials with outward enthusiasm that may lead to messes on herself or someone else. Therefore, when children from different cultural backgrounds arrive at school, they may have had differing prior play experiences and may have already developed definite ideas about when and how they should play. Delpit (1988) warns that making assumptions about other people's children in the absence of cultural understanding leads to misunderstanding children's actions and abilities. Play is one context in which teachers can begin to learn about individual children's strengths and abilities.

Brain Development and Play

Research on the development of the brain indicates that experiences and opportunities afforded to children during the early childhood years are critical to the development of neural pathways that govern cognitive, motor, and socioemotional learning and development (Shore, 1997).

"Connectivity is a crucial feature of brain development, because the neural pathways formed during the early years carry signals and allow us to process information throughout our lives" (p. 22).

Furthermore, timing is crucial. Even though learning continues throughout life, there are critical periods during which the brain is particularly efficient at creating neural pathways, or systems, that facilitate specific kinds of learning (Chugani, 1997). Experiences children have during these critical periods stabilize neural pathways and lay the foundation for optimal development. Lack of experiences during critical periods will likewise result in underdeveloped neural pathways. Therefore, the eventual architecture of the brain reflects the presence or absence of a wide range of physical, cognitive, and emotional experiences during early childhood.

Play is a critical element in early childhood because it provides the context for experiences that are vital to the development of neural pathways. Connections among neurons are formed as children explore their environment, play, and develop attachments to family members and other care providers. In fact, warm responsive care and positive interactions between children and care providers are critical to healthy neurological development (Gunnar, 1996).

Shore (1997) presents broad guidelines, based on brain research, for the care of young children. Among these guidelines are many suggestions that link play to healthy brain development. Here are examples from these guidelines:

- Respond to children's cues and clues—Notice their rhythms and moods . . .
- Play with them in a way that lets you follow their lead.
- Move in when children want to play, and pull back when they seem to have had enough stimulation.
- Talk, read, and sing to children—Surround them with language.
- Maintain an ongoing conversation with them about what you and they are doing.
- Ask toddlers and preschoolers to guess what will come next in a story.
- Play word games.
- Ask children to picture things that have happened in the past or might happen in the future.
- Provide reading and writing materials, including crayons and paper, books, magazines, and toys.
- Encourage safe exploration and play.
- Allow them to explore their relationships as well.
- Arrange for children to spend time with children of their own age and of other ages.
- Help them learn to solve the conflicts that inevitably arise. (p. 26–27)

Defining Play and Playfulness

It is important that all voices regarding play and its role in learning, development, and education be heard and respected when working with families and developing educational strategies for early childhood programs. Divergent positions regarding play certainly exist within our communities and schools. We heard, in the voices from our Get-Acquainted Night group, multiple perspectives, each expressed with conviction and emotion. It seems that whatever people feel about play, they feel it deeply. The National Association for the Education of Young Children (NAEYC) suggests, in its guidelines for developmentally appropriate practice (Bredekamp & Copple, 1997), that the early childhood community move beyond *either/or* positions (e.g., children learn *either* through play *or* through other strategies, including direct instruction) and embrace *both/and* positions (e.g., children learn *both* through play *and* through other strategies, including direct instruction) when designing programs for young children. This statement acknowledges the need for teachers to develop and use many differing strategies that foster learning and development among the children they teach. Applying this guideline to the use of play in educational settings presents a challenge to educators, namely, to develop and implement strategies and curricula that encompass the values and perspectives of all adults and children involved, and to do so without compromising the evidence, accumulated over the past decades, that supports play's important role in learning and development. We will now examine this evidence.

The Unifying Quality of Play

Each of the theoretical approaches we have discussed presents differing views of play and its role in early development and learning. For example, cognitive theorists focus on how play provides opportunities for children to develop their understanding of how the world works through interactions with people, objects, and the environment (Rubin, Fein, & Vandenberg, 1983). Psychoanalytic theorists focus on the affective qualities of play, particularly wish fulfillment (Erikson, 1963; Fraiberg, 1959). Considering each theory separately results in the development of dichotomies concerning the value of play; either play supports children's mental development or play supports children's emotional development. Indeed, adults often see mental and emotional qualities as separate, and school systems divide and subdivide these qualities into curricular areas such as math, language arts, and physical education. However, one of the most significant attributes of play is that it works to unite and integrate the cognitive, language, socioemotional, and motor aspects of learning and development (Nachmanovitch, 1990; Van Hoorn, Nourot, Scales, & Alward, 1993).

Play as a Way of Knowing

Sutton-Smith (1971) draws an analogy between children's play and children's way of knowing their world. He describes four modes of knowing: exploration, testing, imitation, and construction. As children play, they construct an understanding of their world. They explore their environment and the objects and people in it, imitate others they see, and predict the outcomes of their actions and the actions of others. Children's actions alternate between exploring, predicting, constructing new meaning, testing out that meaning, and exploring again. These mental actions occur so quickly that adults cannot always follow them. Through play, children unify their knowledge about the world, their understanding of how people interact, and their beliefs about their own effectiveness in their world.

Play as an Expression of Competence

Elkind (1987) provides further support for the idea that play unifies aspects of mental, physical and socioemotional development. He states that the function of play in early childhood is to give children a means of developing and asserting their sense of competency. This sense of competency emanates from a sense of wholeness. That is, the child does not separate his or her feeling of competency into specific mental, socioemotional, or physical frames. For example, when a child successfully maneuvers her tricycle, she feels good all over. Another example of the generalized feeling of competency resulting from play can be seen as children explore reading and writing. As they play with combining letters to make words that express their ideas, children smile with satisfaction and show extreme pride in the results of

their efforts. Play then has the ability to unify and integrate all aspects of learning and development; this quality is the essence of its definition and its role in early childhood education (Monighan-Nourot, 1997). Play helps children *put it all together.*

Therefore, play is not only an important vehicle for children's social, emotional, and cognitive development (Bergen, 1988; Berk & Winsler, 1995; Fein, 1981; Fromberg, 1992; Piaget, 1952; Smilansky & Shefatya, 1990), but also it unifies learning and development in holistic ways while supporting children's positive beliefs about their own competency (Elkind, 1987; Nachmanovitch, 1990; Van Hoorn et al., 1993). Here are some examples of learning that can be developed and enhanced as children play. Play provides children opportunities to develop a broad range of skills in the following areas.

Creative Expression
- improvising
- thinking flexibly
- exploring new options
- extending and elaborating on ideas
- manipulating rhythm, sound, form, and volume
- testing new materials

Cognitive Competencies and Literacy Skills
- developing symbolic capabilities
- practicing newly acquired skills
- attempting novel or challenging tasks
- solving complex problems
- making predictions
- drawing conclusions

- comparing sizes, shapes, colors
- determining cause and effect
- developing an understanding of time
- enhancing literacy skills
- energizing and organizing learning
- paying attention to a project until it is done

Social Competence
- interacting with others
- expressing and controlling emotions
- taking on new roles
- sharing
- taking turns
- negotiating to resolve problems
- settling arguments
- cooperating
- having and being friends

Healthy Lifestyle
- refining large motor skills
- refining small motor skills
- understanding safety concerns
- understanding nutrition concepts
- developing trust in one's own capabilities

How Play Unifies Learning and Development

The preceding list of accomplishments, all possible when children have multiple opportunities to engage in rich, culturally sensitive and meaningful play, attests to the important contributions play can make in early childhood programs and curriculum. It is important, then, to understand how play promotes learning and development. The constructivist view, which grew from cognitive-developmental theory (Berk, 1994; DeVries & Kohlberg, 1987; Piaget & Inhelder, 1969), offers one explanation. According to this theory, children build knowledge and skills through a continuous and spiraling process of construction. Children are actively learning, transforming prior knowledge into new understanding and new ways of thinking as they interact with people and objects in their environment. With each transformation, knowledge and skills become more sophisticated and more personally meaningful for the child.

Play is a vital part of this process. When children choose to play, they choose to play with something, with someone, or with some concept that is interesting to them and that they have some level of comfort with or knowledge about. As play progresses, children will encounter new problems, elements, or ideas that will surprise or confuse them. They then focus their attention on resolving or mastering these new problems, elements, or ideas. They experiment, hypothesize, and receive ideas from adults or more experienced peers; test new ideas; and revise their initial ideas. As they keep revising, their understanding of their original concepts expands and becomes more sophisticated. They have added a new dimension to their original understanding. As play continues, there will be additional surprises, problems, or elements to resolve. Therefore, new understanding will be constructed. All of this occurs within an environment that feels both safe and challenging.

Using the constructivist framework, let us follow a young child, Jackson, as he discovers the technology of electronic digital pagers.

One day three-year-old Jackson was riding in a car with his mother when they got stuck in traffic behind a large white cement truck. As they were sitting in the car, a beeping noise came from the truck, warning that it was in reverse and backing up. Jackson and his mother were quite upset because they were sure the cement truck was going to hit their car. The truck stopped just in time and all was well. When Jackson arrived home that evening, he pulled out all of his toy cars and trucks, built a road, and played intently. He made beeping sounds continually for every car and truck regardless of whether they were backing up in the play scenario.

The next day, Jackson and his father went to the grocery store. Jackson had been to this grocery story many times, but he was still somewhat intimidated by the size, brightness, bustle, and noise of the place. On this particular day, the store was quite busy, and Jackson and his father had to stand in line for a long time. They stood behind a woman dressed all in white and carrying a pager. Suddenly, the pager sounded. *Beep! Beep! Beep!* Jackson was surprised, anxious, and frightened. His eyes got large and his posture stiffened. He grabbed his father's hand and pulled him backward. "Dad, watch out!" he shouted. "That lady is going to back up!"

The lady turned and smiled at Jackson and his dad, studied a small black box that hung on her belt, and asked the clerk where the nearest telephone was. Jackson was confused by her actions because he had expected her to back into him.

Over the course of the next few days, Jackson became very aware of beeping sounds. He noticed that the microwave made beeping noises, but it didn't back up. The clothes drier made a beeping noise when the cycle was finished, but it didn't back up. When the school bus made a beeping noise, it did back up. Mother's watch alarm beeped one day and she didn't back up. During this time, Jackson's play was full of things that went beep. Sometimes what he was playing with backed up as it beeped, but sometimes it didn't.

Then one night, Jackson was again playing with his cars and trucks. As they headed down the imaginary roadway, one truck, a large delivery truck stopped. Then it started forward again under "Jackson power." Soon it stopped again. It had a load of hay to deliver to the farm. The truck had to back into the field. Before it backed up, it beeped.

A year has passed. Jackson and his mom are pushing a cart in the grocery store. There is a beeping noise somewhere in the store. Jackson looks around. He is now aware of many things that make beeping noises, including pagers, warning devices on automobiles and machines, and security systems. He hears the beeping noise again. Jackson says to his mother, "I think somebody left the store without paying." Jackson's understanding of beeping sounds has certainly changed.

Jackson formed a new understanding of beeping sounds because he had multiple opportunities to construct new knowledge and understanding through play. He was able to follow his interests, received timely information from the adults around when they sensed he needed it, and followed his own learning timetable. Indeed, his play took him further than any adult would or could have planned. We can apply the constructivist framework to this scenario and explain how play facilitated Jackson's learning. When Jackson first heard the beeping coming from the direction of the lady dressed in white, he assimilated that information. That is, he predicted what was going to happen based on his previous experience (prior knowledge) with the cement truck. Jackson's initial understanding of the world (schema) was that when "big white things" go "beep beep," you better get out of the way. Obviously this was a misconception. Jackson expected the lady to back up, and when she did not he was confused (in a state of disequilibrium). This confusion motivated him to develop a new understanding of beeping sounds, and he became more aware of them in his world. Through continuous opportunities to play, Jackson experimented and hypothesized about what objects would beep and under what circumstances. His play centered around his interest in beeping sounds and his understanding of them changed (accommodation).

This example illustrates the developmental process described by Piaget (1952). Play is one important way that children work through this learning process. It is certainly not the only way children learn, but for many children it is a natural way to develop understanding. Vygotsky (1978) also describes play as central to a child's learning and development. Through play, children receive the individualized support (scaffolding) necessary to create new understanding.

Play and Playfulness

Jackson's process of learning about beeping sounds could be described as play. There certainly were playful aspects to his learning. He had fun. He laughed. He was even silly at times. However, there was also a serious aspect to his learning. He was thoughtful. He was intent. He was committed to figuring out when objects beeped and when they did not. Those behaviors might suggest to some that he was engaged in work. Indeed, under certain conditions work and play seem the same. Fortunate is the adult who defines his or her job as fun and goes about work in a playful way. Dewey (1916) described a continuum of activities that ranged from foolery on one end to drudgery on the other. He placed the activities of work and play together in the middle. In this text, we use the terms *play* and *playful* to describe actions and activities that are motivated by personal interest, are exploratory in nature, and lead to an expanded understanding. To some, these same activities might be described as work. The important issue for early child educators is not to get caught up in the either/or dichotomy (*either* work *or* play), but to establish an atmosphere in which work and play are recursive in nature and exist simultaneously.

Playfulness then becomes an important indicator of quality when creating an environment for learning or implementing learning strategies. Csikszentmihalyi (1979, 1993) described several qualities of playfulness in childhood and adulthood. These qualities include having clear goals, concentrated attention, loss of self-consciousness, an altered sense of time, intrinsic motivation, and the belief that an experience is worthwhile for its own sake. Sutton-Smith (1971) said of playfulness, "The most important thing about playfulness is that it makes life worth living" (p.21). Playfulness has the potential to make both teaching and learning fulfilling endeavors.

For the purposes of this book, we will define *play* as actions of the learner that unite and integrate cognitive, socioemotional, and motor aspects of learning within rich, culturally sensitive, child-centered, and supportive contexts. *Playful learning* refers to the process of learning through play and the spirit that encompasses this process. Elements of playful learning will be described in Chapter 2. *Playful teaching* refers to strategies that create the environment and support the process of learning through play and the spirit that encompasses these actions. These strategies will be described in detail throughout the remainder of this book.

The terms *playful learning* and *playful teaching* are not intended to trivialize the actions of learning and the goals of schools, nor is the intention to elevate or inflate the role of play in learning and development. Rather, the use of these terms is intended to draw attention to the reciprocal nature of work and play in the lives of children and the adults who teach and care for them.

Developing Advocacy Skills

The evidence supporting play, both empirical and intuitive, is clear. When children have multiple opportunities to engage in rich, culturally sensitive, child-centered play in meaningful contexts, both in and out of school, learning and development are enhanced. Therefore, play is a vital component of early childhood programs and curricula. However, there are factors that severely limit children's opportunities to play in meaningful, constructive ways. For example, children are spending more time alone while the adults in their families work. These children might spend their time watching television or videos rather than engaging in playful activities. Another hindrance to play is the fact that many neighborhoods are not safe enough for children to play outside without close or constant supervision. Also, many neighborhood playgrounds are often in disrepair. Political and social pressures also threaten children's opportunities to play, as school boards and building administrators push for more structured and measurable styles of teaching and learning. However, one of the most critical issues affecting children's play is the misunderstanding that surrounds the use of play in classrooms. This was illustrated clearly by statements heard in the parent meeting described at the beginning of the chapter: "Play is fun," and "Messing around and having fun with other children, that's play." Therefore, teachers need to work to protect and support the use of playful learning and playful teaching strategies in educational settings. Through advocacy activities, teachers can work to preserve this right of childhood.

Defining Advocacy

Advocacy is a proactive stance taken by individuals in response to particular issues that concern them. In early childhood education, the purpose of advocacy is to promote ideas and seek resolutions that will affect children and families in positive ways. Early childhood practitioners have two primary goals: first, to support the family unit, and second, to help children meet their full potential (Bredekamp & Copple,1997; Melton, 1983). Therefore, early childhood practitioners need to become involved in issues that impinge directly on their obligations to the families and children in their care (Hostetler, 1981; Whitebrook & Almy, 1986).

Providing multiple opportunities for children to learn through play at school or in child care centers would certainly qualify as an important advocacy issue. Advocacy activities that focus on the issue of play include the following:

- A second-grade teacher rearranges one area of her classroom so children have space to produce self-authored plays.
- A videotape designed to show and explain how children learn and play simultaneously is sent home with children.

- Preschool and kindergarten teachers meet with the principal to discuss and redesign the cafeteria schedule so that children have a larger block of time in the morning for classroom activities that include free-choice centers.
- A first-grade teacher lends a book about play in the classroom to a kindergarten teacher and suggests that they meet soon to discuss ideas.
- A parent writes an open letter to other parents describing how his ideas concerning play in the classroom changed after a recent visit to the classroom.
- A teacher presents a session concerning the value of play at a conference sponsored by the local affiliate of NAEYC.

When teachers advocate, they seek to change the perceptions, procedures, conditions, or resources that affect children and families. Indeed, the purpose of advocacy is to improve the life chances for all children and their families.

Becoming an Advocate

Advocacy begins when an individual overcomes feelings of powerlessness or fears of consequences and develops a proactive stance (Jensen, 1986; Lombardi, 1986; Markus & Nurius, 1986). To change other's views (and that is what advocacy is really about), one needs to move from an *"I can't do anything about it"* position to a *"This is what we can do about it"* position. There are many steps along the way. In the beginning, these steps may seem small, tentative, and private as advocates begin to test the waters of change. Over time, as knowledge and confidence increase, advocates network with each other to bring about positive changes for families and children.

Actions that help develop a proactive stance include:

- studying what has been written about the issue
- listening sensitively to different perspectives on the issue, thereby developing multiple perspectives
- brainstorming alternatives to existing practice
- experimenting on a small scale

Once one has overcome feelings of powerlessness and fears of consequences, advocacy can begin.

Personal Qualities of Advocates

Effective advocates have high moral principles, courage, vision, and credibility. Blank (1997) describes many actions that make advocacy efforts successful. Here is an abbreviated list.

- developing a vision
- extending their thinking into the future
- reaching out and working with people and organizations beyond familiar colleagues
- seizing strategic opportunities to move an issue forward
- finding a way to address issues
- making tough decisions and risking being unpopular
- being tough
- knowing how and when to compromise

In the introduction to *The State of America's Children: Yearbook, 1997,* published by the Children's Defense Fund, Marion Wright Edleman offers twenty-five tips for advocating effectively for children. Among these tips are the following.

- Ignore labels and do what you've got to do.
- Talk less and act more.
- Do something personal to help at least one child or family besides your own.
- Don't worry about credit, turf, or critics. Keep doing your work. Stand together.
- Learn to communicate simply.
- Reach out to others. Know how and when to collaborate but do not be afraid to lead.
- Don't take *but* for an answer.
- Don't give up when you fail the first, second, fifth, or tenth time.
- Focus on a few important priorities.
- Do your homework and keep learning new skills.

As mentioned earlier, advocating for playful environments that facilitate children's learning can be an overwhelming task. However, dividing advocacy activities into three broad categories and developing the skills needed to work within each category will make the process of advocacy less complicated. The three categories of advocacy activities are (1) Becoming Aware, (2) Furthering One's Own Understanding, and (3) Taking Action. The first category, *Becoming Aware,* refers to the need to learn about what is actually happening concerning the issue in question. For example, if you were going to begin to advocate for more opportunities for children to play in your community, you would first need to become aware of the current state of affairs concerning children and play in your community. Do children have multiple opportunities to play? Do all children have equal opportunities? Are there safety factors that, if addressed, would increase children's opportunities to play? Becoming aware means tuning in to what is going on around you. Activities that help you tune in include taking walks and observing what is going on around you, reading the newspaper, and engaging parents and other teachers in meaningful dialogue.

The second category, *Furthering Your Own Understanding,* refers to the need to study the situation closely and form multiple perspectives. Building on knowledge you gained from your awareness activities, ask more questions of more people. Do not be afraid to ask questions of community or school officials. You are on a mission to find the facts and understand all perspectives. Supplement your questions with more reading. Become an expert on the aspect of the issue that you find most interesting.

The third category, *Taking Action,* is the ultimate purpose of advocacy. When you study an issue carefully, your actions will be informed and successful. Do not feel that advocacy has to be a great or even a public undertaking. Spending an hour on Saturday morning picking up the trash in a neighborhood playground will enhance the play of all the children playing there that day. Developing a learning center in your classroom that is based on an interest expressed by children is another example of advocacy. Letting families know how and what children are learning in the learning center is still another example of advocacy in action.

Throughout this text, we will further our discussion of effective advocacy practices as they relate to play and promoting play opportunities in early childhood programs. We will concentrate on activities that help parents and administrators understand the value of play and its important role in early childhood programs. We will also provide suggestions for action at each of the three levels of advocacy.

Summary

The meaning and value of play are embedded in one's knowledge about play, past experiences with play, and cultural values regarding play. Perceptions of the definition and role of play are influenced by one's experiences and cultural background. Therefore educators must understand and appreciate the perspectives of parents and colleagues as they integrate play into classrooms.

Play has the ability to unify and integrate all aspects of learning and development, and this quality is the essence of its definition and its role in educational settings. Playful learning refers to the process of learning through play and the spirit that encompasses this process. Playful teaching refers to strategies that create the environment and support the process of learning through play and the spirit that encompasses these actions. Early childhood educators have a responsibility to advocate for conditions that support the family unit and help children meet their full potential. Providing multiple opportunities to learn through play is an important advocacy issue.

REVISITING FIRST IMPRESSIONS

Revisit your first impressions and respond to the following questions: How did your definition of play compare to the definitions voiced at the Get-Acquainted Night? How has your perception of play and its role in early childhood education changed after reading this chapter?

QUESTIONS FOR DISCUSSION

1. Create an example that describes how play unifies children's learning for a three-year-old child and for a six-year-old child.

2. Roman, age four, has been arranging plastic letters on a magnetic board for about ten minutes. He is concentrating intently, lining up the letters in rows moving from left to right. He has not yet attempted to create any words. Roman's father is visiting the preschool for the first time and approaches the teacher to express his concern that Roman is spending too much time "just playing." If you were Roman's teacher, how would you react to this concern?

3. How does dichotomous thinking distract early childhood educators from developing environments that foster learning among all children? Develop an example that explains your ideas.

SUGGESTED READINGS

Bodrova, E., & Leong, D. J. (1996). *Tools of the mind: The Vygotskian approach to early childhood education*. Englewood Cliffs, NJ: Merrill.

Kagan, S. L., & Bowman, B. (Eds.), (1997). *Leadership in early care and education*. Washington, DC: National Association for the Education of Young Children.

Phillips, A. L. (1996). *Topics in early childhood education: Playing for keeps*. St. Paul, MN: Redleaf Press.

Shore, R. (1997). *Rethinking the brain: New insights into early development*. New York: Families and Work Institute.

CHAPTER

2

The Child's Perspective of Play

Prereading Guide

First Impressions.   Describe in your journal how you envision incorporating play into your classroom. Consider the following questions: What types of play can be included in classroom settings? What elements characterize play as opposed to work? What do you think you need to know about the children in your class in order to plan play activities for them?

Revisit
The Unifying Quality of Play (Chapter 1)

Stories from the Field

Ms. Griffith, a first-grade teacher in a suburban public school, expressed mixed feelings when she spoke of her experiences with incorporating play into her classroom. On one hand, she believed that children learned through play, and yet she often questioned the effectiveness of some of the play episodes she created for her class. Here is an account, in her own words, of one such episode.

> I believe in letting kids play and think that they can learn a lot when concepts and skills are presented through games. When there is something I need to teach, I always try to figure out how to present it as a game. For example, until the beginning of this school year, I used to put sight words on flash cards and let the children take turns reading them when I held them up. But they would get restless pretty quickly, and I noticed that many of the children weren't paying attention when it was someone else's turn. So after a few weeks, I decided to create a game that would let them practice reading sight words.
>
> I made a simple Treasure Hunt game board with thirty squares drawn along a curving path decorated to look like an underwater scene, and also constructed a simple spinner. I used some of the Disney *Little Mermaid* characters on both the board and the spinner since I know how popular that video is with children this age. I taught the children how to spin and then move the correct number of spaces. Some of the squares had seashell designs on them, but most of them had treasure chest designs. When children landed on a space with a treasure chest, they got to pick a card from the treasure pile in the middle of the board and then read the word written on the card. If they read the word correctly,

they got to put the card in their treasure pile. If they could not read it, the word card had to go back into the pile. I designed the game to end when the first player reached the end of the path—a ship at the top of the board above the water. At that point, whoever had the most pieces of treasure would be the winner.

I thought this would be a better way to practice sight words, and the children were really excited when they saw the game. They seemed to have lots of fun when I sat with small groups and played with them to teach them the rules. But once children were assigned to the vocabulary center and they started to play the game without me, they just didn't do very well. They argued about everything: whose turn it was, what number the spinner was really pointing to, whether a spin counted or not, even what word someone had actually said when he tried to read a card!

Even worse, they didn't stay focused on the game. I'd see them grabbing the spinner and flicking it to see who could make it go the fastest. Other times, they'd take turns just spinning to see who could get the highest number, and not even move their pieces or try to read the words. Once, I saw them using the cards to try to build houses! They seemed to do everything *but* play the game like it was supposed to be played.

I'd get so frustrated that I'd end up telling them that they had to put the game away. Finally, I just gave up and went back to using flash cards to teach sight words. I know it's not really fun, but at least I know they are practicing the words they need. I wish there were a way for them to play and learn simultaneously.

Bredekamp and Copple (1997) emphasize the inclusion of play as an essential component of developmentally appropriate teaching. The use of play as a learning tool for children and a teaching strategy for teachers is considered one of the basic principles of learning and development. Play is certainly not the only way children learn, but it has been demonstrated repeatedly that it is an effective way of learning.

Yet many teachers have experiences similar to Ms. Griffith's when they attempt to weave play into their daily routines. They may then decide that the idea of learning through play is good in theory, but impractical for *real* children in *real* classrooms. When presented with evidence that theories about learning and play are based on observations of real children, many teachers who have been frustrated in their attempts to foster learning through play begin to suspect that the children they teach are somehow different and, sadly, not able to engage in productive play in a classroom setting.

Frustrations similar to those described here can be alleviated when teachers create play experiences that match children's interests, cultural experiences, and developmental abilities. To create play environments that effectively foster learning and development, teachers need to understand play from the child's perspective. Often, what adults view as play and what children view as play are very different. Furthermore, children's views of play change with age and experience. A greater understanding of the general characteristics of play, the different categories of play, and the factors that influence an individual's play activities will aid early childhood professionals in their effort to plan effective playful learning environments. These characteristics, categories, and factors will be discussed in this chapter. As you read each section, reflect back to Ms. Griffith's experience with the Treasure Hunt game to determine the extent to which these factors contributed to her children's responses.

Characteristics of Play That Facilitate Learning and Development

Although play can take many forms, researchers have identified common characteristics that separate play from nonplay behaviors. Furthermore, some play experiences will support learning and development more effectively than others. Specifically, five elements of play have been shown to support cognitive, language, and social development and learning (Rubin, Fein, & Vandenburg, 1983). These characteristics are process orientation, intrinsic motivation, nonliteral qualities, experimentation with rules, and mental activity.

Process Orientation

During play activities, the child's attention and interest is focused on the process of the play rather than on the product or outcome of the play. This is particularly true when the content of play is novel for the child. For example, while painting, a young preschool child may become absorbed in the very act of painting. The child concentrates on how the paint flows on the paper, how the colors mix together, or how the paint drips off the brush onto the floor. At that point, the interest in the process of painting overshadows the product, the picture itself. This is one reason why novice painters in a preschool, kindergarten, or even first-grade class will often cover the entire paper with paint. When asked what they are painting, they may look a little startled and name the first thing that comes to mind, whether or not they had any intention of representing this in their painting. They forget, or don't yet know, that they are supposed to be painting *something*. What matters instead is the *act* of painting.

Children may in fact get so involved in the process of their play that the initial goal of the play shifts. For example, a group of children may start out to construct a building with blocks, but as they play, they get interested in balance. They do not necessarily know the word, but they are caught up by the phenomenon that is balance. They explore the idea of balance and experiment to see how many blocks they can stack before the structure falls. In this instance, the goal of the children's play shifts from constructing a building to creating balance. They are not aware of the shift; they just follow their interest.

This shifting, or flexibility, of goals because of a focus on the process of play contributes to children's sense of exhilaration and discovery. Some adults, observing the play described in the previous paragraph, may be delighted and introduce the word *balance*. They may even suggest other objects to add to the blocks. Other adults, however, may see children's shifting goals as indicative of short attention spans or lack of persistence. Such adults might suggest that the children go back to building the house. Play in classrooms is often misinterpreted by adults because they lack children's perspectives on play.

Intrinsic Motivation

When play is intrinsically motivated, children instigate or sustain the play purely for the pleasure the activity brings them and not for any kind of external praise or reward. Greater learning and achievement is associated with activities that are intrinsically motivated (Gottfried, 1985; Pintrich & Schunk, 1996). Therefore, play episodes that are child-initiated, freely chosen, or move from an obligation or assigned activity to one that is sustained because the child is enjoying it will provide more effective learning opportunities.

There are times, of course, when teachers have specific learning goals in mind and initiate particular play activities, guide the play's development, and even provide incentives for children to continue playing. However, when the children derive enjoyment and satisfaction from the play and continue to play even after the adult guidance and extrinsic incentives are gone, or when they initiate the same kind of play at another time, then the play becomes intrinsically motivated. Play that is intrinsically motivated is sustained longer and leads children to invest more mental energy. Such play thus provides children with more opportunities to define and refine their learning. As children take charge of the content and direction of intrinsically motivated play, it becomes self-satisfying and thus inherently rewarding and cognitively productive.

Nonliteral Quality

During play, the true meanings and functions of objects may be suspended. For example, a cardboard box may be transformed from a mere container for objects into a space ship. The next day, or even the next play period, this same box may be transformed into a castle. In play, children suspend reality and act as if what is happening in the minds of the players is the same as what is happening in the play area. For example, when children play, a torn dress rescued from a teacher's collection of rummage becomes, in the minds of the children, a beautifully sequined gown. A crude block structure that is barely standing becomes a skyscraper about to be destroyed by alien invaders.

Through play children transport themselves back and forth through the past, present, and future. Children become what they play. In this way they take on new roles and try out new actions in the safety of their classroom. They experiment with new ideas and new language. The teacher observing this kind of play can get a good idea about the children's reality, what they know and what they don't know, what they are trying to work out, and what they are ready to learn.

Experimentation with Rules

Children's play is often simultaneously rule-bound and rule-free. That is, the play is bound to the implicit rules the players bring to it: rules of language, rules of role requirements, and rules of social negotiation. These rules are dependent on the players' prior knowledge, cultural background, and experience. While children play, each individual's implicit rule structures begin to surface and in some cases clash with those of the other players. The players then have to negotiate and design a set of rules that are workable for them. Therefore, new rule structures emerge from play as children experiment with rules.

Examples of experimentation with rules can be seen when children play together in a dramatic play center such as a post office. Each child brings to this play his or her prior understanding of post offices and mail carriers. These prior understandings become the implied rules for each player. If each player has the same understandings regarding the work of the post office and mail carriers, there will be few conflicts, and the roles of the individuals will be mutually constructed. However, if the players have different understandings of the working of a post office, the names of the objects in the post office, or the work of mail carriers, their implicit rules will be in conflict, and they will need to experiment with these rules or negotiate and come to a mutual understanding in order to continue their play. This experimentation with rules provides opportunities for cognitive and social learning.

Explicit rules are imposed on children by adults and often hinder the play of novice players because they block or prevent the process of experimentation and negotiation, an important aspect of social learning. Children will learn with time and experience to deal with, appreciate, and apply explicit rules. Novice players need to create and change rules to control the direction of their play, whereas children with experience related to a particular concept are able to accept predetermined rules.

Mental Activity

When children explore, probe, experiment, investigate, and inquire during their play, their minds are active in the process of constructing and reconstructing meaning and understanding about their world. It is a myth that children are always noisy, boisterous, and physically active when at play. Indeed, a playful classroom could be very quiet. Children can be physically inactive while playing. For example, a board game such as chess involves little physical activity; but chess players must be mentally active while engaged in the match.

Children's play is often characterized by concentration and unwillingness to be distracted. A young child crooning softly to a baby doll may be totally oblivious to the trio of boisterous classmates galloping through the dress-up area and rearing up as they pretend to be wild horses. Older children may be just as focused as they engage in fantasy play through day dreaming. The physical activity levels of each are very different, but they have high levels of mental concentration.

Revisiting the Treasure Hunt Game. It might be helpful at this point to revisit Ms. Griffith's attempt to incorporate play into her children's learning of sight words. Given the preceding discussion of characteristics of play that support learning, Ms. Griffith's experience with her Treasure Hunt game begins to make sense.

First, the focus of the play was determined by the teacher—children were to practice reading sight words. It has been demonstrated that play is most likely to be sustained when it focuses on process rather than product. The ultimate goal of the Treasure Hunt game, however, was mastery of a predetermined vocabulary—clearly a product. Given this rationale for the play activity, it is not likely that the children were actively encouraged to enjoy the game for any inherent pleasure it might provide. Indeed, when the children did find pleasure in exploring the speed of the spinner, and the construction possibilities of the word cards, their play was viewed as inappropriate.

A related problem was that the play and its intended focus were extrinsically rather than intrinsically motivated. The goals were the teacher's, and they apparently never became the children's. Although some children might have come to enjoy the game if left to explore it on their own, they were instead assigned to play the game in a center not of their choosing.

Furthermore, the play was mainly literal. Although the design of the game board had the potential to invite children to imagine that they were moving along the ocean floor in search of treasure, this feature was a relatively minor aspect of the game. The children's need to break away from literal use of the game pieces was evident in their attempt to construct houses out of the word cards (also a shift in focus). Yet, as noted earlier, this shift into imaginative play was regarded as a misuse of the game.

Finally, the format of the game precluded significant experimentation with rules. Rather, children were presented with a set of rules that governed how the game should proceed, when it should end, and how a winner was to be determined. Children had no opportunities to negotiate rules among themselves, or to determine in collaboration with each other and the teacher which rules were needed.

The only critical element inherent in the game was its focus on mental activity. But even that aspect of the game was somewhat problematic, mainly because the parameters of the mental activity were so narrowly defined. The primary challenge of the game was to recognize and read aloud specified words. While that might be a worthwhile endeavor, it may not have been sufficiently rewarding to sustain children's interest.

Clearly, Ms. Griffith did not take into account children's perspective on play when she created the Treasure Hunt Game. However, there are many ways that Ms. Griffith could have adapted her game to incorporate characteristics of play that encourage learning and thereby could have established a better match between the children in her class and the play experience offered.

First, Ms. Griffith could have attempted to emphasize the process of playing the game rather than the product by making the game more appealing. This might have been done by incorporating dramatic play into the experience. Something as simple as providing appropriate "Under the Sea" props, such as shark fins, mermaid or mermen props, and swim masks and fins for children to wear, would invite them to imagine themselves as underwater inhabitants discovering buried treasure. Writing the words to be practiced on coin-shaped cards and hiding them around the center (or outdoors in a fairly confined space) would further the imaginative play and would also render the game less literal than it was originally designed. In this way, incidental learning of words would be a natural outcome of a more process-oriented, dramatic play experience.

The game's focus on extrinsic rather than intrinsic motivation would also be addressed, because children are naturally drawn to sociodramatic play. They would be intrinsically motivated to play and would continue to do so because they like dressing up and imagining themselves moving through an underwater world. Their intrinsic motivation could have been stimulated even more, though, had Ms. Griffith involved the children themselves in the construction of the game. She could have briefly laid out her ideas for the game, then invited the children to flesh out the details. They could have selected from among the variety of sight words first graders might be expected to master, both those that most appealed to them and those they felt the strongest need to learn. Equally important, they could have been encouraged to add additional vocabulary that interested them, possibly related to thematic studies under-way in their classroom. It is likely that the children would have included words that were infi-nitely more challenging than the basic sight words that often comprise first-grade words lists. Perhaps they would have felt more motivation to master these self-selected grown-up words.

Involving the children in constructing the game would also have addressed their devel-opmental need to negotiate rules. Given the opportunity to determine for themselves how the game should be played, the children probably would have created fairly simple rules that were well within their understanding and experiences with social negotiation. Ms. Griffith then could have played the game with the children, offering assistance as they internalized the rules and became able to sustain the play on their own.

Categories of Play

The characteristics of play described thus far can be applied to all kinds of children's play. Piaget (1962) described three distinct categories of play, including functional play, symbolic play, and games with rules. Smilansky (1968) expanded Piaget's cognitive stages based on her studies with lower socioeconomic Israeli children and developed her own categories of play. Such categories are useful because they clarify the kinds of play that can be incorporated into classrooms. These categories of play are briefly described here. We will discuss how each can be implemented and managed in the classroom throughout the chapters that follow.

Functional Play

Functional play is also known as exploratory play or practice play. It is something that chil-dren do over and over purely for pleasure. For example, young children, enjoy pouring sand from one container into another. Because they are mentally engrossed in the activity, it sus-tains their interest. As they practice, they refine their motor skills while gathering some basic understanding of concepts related to velocity, speed, and mass, even though they obviously do not label these concepts as such.

Children also engage in functional play when they practice newly acquired motor skills. They run for the sake of running, jump for the sake of jumping. Older children kick soccer balls, play jacks, skate, or shoot baskets, again only to derive pleasure from the activ-ity. In the process, they refine their motor skills and learn about balance.

Functional play is further evidenced in more cognitive pursuits. When children first learn to write their names or spell a word that has meaning for them, they can be seen filling up a whole page with print. They do not intend their writing to communicate a message, nor do they expect others to read it. Rather, they simply derive pleasure from practicing a newly discovered skill.

Other outcomes of functional play are automatic response and memory. For example, when children first learn a song, they may practice it over and over. This leads to their under-standing of the song and memorization. The song becomes automatic. This is a voluntary way to practice, refine, and test their own abilities.

When teachers allow children to choose from among several ways to practice a skill, they are involving children in functional play. For example, when children who are ready to memorize addition or subtraction facts are allowed to choose from several options for practice, the practice itself will become more playful, and they will be more intrinsically motivated to sustain the activity. One child might choose to work with flash cards. Another might choose to take timed tests. Both children will become engrossed in their playful practice, and their attention will be focused, resulting in a productive use of time and effort.

Constructive Play

Constructive play refers to building or creating. It includes the manipulation of objects with the goal of creating something new or imagined, as well as putting things together to make representations of reality. Forman and Hill (1984) define constructive play as "open ended, 'playing around' with alternative ways of doing things" (p. 2). Piaget (1962) placed constructive play on a continuum, midway between work and play. Constructive play is not limited to traditional building toys like blocks, Legos, and Tinkertoys. Paintings and collages can also be considered constructions, as can objects formed from blocks of Play-Doh.

When children are allowed to construct, they expand their ideas and understanding of the world. Teachers interacting with children engaged in constructive play can extend language and concept development. An example of this can be seen in a second-grade class that has been studying the habits of bees. Several children have chosen to construct a model of a beehive. As they discuss ideas related to forming the hive, the teacher intervenes and scaffolds a greater understanding of the concepts involved.

Rough-and-Tumble Play

Recent research on play brings to light another category of play not specifically mentioned by either Smilansky or Piaget. Rough-and-tumble play frequently accompanies pretend play. This is a positive socializing experience for young children, particularly boys. Rough-and-tumble play shares aspects of functional play and dramatic play. It is likely to occur in soft spaces such as a rug area indoors or a grassy area outdoors. It is important that teachers do not misinterpret rough-and-tumble play as aggressive or violent play. In rough-and-tumble play, children are laughing and frolicking and pretending to be someone or something other than themselves. They are able to separate from one another at any time during the play and joust open-fisted. They also take turns being the aggressor and the victim. Negotiating these role exchanges exercises children's perspective-taking abilities (Corsaro, 1985). This is unlike fighting, aggression, and violent play.

Dramatic Play

Dramatic play begins when children engage in symbolic representation, as when children use one thing to represent another. It develops from simple representations of objects to dramatic representations of events and people. When children begin to play out their ideas of the way the world works with other children, then dramatic play has turned into sociodramatic play. Like functional play, dramatic play (also called pretense or pretend play) starts in early infancy when children interact with adults or mimic adult behavior. For example, a toddler might pretend to be talking on a toy telephone because she has seen her father talk on the phone.

Games with Rules

Games with rules are a form of play requiring children to conform to the structure of external rules and control of the play by authorities. The youngest children and the most novice of players will become frustrated with many games with rules because their inclination is to dismiss the rules and invent their own. However, motor activities such as "Duck, Duck, Goose" and singing games such as "Ring Around the Rosy" allow young children to experience rule-bound activities in a casual and intrinsically motivating situation. As children get older or have more experience playing, the rule structure of the game becomes more intriguing. Older children and more experienced players enjoy board games, computer-generated games, and sports in which they have to learn to follow a prescribed format. In this way, children reach a stage at which they are better able to apply their thinking to the real world.

One task for teachers who wish to facilitate a good match between children and the play experiences they embed into their programs is to ensure that children have opportunities to engage in all categories of play that are appealing to them. This does not mean, or course, that children should have totally free rein to decide what constitutes acceptable play in a classroom setting. Teachers will need to monitor play in the dramatic play center, for example, to be sure that children are not engaging in pretend scenarios that might humiliate a classmate, or role-plays that include the use of pretend weapons if that type of play is forbidden in the school setting. As noted earlier, each type of play should incorporate characteristics that have been shown to enhance learning. Equally important, the play should be tailored to fit the individual differences of all the children in a program.

Revisiting the Treasure Hunt Game. Returning once again to Ms. Griffith's Treasure Hunt Game, we note that all of her efforts to incorporate play into learning vocabulary words were centered on the development of a game with rules. It could be that many of the children in her class were not developmentally ready to handle such structured rules. Ms. Griffith could have incorporated other forms of play into the classroom routine and still have met her goal of developing vocabulary skills. For example, working with flash cards, alone or in pairs, could have been intrinsically motivating for some children, and if using flash cards had been a choice rather than an assigned task, then these children would have approached the use of flash cards playfully. This would be an example of functional play, and using flash cards and keeping track of correctly read cards would become a game. Other children might enjoy drawing a map of a buried treasure and labeling all of the parts. They would extend considerable effort to use the right word in the right place. This would be considered either constructive play or even dramatic play. There would be, of course, some children in Ms. Griffith's class who would enjoy the Treasure Hunt Game, if it were an option. The way to provide playful learning experiences for children is to provide many choices and be flexible enough to consider children's differing interests and abilities when developing teaching strategies.

Individual Factors That Influence Play

Within any given classroom, and certainly across grade levels, there will be profound differences in the way children play and the way they use play as a mode of learning. These differences are related to social participation, age, experience, social class, cultural variation, gender, health, and mental and physical abilities. To develop effective play environments, teachers must take into consideration both the similarities and the diversity that exist among the children in their classrooms.

Social Participation

Children play alone, with one or two partners, or in groups. Their participation depends on their age, prior experience, and individual learning style. Parten (1932) described the following levels of social participation in play.

- *Solitary play.* Child plays alone and is oblivious to others in the room.
- *Onlooker play.* Child plays along, watches an ongoing play episode, may interact some.
- *Parallel play.* Characterized by individual play, close physical proximity with others, nonverbal communication, shared materials, and no attempt to coordinate play.
- *Associative play.* Characterized by physical proximity; verbal conversation; sharing and coordination of materials; pursuing individual goals, process, and product; and no agreed on roles by players.
- *Cooperative play.* Characterized by physical proximity; verbal conversation and negotiation; sharing and coordination of materials; and joint and ongoing negotiations to determine group goals, themes, and constructions.

Children of all ages gain from playing alone and watching others, as well as playing with others. When children are engaged in onlooker play, they are often "scoping out" the group play of others to see if they would enjoy it and feel comfortable being involved. They may also be looking for ways to enter ongoing play episodes. Children engaged in solitary, onlooker, and parallel play may be simultaneously watching the play of others, and will later incorporate observed actions and ideas into their ongoing play.

As children grow older, or as they have more opportunities to observe and engage in group play, we expect to see more frequent involvement in associative and cooperative play. However, the pattern of participation is a matter of personal style. Some children do prefer to play alone, and that is fine, if the child is also able to play successfully with others when he or she chooses. The important issue is determining if a child is developing the ability to enter associative and cooperative play situations and carry through the episode successfully. Carefully tracking the participation patterns of children enables teachers to know which children may need additional guidance and support to further develop social competence.

Age

Bredekamp and Copple (1997) point out that there are some common characteristics of age groups that indicate experiences, activities, materials, and interaction strategies that will generally be safe, healthy, interesting, achievable, and challenging to most children. The interests of three- and four-year-old children tend to be more similar to each other than to the interests of five- and six-year-old children. Although children in both age groups enjoy dramatic play, the younger children are more apt to enact dramas related to their own experiences, playing mommies and daddies, or baby-sitters and babies. Five- and six-year-old children, however, love to engage in pretend play that casts them in the roles of superheroes. Unlike younger children, they act out dramas that are far removed from their own experience. Thus we can expect that infants, toddlers, preschoolers, and primary-grade children will play differently.

Keep in mind, however, that particular types of play, although perhaps more prevalent at certain stages of development, are certainly not exclusive to any particular age. Research suggests, for example, that symbolic play and games with rules can be found in rudimentary forms in infants, whereas solitary and parallel play, generally regarded as representative of the play of toddlers and preschoolers, may not necessarily be immature behavior for six- and seven-year-old children. Still, the existence of all forms of play at all ages does not negate existing developmental hierarchies, as there appears to be a difference in the quality of particular types of play at different age levels (Krasnor & Pepler, 1980). For this reason, common interests and characteristics form one basis for selecting materials and planning experiences that will be both interesting and challenging to children. A closer look at the characteristics of play associated with different age groups will help determine what types of play are most likely to appeal to children in various chronological groupings. Even though developing playful curriculum, supportive environments, and interaction strategies for infants and toddlers is beyond the scope of this text, it is an appropriate way to begin examining the development of play in young children.

Infants and Toddlers: The Play of Children from Birth through Age Three.   Much of the playful behavior of infants is characterized by exploration. Infants engage all of their senses when in the process of figuring out their world. They examine an object from every angle. They manipulate and move objects any way they can. At one time or another, most objects will end up in the baby's mouth. When infants and toddlers are in the act of exploring an object, a person, or a new environment, they often appear very serious. Their affect is not what we normally associate with play. However, as an object, person, or environment becomes more familiar, the child's actions are likely to become more spontaneous and relaxed, more playful. It is in this context that infants and toddlers are most likely to experiment and develop new ways of interacting with the objects and people in their environment.

Infants and toddlers spend much of their waking hours involved in practice play. As they learn to do interesting (to them) things, they repeat them over and over just for the pleasure of it. For example, babbling can be seen as a baby's way of experimenting with his or her ability to produce sounds. This production feels good, is interesting, and brings positive responses from care providers. Therefore the baby repeats and repeats these babbles, and in the process, the babbles become more complex. They eventually grow into words, then into phrases, and then into sentences.

Another example of the effects of practice play relates to the motor development of both infants and toddlers. As children learn to coordinate their movements, they practice, and as they practice, their motor abilities become more refined. Soon toddlers are walking, running, and climbing for the pure pleasure of it. These actions put them in situations where they have opportunities to develop cognitive, language, and social skills.

A third characteristic of infant and toddler play is the development of symbolic understanding. As they play with the objects and people in their world, infants and toddlers develop object permanence, the idea that something or someone still exists even when out of sight. Children then learn to represent an object or person with the mental idea or symbol of that object or person. This understanding sets the stage for the development of language and the use of pretense and fantasy.

Preschool: The Play of Three- and Four-Year-Old Children.   The play of preschool children is dominated by exploration and fantasy. The main purpose for their play seems to be to refine their skills and act out the scripts of their lives. Young three-year-old children or novice players of any age will spend much of their play time in solitary or parallel play as they work out their own ideas. This solitary or parallel play may be exploratory, or it may involve pretense or construction.

In exploratory play, the process of playing is more important to the child than any product he or she might produce. It is common to see three- and four-year-old children gleefully mixing all colors of modeling clay until they have one big grayish wad. The resulting creation is of little interest. Rather, the process of mixing and wadding is in itself immensely satisfying. Much of the child's exploratory or practice play will take the form of motor play. Three- and four-year-old children will run, hop, jump, climb, and wheel tricycles purely for pleasure. In the process, they practice and refine their skills and test their personal abilities.

The preschool period could be called the golden years of pretend or fantasy play. This play evolves from simple symbolic representations such as using a block to represent a telephone. Soon the child is using the block to represent the telephone and acting out a scene in which he or she is calling his or her mother at work. This would be called dramatic play. When children begin to involve others in their dramatic play, sociodramatic play has emerged. The complexity of this play grows as the players become better able to think abstractly and as they gain experience as social negotiators.

Generally, three- and four-year-old children do not initiate games with rules and are frustrated when they are expected to engage in them without close adult support. Motor and music games that have implied rules and structures can be fun for the youngest or the most novice players only if the action of the game satisfies the children's urge to practice motor skills or engage in pretense. It is interesting to watch a group of young players recreate a motor or music game. They generally will revise the rules and develop a version of the game that only slightly resembles the original form introduced by the teacher. Thus, "Duck, Duck, Goose" may become "Cat, Dog, Moo." With time and experience, children's made-up rules come closer and closer to the external rules of the games they play.

Early Primary Grades: The Play of Five- and Six-Year-Old Children.   Kindergarten and first-grade children engage in practice play to help them refine their skills and use them to accomplish self-set goals. Practice play abounds with the memorization of songs and simple action games. Physical activities such as running, skipping, jumping, and hopping are practiced in the context of musical action games. Exploration with art materials continues, and children begin to shift their attention from enjoying the process to creating a recognizable product that represents their ideas. In this way, children focus back and forth from the process of play to the goal or product of play. When they are first learning a skill or refining an ability, their goal is more focused on the process. As they gain ability, they enjoy using this ability to create something else. Erikson (1963) would describe this as the quality of initiative. For example, while playing with modeling clay, children might initially enjoy rolling out long strings. They may spend all of their time at the art table rolling one string after another, then setting aside and ignoring each one. After rolling strings is mastered, however, the strings are created more intentionally to serve as snakes, handles for baskets, or hot dogs and fries for a pretend restaurant.

This shifting from process to product is also evident in the constructive play of children in the early primary grades. Children build structures with a play goal in mind and are often successful in meeting that goal. For example, a group of children may begin play with the intention of creating a space station. Over the course of a few days, they are able to transform a large cardboard box into a facsimile of a space station with the help of paint, paper, other boxes, and glue. The focus of their play moves back and forth from the process of making the station to the goal of construction. They probably do not spend too much time thinking about how they are going to play with the station once it is finished.

The sociodramatic play of children in kindergarten and first grade generally becomes more cooperative in nature. Children develop the ability to take turns and negotiate roles and plots. Children will often gather their own props for play. Whereas younger children are very literal in their use of props, five- and six-year-old children do not necessarily need to be quite as literal. At this age, there is a tendency for hero play; it is common for a particular play scenario to have two or even three children pretending to be the same superhero character.

In regard to games with rules, kindergarten and first-grade children are in the process of developing an understanding of rules. Many times, as they develop this understanding they will become very rigid when enforcing rules. As a result, rules often distract children from their play and become a source of conflict among players. This is one reason teachers see so many tattletales in kindergarten and first grade. Children understand that there are rules, but they are not yet able to apply rules in a flexible, reasonable manner. What they need is to have the support of adults as they play to model how to apply rules and how to understand rules.

Middle Childhood: The Play of Seven- and Eight-Year-Old Children. The middle childhood years generally correspond to second and third grade in schools that use the traditional approach to grouping by chronological age. At this age, children display a need for order, a need to belong, and a need to master the tools for literacy and numeracy. This corresponds to Erikson's fourth stage of development, *industry versus inferiority* (1963), and children's play reflects these needs. Through practice play, children in middle childhood consolidate their knowledge and skills. Playing jacks or marbles, jumping rope, or playing board games gives children opportunities to consolidate knowledge, refine skills, and commit facts to memory (Casbergue & Kieff, 1998). Not all practice play is of a physical nature. For many children, reading and writing their own stories transcends the dichotomy of work and play created by teachers.

Constructive play may not be as visible at this age, at least in a classroom context. This may be partly because of the lack of opportunities provided in schools. It is rare to see blocks in first-grade classrooms, not to mention second- and third-grade rooms. Children at this age do engage in constructive play, however, as evidenced by the popularity of Legos, erector sets, and other construction toys. In school, children's creative efforts take on a constructive tone as they strive to recreate their reality or explore their interests through art, music, and drama. When children are supported in project work, they often construct models of objects that are related to the topic they are studying.

In middle childhood, the themes and scripts of children's fantasy play become more realistic and correlated to their life experiences. Their growing knowledge of the outside world readily informs their drama, and at the same time, their dramas serve to create a refined understanding of their own world.

This is the age at which games with rules become very important. Children become able to negotiate with others concerning existing rules and are able to apply rules in a more flexible manner. Athletic ventures such as soccer and softball become important because they allow children to combine their physical talents and their need to expand their social world. Board games and computer games have the same effect, as they allow children to combine their intellectual and social abilities.

Experience

Although the play of infants, toddlers, preschoolers, and primary-grade children differs according to age, the stages of the play often overlap. One reason for this overlap is children's level of experience, or the opportunities the child has had or has been denied. For example, many kindergarten children are able to engage successfully in associative or cooperative play. However, their ability to do so is related directly to the opportunities they have had to play with other children. If a child has several brothers and sisters, both older and younger, his or her opportunities to play with siblings affects both the rate and quality of his or her development of associative or cooperative play.

Similarly, some children enter group child care situations or preschools at an early age and have had significant opportunities to play with other children, whereas others have not. Even though onlooker or parallel play is more common among three- and four-year-old children, it would not be unusual to see a five-year-old engage in onlooker or parallel play if this child has not had opportunities to play with other children.

It is often useful to think of each child's experience on a continuum from novice to expert. A child who is a novice at playing with blocks has never seen blocks before or at least has never had the opportunity to engage in block play. This child's play will be qualitatively different from that of a child who has had many opportunities to play with blocks in many situations. In this way, experience is a factor affecting the quality of children's play.

Gender

Traditional literature in child development portrays the play of boys and the play of girls to be qualitatively different. In recent years, there has been much discussion regarding the accuracy of this portrayal (Schlank & Metzger, 1997). Researchers have tried to determine if the difference between the play of girls and the play of boys is inherent (biologically driven) or due to environmental factors such as opportunities provided by families and schools.

Generally, research indicates that "girl toys" and "boy toys" and each gender's themes and topics for play have not changed much in the last fifty years, despite concerted efforts on the part of some parents, teachers, and the feminist movement. Boys tend to engage in more rough-and-tumble play, develop aggressive themes in their fantasy play, and use vehicles and building materials in constructive play, whereas girls are more likely to engage in sedentary indoor play, develop domestic roles for themselves in fantasy play, and engage in their need to construct through engaging in art and craft projects (Cunningham, Jones, & Taylor, 1994; DiPietro, 1981; Johnson & Ershler, 1981; Powlishta, Serbin, & Moller, 1993; Smith & Inder, 1993).

Today we encourage teachers and families to adopt a gender-free attitude when selecting toys and providing play opportunities. Studies agree that cross-gender toys and activities are more commonly observed in girls' play than in boys', suggesting that girls may be more flexible in their gender-stereotyped play (Halliday & McNaughton, 1982). Halliday and McNaughton also suggest that the structured nature of teacher-guided tasks may, in fact, limit girls' opportunities to use materials in novel ways and to negotiate conflicts without reliance on adults. It is important that both boys and girls have these opportunities.

It is also important for children to understand that no longer does gender serve as a hindrance for certain occupations and professions. Women certainly have proved to be successful astronauts and physicists, and men have proved to be successful nurses and secretaries. Therefore, both boys and girls need multiple opportunities to select their own themes when they play, be they traditional "boy" themes or traditional "girl" themes.

Culture

In addition to age, experience, and gender, the complexity of play is affected by socioeconomic status and cultural factors. In a seminal study, Smilansky (1968) found that the play of children from Israeli middle-class families was more complex than that of children from Israeli lower-class families. Similar differences in complexity were also found in studies in the United States and England (Fein & Stork, 1981; Griffing, 1980; Rubin, Maioni, & Hornung, 1976). One premise that may account for this difference is that children of poverty may be provided fewer opportunities to play because of parents' belief that play is not essential or even important (Tizard & Hughes, 1976). This parental attitude is reflected in the amount of private space provided for play, parental modeling, and make-believe activities and in efforts to help children make sense of experience (Udwin & Shmukler, 1981).

As noted in Chapter 1, several factors have been found to contribute to differences in play observed across cultures. Sutton-Smith and Heath (1981) describe two major modes of imaginative expression seen in play; the first is oral style and the second is literate style. Oral style refers to the fact that children's expressions are related to real life events and coordinated with the responses of others in the group. Therefore, children from different cultures will not only use different verbal expressions but also accompany those expressions with different nonverbal cues. Furthermore, the language patterns of culture differ.

Literate style refers to the way children express themselves regarding experiences that are distant from real life. Some children come to school with the ability to think in abstract terms about concepts they have not physically encountered. They begin to display these abilities in ways that most resemble school literacy tasks, such as reading and writing. Other children may bring to school abilities that are not as easily recognized and valued, such as the ability to tell long, circular stories comprised of episodes that all revolve around a central theme. Teachers who do not recognize this literate style may believe the child is talking aimlessly, not recognizing that the linear narrative style of western cultures is foreign in many other cultures.

Another cultural factor that creates differences in the way children play is the setting and environment of the play. Griffing (1980) found that children who are capable of engaging in complex play may not do so in settings such as the traditional classroom. In other words, children may be very capable of complex constructive or dramatic play in one setting, say, at home, but do not transfer that complexity to play that occurs at school. One reason might be that these children are given the strong message at home that school is not a place to play. Tizard and Hughes (1976) reported that children in England from low socioeconomic backgrounds exhibited more complex levels of play outdoors than indoors. Curry (1977) told of Navajo children who did not play in the housekeeping corner until the furniture was moved next to the walls for cleaning. Only then did the room resemble the familiar context of their round hogans, allowing them enough comfort to relax and play. The presence of adults in some settings may make some children wary of playing in fully expressive ways (McLoyd, 1982; Pellegrini, 1984); other children find the presence of an adult to be stimulating and supportive.

The important thing for teachers to remember is that differences in play abilities and styles among children are just that—differences, not deficits. Because of cultural background or socioeconomic levels, children may display diverse content in their imaginative play or a difference in preferred social structure while playing. This should not be taken as a disability or deficit that needs to be corrected or remediated, but should be viewed instead as a difference to be valued and respected.

General Health

Another consideration regarding the differences we see in the play of children is their general health and well-being. Play is considered by most leaders in special education as an important element of children's lives and education (Fewell & Kaminski, 1988; Linder, 1990). However, children with special needs may require more structure or more guidance during play activities. Special considerations such as adaptive equipment, specialized instruction, and structured adult intervention may be necessary to make sure that learning, development and enjoyment result from play episodes.

Children with special needs may lack the experiences or abilities to initiate, enter, or sustain play with typically developing playmates. Teachers may need to design strategies that facilitate play between typically developing children and children with special needs. All children need to be guided as they learn to reciprocate overtures that lead to associative and cooperative play. Supporting play in inclusive settings is beneficial to all children and adults involved. We will continue to discuss, throughout the text, ways to embed play into inclusive early childhood settings.

Embedding Play into the Culture of the Classroom

The possibilities for improving Ms. Griffith's game suggest that with an understanding of the theories and categories of children's play, as well as a sense of how to match play experiences to children's perceptions and needs, a teacher has the tools to facilitate learning and development by creating a classroom culture that accepts play and playfulness as a powerful teaching and learning tool. Mrs. Griffith's experience also highlights the fact that embedding play into the culture of the classroom is often confusing and difficult, in large part because play is so multidimensional, and therefore does not fit neatly into distinct curriculum areas. The relationship of play to the learning domains is so integrated that within a single play episode, cognitive, social, and motor learning can all be observed by the teacher. Different children will exhibit different learning in the same episode.

A second difficulty in developing a classroom culture oriented to playful learning results from conflicting views about where to focus children's time and energy. Should children's energy be focused on activities that result in understanding a process for learning, which often looks to adults like play? Or should children's energy be focused on developing a product that results from learning, which often looks to adults like work? This is an example of how adults' organization and analytic view of play may be at odds with children's perceptions. Teachers often feel pressured by parents and administrators to define their jobs in ways that emphasize a dichotomy between work and play. This dichotomy reinforces teachers' beliefs that there must be tangible products in order to demonstrate that the work of learning (and teaching) has been accomplished. It can be difficult to find a product, especially an academic product, in the types of play we see in classrooms.

A final difficulty teachers encounter when attempting to develop a classroom culture that is oriented toward playful learning is that play is so different for different children. As has been noted, these differences are a product of age, experience, cultural expectations, and special needs. Play reflects the development of individual children and is influenced by the culture of peers in the classroom, the culture of the families represented, and the culture of society at large. Play can be both social and private. It can be a difficult task for teachers to structure classroom play that accommodates the needs of the diverse population of students in their classrooms.

Placing play at the center of the curriculum for young children has historically been a focus of early childhood education. No research exists that diminishes the importance of play to the learning and development of young children. However, new information regarding multiple ways of knowing and cultural contributions to learning and the recognition of the diversity that exists within any classroom of young children requires early childhood educators to question any singular approach to curriculum development. In 1997, the National Association for the Education of Young Children (NAEYC) published revised guidelines for developmentally appropriate practice (Bredekamp & Copple, 1997). These guidelines were revised based on new information about children's growth and development and a rethinking of the factors that affect growth. They guide the process by which professionals make decisions about the well-being and education of young children. They do not attempt to prescribe actual practice, because important factors that affect children's learning and development vary greatly, both among children in any given classroom and across the spectrum of programs and classrooms serving young children. The guidelines state that decisions concerning practice should be based on three important kinds of information and knowledge:

1. What is known about child development and learning—knowledge of age-related human characteristics that permits general predictions within an age range about what activities, materials, interactions, or experience will be safe, healthy, interesting, achievable, and also challenging to children;
2. What is known about the strengths, interests, and needs of each individual child in the group to be able to adapt for and be responsive to inevitable individual variation; and
3. Knowledge of the social and cultural contexts in which children live to ensure the learning experiences are meaningful, relevant, and respectful for the participating children and their families.

Furthermore each of these dimensions of knowledge—human development and learning, individual characteristics and experiences, and social and cultural contexts—is dynamic and changing, requiring that early childhood teachers remain learners throughout their careers. (p. 9)

Therefore, considering age-appropriate activities, individually appropriate activities, and culturally appropriate activities is essential to developing appropriate curriculum and classroom cultures that facilitate learning and development for all children.

There is no question about the importance of play in the lives of young children and in the classrooms that serve them. The question is one of degree and perception. Should play be the center of early childhood curriculum? Are art experiences and music experiences always to be considered play? Are experiences that drive children to count and write always to be considered work? Again, we, as educators, seem to be facing dichotomous choices. However, the guidelines for developmentally appropriate practice (Bredekamp & Copple, 1997) attempt to avoid strict dichotomies by stating the need to move from an either/or position to a both/and position. Young children need to both play and work in classrooms. And yet, because of diverse backgrounds, the play of one child may be the work of another. It is therefore important to view play and playfulness as a necessary aspect of appropriate early childhood classrooms. It is also important to accept the role of play in early childhood curricula as variable, dependent on the individual and cumulative needs of a particular classroom. In many classrooms, it will be important to center the curriculum around the play of the children.

In other classrooms, it will be more feasible to tear down the dichotomy of work and play by embedding the curriculum with multiple, rich opportunities for play. The chapters that follow offer specific suggestions for embedding play and playfulness into the culture of classrooms so that the needs of all children can be met. We offer a view of play that is flexible, integrated, and supportive of learning goals common to the teachers and care providers of children enrolled in preschool and primary programs.

Developing Advocacy Skills

In the introduction to *The State of America's Children, Yearbook 1997,* Edelman gives suggestions for those who advocate for children: "Ignore labels and just do what you've got to do." (p. xix). She is referring specifically to the labels used in political circles to identify and qualify a person's actions or beliefs. Examples of these labels include *liberal*, *conservative*, *radical*, and *extreme*. It is important to note that all labels tend to be subjective in nature. We see labeling in early childhood settings too, and these labels are also subjective in nature. For example, in one setting, a teacher who works to embed into curriculum opportunities for play and playful learning may be called progressive, whereas in another setting, this same teacher may be called permissive. The problem with labels is that they narrowly define the actions, attitudes, and abilities of those they are meant to describe. Narrow descriptions create narrow judgments. Narrow judgments prevent important discussions concerning possible actions and abilities. Therefore, labels trap us by creating barriers that prevent problem-solving. Teachers and care providers who wish to advocate for embedding playful opportunities into early childhood curriculum first need to recognize when labels are preventing new ideas from emerging. Then they should choose to ignore labels and keep doing what they need to do.

We also use labels in early childhood settings to describe children. Children are defined by age, race, ethnicity, social class, gender, and ability. Early childhood practitioners must guard against letting labels define children's possibilities. The best way to know about a child's abilities and possibilities is to watch the child in many situations, and ask questions—many questions—of those who know the child best: the family. Isn't it wonderful that children naturally follow Edelman's advice? They just do what they've got to do. They play.

You can learn to advocate for children and their need for play by recognizing when labels trap you and prevent you from engaging in problem-solving activities. You will also need to learn to ignore labels others might attach to active learning environments and forge ahead by informing others about the benefits of learning through play. Specific activities that will help you do this are outlined in Table 2.1, which suggests ways for you to become more skillful at informing families and administrators about children's needs for play.

Summary

There are five essential elements of play that impact the extent to which it contributes to children's learning: a focus on process over product; degree of intrinsic motivation; a tendency toward nonliteral play; freedom to experiment with rules; and degree of mental activity involved. To foster learning and development through play, teachers and care providers need to develop an understanding of how to match children's play experiences with a variety of factors, including level of social participation, children's ages, levels of experience, gender, social class, cultural background, and special needs. Advocates for children's right to play must guard against becoming trapped by labels that prevent problem-solving and positive action.

TABLE 2.1 Advocacy Activities: Informing and Involving Families and Administrators

	Ignore Labels	
Becoming Aware	*Furthering Your Understanding*	*Taking Action*
1. Observe children playing both at home and in a school setting. Note the differences in their play and in their play opportunities in both settings. What elements of play do you observe? What categories of play do you observe?	1. Focus your attention on one of the categories of play outlined in this chapter. Find journal articles that discuss how this type of play facilitates learning and development, and how it can be incorporated into the classroom.	1. Gain permission from a teacher and parents to photograph or videotape children engaged in different kinds of play at school. Prepare a slide show or video presentation to be made at a parents' association meeting or school open house session. Explain to parents the benefits of such play to their children's learning and development.
2. Participate with children while they are playing in a school setting. Compare this experience to your observations of the children playing without adult participation. In what ways does your interaction with the children change the nature of the children's play?	2. Interview several parents concerning their beliefs about the importance of play and the use of it in classrooms. What similarities and differences in attitudes and beliefs do you notice? Do you hear any labels as they talk about play and their children's schools?	2. Volunteer to visit a classroom with limited resources for play on a regular basis. Bring with you materials (props, portable play equipment, etc.) that you can use to engage the children in play. Leave a written account of what learning and development children exhibit as they play.
3. Observe children with special needs in an inclusive setting. What opportunities do they have for play? How do teachers or caregivers facilitate their play?	3. Interview teachers and administrators about their views on the place of play in the school curriculum. What are their concerns about embedding play into the culture of classrooms? What labels are used?	3. Organize a neighborhood play group and schedule regular play sessions that facilitate children's engagement in different kinds of play. Invite parents to stay and play with the children or watch them play. Use this opportunity to point out to parents new concepts, skills, and abilities the children might be acquiring as a result of their play.
4. Observe the play of a group of children from a culture different from your own. In what ways is their play the same as that of children from your culture? In what ways is it different?	4. Interview an early intervention teacher. What are his or her experiences with facilitating the play of children with special needs in inclusive settings?	

REVISITING FIRST IMPRESSIONS

In your initial reflection, you were asked to envision how you would incorporate play into your classroom. Reread this reflection and revise it based on new information you gathered from reading and discussing this chapter. Pay particular attention to the kinds of information you need to know about children to build on their play and learning style in your classroom. Be sure to use specific terms for different kinds of play and concepts related to play.

QUESTIONS FOR DISCUSSION

1. Use the five elements of play that facilitate learning to analyze each of the following experiences. Determine the degree to which each element is evident in the play described. Based on your analysis, which experience is most likely to enhance learning? Explain why.

   a. Three-year-old Daniel is standing in front of the refrigerator playing with magnetic letters while his mother fixes breakfast. He lines up an M, an H, and an O, then says, "L, D, T says eggs and bacon!" He slides five more letters into a row and repeats the process of calling out random letter names and "reading" the "words" he has formed. He continues this process until his mother calls him to breakfast.

   b. A class of seven-year-old children is playing a game of math facts Bingo. Each child has a card with five columns of five numbers. The teacher calls out, "Seven plus three." All those who have the number ten on their cards cover it with a marker. The game ends when someone gets five in a row and calls out, "Bingo!" The teacher then checks to see that all of the numbers marked were in fact called. She then decides if there is enough time for another round. If so, the game is repeated.

   c. A kindergarten class is busy at centers. Joy has chosen to work at the manipulative center. She has a box of buttons and is sorting them by color. When she finishes, she counts the buttons in each category. Then she mixes all the buttons together again and starts over. Winston has been watching Joy sort the buttons and sits down across the table from her. Winston says, "Let's sort the buttons together. I'll find all the big ones and you find all the little ones." The two work together for the next ten minutes discussing the size of each button to determine if it goes in the pile with the big buttons or the pile with the little ones. As they work they develop a pile of medium-sized buttons.

2. As a preschool teacher, you have noticed that several children in your class are unable to identify colors. You work with them individually and provide direct instruction related to learning color names. However, you want to provide other experiences that will help them develop an understanding of color and color identification. Devise three playful strategies that might support these children's learning.

3. Paul is a first grader. He enjoys constructing buildings from unit blocks and prefers to play alone. He does not choose to draw, paint, or play with clay. John is in the same class. He builds roadways and bridges with unit blocks and usually involves several other children. Their constructions often lead to dramatic play using cars, trucks, and figures of construction workers. John does occasionally choose to draw, paint, and play with clay, and when he does, his work often reflects road construction themes. Invent histories for Paul and John that account for the differences in their play.

SUGGESTED READINGS

Delpit, L. (1995). *Other people's children: Cultural conflicts in the classroom.* New York: New Press.

Schlank, C.H., & Metzger, B. (1997). *Together and equal: Fostering cooperative play and promoting gender equity in early childhood programs.* Boston: Allyn & Bacon.

Spodek, B., & Saracho, O.N. (1994). *Dealing with individual differences in the early childhood classroom.* White Plains, NY: Longman.

PART TWO

Connecting Play Theory and Practice in Preschool Programs and Primary Classrooms

CHAPTER

3 Embedding Play into Curricula

Prereading Guide

First Impressions. Visualize a typical day in your ideal classroom. What are your students doing today? What is the general mood of the class? What is the worst thing that happened today? What is the best thing that happened today? How do you feel as the day comes to an end? How do your students feel? What do you think they learned today? Write several paragraphs describing this day.

Revisit
Characteristics of Play That Facilitate Learning and Development (Chapter 2)

Stories from the Field

The following is taken from the transcript of an interview with a second-grade teacher, Mrs. Gonzales. At the time of this interview, Mrs. Gonzales had been teaching for five years in a public elementary school in the southwestern United States.

INTERVIEWER: Mrs. Gonzales, would you please describe your class and classroom.

MRS. GONZALES: Well, I have a regular size classroom. I suppose it would seem cluttered to most people because we have both tables and desks, three computers, our own library, and I insisted on keeping the sand/water table I used when I taught kindergarten. The other second-grade teachers raise their eyebrows a little when they see these big kids at the water table, but the children enjoy it so much and are always improvising new ways to use it. I also kept my puppet stage and puppets. I have twenty-two students. Their abilities range from kindergarten-level reading, just knowing the alphabet and beginning to write their names, to reading at fourth- and fifth-grade level. All my students feel comfortable with basic adding and subtracting. Some are interested in learning to multiply and divide, while others are working on memorizing addition and subtraction facts. I have two students that are mainstreamed into my classroom. Sarah, has cerebral palsy and is in a wheelchair. It is hard for her to speak so she communicates through a computerized device. David has emotional problems. He is difficult to motivate at times and often creates a fuss when he doesn't get his way, but most of the time I can get him involved with a project or activity, and he is delightful and adds a lot to the group.

About half of the students in my class are eligible for free or reduced lunch so I know many are coming from poor families. My students are certainly not all from traditional two-parent families. In fact, I think less than half of them are living with both biological parents. I know two are living in foster homes and one child is living with her grandmother.

INTERVIEWER: How would you describe the culture of your classroom?

MRS. GONZALES: I am not sure exactly what you mean. There is quite a mixture of cultural backgrounds represented by the families of the students in the class. Probably half the students are Hispanic. Three families recently immigrated from Mexico and one from Cuba. The others are native to the United States. We have twins whose family is from Vietnam. We also have several African American children, and I guess the rest are European American.

INTERVIEWER: What I was really trying to get you to discuss was the culture, the ambience of your classroom. Classroom culture refers to some of the assumptions and unwritten rules that influence how everyone interacts with each other. What is the feel of the classroom? How do you all get along?

MRS. GONZALES: I see what you mean. Well, let's see. You know it is really hard to describe a culture, as you call it, when you are a part of it. Having observed my class the past few days, you could probably describe it better than I. We all get along very well. I work hard at that. It is important to me that the students develop tolerance, even appreciation for each other. I want them to understand how they are alike, and how they are different. We have a lot of fun during the day. I work hard at that too. I want them to want to come back tomorrow. I want to want to come back tomorrow!

We usually start the morning with a planning session. Each child makes a schedule for the day that fits into our overall schedule. They set daily goals for themselves. Because they are so different in their reading and their math abilities, all the activities we do together have to be very open-ended. I mean, we can all be studying the same general concepts, ideas, themes, but going about it in different ways and finding different ways to contribute to each other's learning and understanding. I use centers and organize group activities around a theme. That way we have some common goals that we work towards together. Right now we are studying emergency rooms, ambulances, and emergency medical technicians because Joey fell down a flight of stairs and had to go to the emergency room. Everyone was intrigued by all the stories he told after this experience, and I wasn't quite sure whether everything he said was quite accurate, so we started piecing together bits of information. I encourage the children to work together in pairs or in trios on projects that interest them. Several students wanted to create a little emergency room right here in the classroom. We improvised with the sand/water table and are using it for an examining table.

So you can see there is a lot of movement and conversation in my classroom. Someone walking by might think the children were playing most of the time. Maybe we are. I can't always tell whether the children are working or playing.

That used to bother me. I was concerned that they were playing too much and would not do the "real learning" they needed to do. However, I spend a great deal of time observing them. They seem to switch back and forth from work to play so often that I stopped trying to categorize their activities. Now I trust that they learn when they are engaged, so I just look for engagement. As I walk around, I watch and listen to see if they are engaged. If they are, I listen to see what I can do to support them or challenge them so that they extend their thinking and understanding. If they are not engaged, then I find a way to engage them.

INTERVIEWER: I assume that your school, like most schools, has a required curriculum. With all that is going on in your classroom, do you have time to meet the mandated requirements?

MRS. GONZALES: Well, of course. It isn't an option. I certainly have to be flexible and I certainly have to be organized. In fact, I generally reorganize the mandated curriculum by combining skill and content requirements into themes or content studies. I find that curriculum guidelines and goals put forth by the school board and the state are just minimums—the place to begin planning. As far as the mandated goals are concerned, they are generally written in the form of skills that should be mastered or knowledge that should be acquired during a certain grade. When I pretest students, I find that some already have mastered many of the skills or know the information required. Some, of course, are not quite ready to study these things or acquire these skills. So, the required curriculum does not necessarily match the needs of my students. It is just a place for me to start thinking about what the children need. Like I said, I have to be very organized and keep careful records so I know who needs to be working on what skills.

I certainly make sure I include the school's goals in my planning, but I always go beyond these goals. I think about what I want the children to be like when they grow up, what attitudes and dispositions they will need to continue learning and to be successful in the future. I talk with their families about what they value for their children and then plan the activities that pull it all together. I have learned to trust the power of play. Through play, children have the opportunities to practice their skills, learn useful information, and develop the dispositions that are important to their future success. For example, with this emergency room theme we are developing right now, the children wanted to make an x-ray machine, but none of us knew anything about x-rays or what machines looked like. Some of the children drew pictures of what they thought the machines would look like. It seems that our idea of x-rays was a bit outdated. Some parents took four of the students to a radiology lab one Saturday. The students were able to bring back pictures, diagrams, and sketches of an imaging machine.

Again, it is hard to tell whether they were working or playing when they are engaged in all of this, but it isn't hard to see that they are learning. There is no mistake about that. I love to see them exercise such initiative.

INTERVIEWER: From listening to you talk about your classroom, it seems that one could say that one characteristic of the culture in your class room is playfulness. Would you agree with that assessment? Do you find that you are criticized for taking this playful approach? How do you handle that criticism?

MRS. GONZALES: Well, yes, I guess you could call my class playful, and, yes, I was criticized when I first started teaching second grade this way. I moved to second grade three years ago. I had completed my student teaching in kindergarten and then found a temporary position as a kindergarten teacher in another school. I loved teaching kindergarten, but in order to get a permanent position, I had to take a second-grade classroom. In the beginning it was really stressful. It seemed that I forgot everything I knew about children and child development. I forgot about the power of play. Well, I didn't really forget, I just didn't think it applied to second grade. I pushed the kids and would only let them play after they had been working for a scheduled amount of time, and then I just let them alone when they played. I did a lot of direct teaching and a lot of whole-class instruction the way it seemed the other second-grade teachers were teaching, but it just didn't work for me or for the children in that class. None of us were particularly happy.

One day, towards the end of the first year, the physical education teacher was absent and I took the class out to the field for exercise. As we were walking back to the classroom, we discovered a beautiful patch of wildflowers. We were all intrigued and we spent more time there than I had planned. When we got back to the classroom, I gave up the next activity I had planned and let the children draw pictures of the wildflowers they had seen. This was a radical departure from my lesson plans and I remember feeling guilty about it at the time. The next day, three of the students brought bouquets of wildflowers to class. We couldn't resist. Together, we developed a project centered on the wildflowers we had found in our field. We played with all the possible ways we could learn about these flowers. We even set up centers, in a second-grade class! Now that was considered somewhat radical for this school. But in the process, I rediscovered what I always knew about children. If I allowed children to lead then I could incorporate the skills and knowledge they needed as they went along.

Looking back on it, I have to say that something magical happened to that class that day. We had been together nearly a full year but had never really become a group, a community, but because they began to share an interest and information, and because they had more time to talk and play together, they began to appreciate each other in a very special way.

Yes, I did get criticized when I began to use themes, projects, and centers, and when my students began to look like they were spending a great deal of time playing. Much of the criticism came from the other teachers. I remember hearing one teacher say to another, "Well, she's young. She will learn." The principal did call me in and we had a long chat one day. She was concerned about the children's preparation for the standardized tests that would begin in third grade. But I had charted the students' progress on the mandated goals and I had incorporated the knowledge goals from several of our science units into the wildflowers theme. She was satisfied with my planning and the documented progress of my students.

Generally parents have always been supportive, because I keep them informed as to how their child is progressing and what we are learning together. Sometimes, a parent will express concern that their child is playing too much. I discuss my understanding of learning and how that might look like play. I try to find out how they define play and why they are worried. Generally, these open discussions resolve their concerns. I think that relieves some pressure on the children too. They want to please their parents and their teachers, and they want to learn and have fun too.

After the experience with the wildflower project, I was hooked and now I am refining this, as you put it, playful approach to teaching and learning. I do not feel the criticism of others much any more. Actually, I am my strongest critic. Sometimes I get hassled and worry about test scores and if the kids can make it in the next grade. But then, all I have to do is watch them and I know that because they are learning how to learn and when to apply their skills, that they will be ready for anything. It is interesting, but this year two of the other second-grade teachers are working with the idea of centers and projects in their classrooms.

Learning Goals for Young Children

The power play has in facilitating the learning and development of young children has been well documented in the literature (Brunner, 1966; Fromberg, 1992; Piaget, 1962; Vygotsky, 1978). Creating a classroom culture that is characterized by playful attitudes and opportunities to learn through play takes imagination and dedication. It also requires trust in oneself and trust in children's ability to initiate and guide their own learning. A closer look at Mrs. Gonzales' teaching style will reveal some essential characteristics of playful learning and teaching.

Mrs. Gonzales is able to *visualize long-term as well as short-term goals* for her students. Much thought is given to the qualities and characteristics that the children will need to become lifelong learners. She *adapts* mandated curriculum and learning goals to fit the needs of individual students in her classroom and to foster those qualities and characteristics she values.

Mrs. Gonzales *understands and uses knowledge of child development* as she plans for learning. She knows that children have different abilities and different interests and she takes these into account when planning. She *respects families'* differing attitudes toward play and provides multiple opportunities for children to work and play in their own way. She *articulates and demonstrates* to families and administrators how the curriculum goals are being met even when her classroom does not look or sound like other classrooms.

Mrs. Gonzales is not afraid to have fun with her students or let students have fun. She *values play for the sake of play* and is willing to wait for the long term to see the positive effects of play. She sees learning as engagement and recognizes that different children engage in learning in different ways. Sometimes this engagement looks like play and sometimes it looks like work. Therefore, she does not worry about whether the child is working or playing, but appreciates the consistent movement back and forth from work to play.

Mrs. Gonzales *displays confidence and high self-esteem.* She sees herself as a lifelong learner and is anxious to learn with her students. She creates situations in which she and her students plan together. She *can live with ambiguity,* not knowing exactly what will happen or how things will turn out. She recognizes teachable moments and is able to *improvise activities* that capitalize on these moments. She *trusts* herself to figure things out and she trusts that children will figure things out when given the opportunity. She visualizes her role as teacher as a guide, a facilitator, a record keeper, and a resource person.

Mrs. Gonzales *welcomes cognitive dissonance.* In fact, she creates it when planning learning opportunities and when interacting with the children as they work and play. Dissonance, you will remember from the story about Jackson and the pagers in Chapter 1, is finding the unexpected and thinking one thing will happen, when actually something else happens. These surprises create disequilibrium and thus drive adaptation and learning.

Mrs. Gonzales is *flexible.* She *provides open-ended tasks* and opportunities for children. She will rearrange her schedule if an opportunity arises. She is willing to switch courses if a better plan presents itself. She is not stuck with the tradition of doing things the way they have always been done, because she understands that there is more than one way to reach learning goals.

The first step toward developing the characteristics displayed by Mrs. Gonzales and creating a culture of playfulness is understanding how play facilitates the satisfaction of both long-term and short-term goals common to early childhood programs. A second step is to develop a way to organize curricula that provide children opportunities to learn in playful ways. In this chapter we will first examine goals common to early childhood programs and then discuss how these goals can be satisfied when children have multiple opportunities for meaningful play. We will also examine different models of integrated curriculum and demonstrate how combining elements of these models provides a framework for planning a curriculum that fosters playful learning while preserving and respecting the right of each child to develop and learn in his/her own unique way.

Knowledge Goals

There are many ways to categorize the learning that takes place in early childhood. One common goal we have for young children is that they learn new information, or that they gain knowledge. Piaget (1952) identified three types of knowledge useful to young children's attempts to organize and understand their world: physical, logico-mathematical, and social knowledge. Physical knowledge includes information and understandings that children gain about physical properties of objects as they interact with materials and objects in their environments. For example, after many opportunities to work and play with natural materials such as rocks, a child will come to understand that generally rocks are hard, relatively heavy, and will probably sink when put into water. Of course, a child could simply be told this information, but until he or she has constructed that understanding of hardness and heaviness and *sinkingness,* this information in not usable to solve problems or transferable to other situations.

Logico-Mathematical Knowledge.   Logico-mathematical knowledge is the knowledge and understanding of relationships. Children construct this knowledge as they encounter and reflect on similarities and differences among the objects or people in their environment. For example, shortness is a property that is relative to the actual objects being compared. A particular twig may be the shortest twig in one group of twigs but the longest in another group. Therefore, a child needs to construct an understanding of this relationship if he or she is to be successful at labeling the twigs as long or short. Logico-mathematical knowledge allows children to successfully organize, categorize, and use information about their world. Again, a child can be taught labels such as longest, shortest, heaviest, and lightest, but the ability to transfer this understanding to different contexts is constructed through repeated opportunities to compare objects and ideas in his or her world.

Social Knowledge.   Social knowledge is information and understanding gained through interaction with others. Social conventions such as sharing, being polite, or waiting for a turn are examples of social knowledge. Vocabulary is also an example of social knowledge. Children learn a great deal of social knowledge as they imitate the models around them. However, the use of social knowledge is dependent on the mental structures created through logico-mathematical knowledge (Kamii, 1982). For example, a child may be asked to set the table for snack time. He knows that he will need to have enough napkins, glasses, and forks for sixteen children, but in order to complete this social task correctly, he will need to understand one to one correspondence as it relates to *sixteenness.*

It is important to distinguish between knowledge (understanding concepts related to physical, logico-mathematical, and social knowledge) and facts and information. Examples of children's understanding of facts and information include naming colors, stating the days of the week, reciting the names of the letters in the alphabet, learning the names of farm or zoo animals, and describing facts about their lives, such as what they eat. Facts and information can be learned in many different ways, including direct instruction and memorization activities. However, the ability to apply and use facts and information to solve new problems is related to children's constructive understanding of relevant physical, logico-mathematical, or social knowledge. For example, a child may have memorized the names of the days of the week in the conventional order—Sunday, Monday, Tuesday, etc.—however, the correct answer to the questions, "What is tomorrow?" and "What day was yesterday?" will depend on an understanding of the relationship between the conventional labels for the days of the week and of the concept of "day" and "week." The understanding of this relationship and the concepts involved cannot be taught directly, and cannot be inferred through the memorized order, but must be constructed by the child.

Play provides a context in which the child encounters a need to understand this relationship. For example, when children play in the home-living center, they often take on the roles of adults and carry on dialogue that causes them to experiment with logico-mathematical relationships and work out meaning. The following dialogue is typical of the kind of thinking and problem-solving children encounter as they play.

Make-believe mother to child: "Today is Thursday and you know what that means. You have to go to the dentist."

Make-believe child to mother: "Oh no. Look at the calendar!" The child points to designated space for Tuesday with one hand and the designated space for Thursday with the other. She then counts the Tuesday and Wednesday spaces. "It is only Tuesday. I have two more days before I have to go to the dentist. Can I have an apple?"

Skill Goals

It is also common in early childhood programs to set skill goals for young children. Skills are things children can do—small units of actions. Examples of skills included in most preschool and kindergarten curricula include cutting, running, reciting the alphabet, identifying colors and shapes, and writing one's name. Examples of skills that are most often included in first- and second-grade curricula are using appropriate punctuation when writing, spelling conventionally, and being able to add subtract, multiply, and divide. Children develop and refine skills in many different ways, such as exploration, direct instruction, peer or adult coaching, and watching others. The quality of any skill will improve through practice and repetition. Drill is practice that is perceived by the child as tedious and is often disconnected from the relevant use of the skill. Children can also improve and practice their skills through play. For example, most second graders understand simple addition and subtraction computation and are ready to memorize math facts. Drill will help them memorize these facts. However, if children have a choice in how they practice, they will concentrate for a longer period of time and show a greater dedication to the process of learning math facts. One child may choose to practice math facts by giving him- or herself timed tests. Another child may prefer working with flash cards. In either case, the child was given the opportunity to choose, and choice adds a playful element to learning.

Disposition Goals

Another category of learning goals is dispositions. Dispositions are mental habits or tendencies to react in consistent ways under similar circumstances (Katz, 1985). For example, when a particular child encounters a new object in his or her environment and he or she generally reacts by examining it, asking questions about it, and expending relentless energy aimed at figuring out what this new object is and what it is used for, we could say that the child is demonstrating the disposition of curiosity. That is, curiosity is a mental habit or an inner motivation for this child.

It is important to distinguish between dispositions and automatic habits such as fastening a seat belt or looking both ways before crossing a street. Automatic habits are certainly important, but they do not describe or contribute to the process of learning in the same way as dispositions. Dispositions describe ways in which one generally goes about making sense out of the objects, people, and situations one encounters in the world. Examples of dispositions that generally support learning and development include creativity, curiosity, humor, independence, initiative, interdependence, persistence, playfulness, resourcefulness, risk-taking, responsibility, and sociocentric thinking.

Of course, not all dispositions represent positive traits, nor will they all support learning. Dispositions that often detract from the learning process include aggressiveness, callousness, impulsivity, and pessimism.

Many dispositions not only support the development of knowledge and skills but also support the application of knowledge and skills in problem solving. For example, most children have listening skills but do not necessarily have the disposition to use them; therefore, they may not be good listeners (Cantor, 1990). In regard to literacy, having word attack skills and comprehension skills does not in itself insure that children will use these skills. However, children who have the disposition to be readers and writers use their skills to learn, to solve problems, and to entertain themselves.

Katz (1985) suggests that some teaching practices employed with young children, specifically extensive drill and practice of unrelated skills and information, may damage the disposition to use those skills and that information. Knowledge and skills not acquired early in life might be acquired later, but dispositions are less amenable to reacquisition once they are damaged.

Dispositions may be innate, inherited characteristics, born into the nature of a child, or they may be learned. Even when a disposition is innate, a child must have opportunities to display it, and it must be recognized and valued in order for it to develop. With supportive experiences, dispositions become robust. Without supportive experiences dispositions may weaken or disappear (Rogoff, Gauvain, & Ellis, 1990). Therefore, if a child has an innate tendency to be curious, but this curiosity is not recognized, valued or supported during the early years, then the disposition will not strengthen and may even be lost to the child.

Katz (1988) maintains that dispositions are not learned from direct instruction or drill and practice the way that facts, information, and skills are learned. Children learn dispositions through the process of modeling. Children learn to be curious by being with adults and peers who are curious. Children learn to be responsible by being in the presence of responsible peers and adults. Therefore it is important for educators to create situations in which they themselves display positive dispositions for learning. This supports the idea of a community of learners—teachers learning with students, teachers writing with students, teachers reading with students. Displaying positive dispositions for learning implies that at times teachers need to think out loud. For example, to model curiosity an educator might say out loud what he or she is thinking: "I wonder what would happen if we did this?"

A second way children learn or strengthen dispositions is by having the opportunities to display dispositions and have them acknowledged. For example, a child may learn to persistently pursue a goal by observing a significant adult pursue goals and then having multiple opportunities to set and pursue his or her own goals. It is important that positive learning dispositions be recognized, valued, and reinforced during the early years in order for them to become a stable part of the child's repertoire of behavior.

The Teacher's Role in Fostering Learning Goals through Play

Play is certainly not the only way children learn. However, when children's play is focused on the process, is intrinsically motivated, does not necessarily require literal interpretation, allows experimentation with rules, and promotes mental activity, a context for meaningful learning is formed. In this context children have the opportunity to

- explore phenomena and develop an understanding of relationships
- develop a repertoire of useful information and facts
- practice skills in meaningful and authentic contexts
- transfer and apply skills to problem-solving situations
- develop dispositions that support learning and the use of knowledge and skills

The context of play is also an efficient use of time in early childhood programs. Through play and playful activities, teachers can meet the individual learning needs of a diverse group of children. When children have the opportunity to play, they tend to choose activities that challenge their current knowledge and understanding. They link prior knowledge and develop new understanding, thus unifying the development of knowledge, skills, and dispositions. As a teacher interacts with the players in the classroom, she or he can challenge the current thinking of one child, suggest a way another child can practice a developing skill within the context of play, or recognize and support a positive disposition being demonstrated by a third. Table 3.1 gives examples of how play provides a context that supports learning goals.

Play is a very powerful and efficient learning and teaching strategy. However, it is not enough for teachers simply to provide opportunities for play. Teachers need to engage with children while they play to facilitate optimal development. Early childhood educators have three major roles regarding young children and play. First, teachers must plan for play by creating environments and schedules, developing and modifying curricula, and advocating for the use of play as a context for learning.

The second role teachers have regarding children's play requires teachers to engage and interact with children as they play. Teachers certainly need to observe children at play, but there are times when more than observation is necessary to promote optimal learning and development. Teachers must be prepared to move in and out of play activities, constantly making decisions about interactions. There will be times when teachers need to observe and record the mental processes children are using as they play. There will also be times when it

TABLE 3.1   Play as a Context for Learning

The learning that takes place in the context of children's play can be illustrated by the following examples. What is listed here is just a small sample of the possible learning outcomes in each scenario.

Three first graders are playing Chutes and Ladders, a board game, during center time.

They are practicing the skills of counting, color matching, and recognition.
They are developing the social skill of taking turns.
They are developing social knowledge through conversational turns.
They are developing the disposition of collaboration.

Two kindergarten children built a space ship with hollow blocks two days ago. They created a scenario depicting life on a space station. Four other children join them. This is the third day of the joint play.

They have experienced solving problems that deal with weight, height, and balance.
They are developing schema and event scripts by experimenting with language concepts and dialogue.
They are developing the disposition of persistence.

Two three-year-old children are playing side by side at the sand box. One fills a bucket with dry sand and dumps it upside down. When he takes the bucket away, the sand forms a soft hill. The second child's actions mirror the first's. The teacher pours a bucket of water into the sand box. Now when the children dump their buckets, they have a very moldable mountain.

They are experimenting with sensory material.
They are developing concepts of wet and dry.
They are experiencing the relationship of cause and effect.
They are learning to share space.

Second-grade children have initiated an impromptu game of dodge ball on the playground at recess.

They are developing and refining motor and perceptual skills.
They are developing an understanding of rules.
They are developing an appreciation for each other's skills and abilities.
They are developing the disposition of initiation and follow through.

Two four-year-old children are at the computer listening and interacting with a software version of *Green Eggs and Ham* by Dr. Seuss. After hearing the story, they play several games and then choose to hear the story again. This time they find a hard copy of the book and follow along.

They are developing computer skills.
They are developing a relationship between print and spoken words.
They are collaborating and taking turns using the mouse.
They developing dispositions to read and to use computers.

is appropriate, even necessary, for teachers to ask children questions that will extend their children's concept knowledge and language. There will be still other times when teachers will need to demonstrate the use of new materials or provide models for positive interactions.

The third role teachers have in children's play is to be accountable for the time children spend playing. Teachers must assess, record, and display children's learning no matter what form that learning takes. Teachers can utilize play as a context for assessing developing knowledge, skills, and dispositions. Teachers will also need to assess play environments to maintain their viability as appropriate contexts for learning. We will now focus on the first role teachers have regarding play: planning for playful learning.

Developing Curricula That Foster Playful Learning

Curriculum is the design of experiences and activities used by teachers to foster children's cognitive, motor, social, and emotional growth and well-being. It encompasses everything that happens to children during the time they spend in school or child care settings (Hendrick, 1998). Some learning is planned through the use of curriculum guides, scope and sequence plans, or prescribed goals and objectives, but much learning happens spontaneously or in an incidental way. Spontaneous learning simply happens in the course of the day. For example, during a storm that flooded the entry to their classroom, kindergarten children learned that they could use the long planks and hollow blocks to create a bridge from the door to the sidewalk so that they could get to the buses without getting their feet wet. Incidental learning occurs in the process of learning something else. For example, while learning the names of the fish in the aquarium, a child might also be learning to recognize the differences in fins, scales, and gills that distinguish each species. Appropriate early childhood curriculum is developed to create a context that supports prescribed, spontaneous, and incidental learning.

Content areas can be defined as unified bodies of concepts, information, and knowledge. In the story that began the chapter, Mrs. Gonzales used content areas related to the emergency room and wildflowers when developing learning experiences and activities. When teachers organize and develop curricula around rich meaningful content, they are able to create a seamless learning environment in which prescribed learning, spontaneous learning, and incidental learning occur in a reciprocal manner. There are many advantages associated with content-driven curriculum. Among these advantages are:

1. Content-driven curricula match the way children think and learn. Because children see the world in a holistic way, not separated into individual domains, skills, facts, or disciplines (Piaget, 1952), they learn best when they have the opportunity to explore information that is presented in relevant wholes, related directly to their lives. In content-driven curriculum, skills develop naturally as children go about the process of making sense of their world, because the skills are necessary and relevant to pursuing questions concerning the theme.

2. Curricula organized around content areas allow efficient use of classroom time because they provide opportunities for children of different abilities to work together on the same subject and learn from each other. This organizational strategy also provides teachers with the opportunity to incorporate mandated curriculum and individualized instruction into a context that is meaningful and relevant to the children in their classes.

3. Curricula organized around rich, meaningful content provide many opportunities to create cognitive dissonance. Cognitive dissonance, sometimes referred to as cognitive conflict or disequilibrium, is that element of surprise that occurs as children interact with objects and people in their world. For example, in Mrs. Gonzales's classroom, the children were surprised to find flowers growing in a field dedicated to play. That surprise created disequilibrium and motivated the children to learn more. Organizing learning experiences around content can lead to collaboration between students and the adults in the classroom around an area of interest. Collaborating with others provides an important source of cognitive dissonance and therefore promotes the restructuring of children's ideas (Brunner, 1986; Donaldson, 1978; Dunn, 1988; Vygotsky, 1962, 1978; Wells, 1988).

4. Content-driven curricula provide children with opportunities to study a topic in-depth, attend to details, and develop the disposition to be thorough and follow through on projects. In-depth learning accounts for some children's expertise in subjects such as environment, recycling, and dinosaurs. When children share their expertise with family and friends, they develop an appreciation for their own intellectual ability. They learn to love learning.

5. Curricula organized around content areas provide more opportunities for meaningful play. Teachers can design play and playful activities that provide children with opportunities to develop understanding of related concepts, expand and unify learning across domains, practice skills in a meaningful way, and develop dispositions that will support lifelong learning.

Models of Content-Driven Curricula

There are many ways to develop content-driven curricula. We will discuss three models commonly used in early childhood education: emergent curriculum, theme exploration, and the project approach.

Emergent Curriculum.   Emergent curriculum is based on the belief that curriculum planning needs to emerge from the daily life of the children and teachers in a learning community. In this model, curriculum is not prescribed in advance, but develops day to day, week to week, based on the observed needs and interests of a particular group of children. According to Jones and Nimmo (1994), "[e]mergent curriculum is sensible but not predictable. It requires of its practitioners *trust in the power of play*—trust in spontaneous choices among many possibilities" (p. 1). Therefore, emergent curriculum is a dynamic process of planning curriculum that relies on the teacher's ability to capitalize on spontaneous events that happen in the course of the children's daily experiences living and playing together.

It is not correct to think of emergent curriculum as an "anything goes" approach to teaching. On the contrary, in this model, curriculum results from negotiating an intricate balance between children's interests and teachers' understanding of what knowledge, skills, and dispositions children are ready to learn. For example, as a teacher of three-year-old children, Mr. Burton understands that the children in his care need to be engaged in concept and vocabulary development, constructing relationships between objects and numerals, and developing the disposition of cooperation (among other things). One morning, Joseph brings to school a bucket of seashells that he and his grandfather had gathered from the beach. Several children show an interest in Joseph's treasures, and they begin to play as if they were all at the beach collecting shells. Mr. Burton quickly makes a decision to foster this interest and interact with these children as they play, engaging them in conversations that will promote concept development, counting, and cooperation. These activities may displace or supplement other activities planned for this particular day. At the end of the day, Mr. Burton will rethink his current curriculum plans and decide exactly how to capitalize on the children's interest in the seashells. As he negotiates the balance between the needs and interests of the children, the curriculum that emerges will certainly be sensible but not predictable.

Thematic Instruction.   A thematic approach to curriculum organization focuses study on a central content area. One of the great advantages of theme study is that it creates a context for shared ownership of curriculum and of learning between students and teacher. Weaver (1994) suggests that learning to share the ownership of curriculum with students is a developmental process for teachers. Commercial prepackaged theme units and themes developed by

teachers without input from the students represent the highest degree of teacher-centered learning and curriculum. In these units, activities, experiences, and goals are organized around a single theme, generally chosen by adults to meet the demands of a mandated curriculum. Theme units often provide a step-by-step approach to teaching, offering a variety of traditional activities designed to teach isolated skills and facts. Theme units may be helpful in providing novice teachers, or teachers new to the art of developing integrated curriculum, ideas and experience in organizing curriculum, but because they are prepackaged, they will require much modification to fit the developmental needs of any specific class.

Theme explorations (Weaver, Chaston, & Peterson, 1993) represent a higher degree of shared ownership of the choice of study themes and activities. In this model, the teacher, in the beginning of the school year, chooses several broad topics that correspond to district or school mandates. The teacher introduces each of the topics. Students, through subsequent discussions, suggest possible subtopics. Then students, often working in groups or pairs, choose their subtopic and plan, day to day, with the teacher. Together they develop activities that facilitate their studies and make plans to organize and present their findings. Skills are developed as they are needed to carry out the activities related to the theme exploration.

Theme cycles (Edelsky, Altwerger, & Flores, 1991) represent a way to develop beyond shared ownership to student ownership of curriculum and learning experiences. In this system, students and teachers brainstorm possible topics for extended study. After choosing a topic, students decide what questions to pursue. As the study proceeds, new questions arise, and the study cycles into another related topic of study. For example, Mrs. Gonzales noticed that many children had become interested in the wildflowers growing in their play field. She worked with the children and developed a list of concepts and questions related to wildflowers. The list might have included the names of the flowers in the field, the names of other flowers children found around the neighborhood, the origins of each flower, and the requirements for survival of each kind of flower. The children then chose which concepts to study and developed a more detailed list of questions to pursue. As the study progressed, the children's questions led them not only to new information, but also to new questions. Eventually, the theme of wildflowers cycled into a study of local vegetation. In pursuing their chosen line of inquiry, the children replaced teacher-structured activities with authentic experiences developed by the students themselves. "In short, theme cycles involve authentic learning experiences that are typically missing from theme units, though not necessarily missing from theme explorations" (Weaver, 1994, p. 433).

Project Approach.   A project is an in-depth study of a topic by an individual child, a group of children, or a whole class (Katz & Chard, 1989). Often projects develop from the themes being studied. Students and teachers work together to determine the course of the project, the questions, and the way the learning will be displayed. Students are encouraged to interact with people in their communities and objects in their environment. Project work provides a context for the development of knowledge, skills, and dispositions. The benefits for the child include active learning, intrinsic motivation, self-esteem, independence, self-direction, and initiative.

Teachers also benefit from using the project approach. They are able to provide opportunities for children to pursue their own interests, and they are able to provide individualized instruction. For example, during the project that focused on local wildflowers, which students from Mrs. Gonzales's class developed from the general study of wildflowers, Mrs. Gonzales was able to work directly with two students and help them develop their writing skills. Simultaneously, another child received direct guidance aimed at developing her ability to categorize the flowers.

Katz and Chard (1989) describe three phases in the life of a project: initial, developmental, and concluding. In the initial phase, the teacher assesses children's current level of experience and prior knowledge. Children share memories and thoughts about the topic through various forms of representation. Afterward, children develop questions for investigation. In the developmental phase of the project, the teacher helps children gain new firsthand experience with the topic through field work. In the concluding phase of the project, the teacher draws the project to a close, and children share their learning with others through displays, constructions, or plays.

Are projects to be considered play? There are similarities and there are differences. Similarities include the fact that there are many choices of topics and method of study. Therefore, investigations are voluntary and intrinsically motivated. Project work also will involve many of the same materials traditionally associated with play—sand, clay, paint, and wood. However, Katz and Chard (1989) point out several differences between project work and play. They maintain that project work is more purposeful, children's activities are more focused, and longer periods of time are spent investigating the topic. Unlike spontaneous play, projects require advanced planning by children, and projects continue over several days or weeks. However, it is important to remember that work and play are not opposites; rather, they are elements of learning that often resemble each other (Csikszentmihalyi, 1988; Dewey, 1933). It is therefore important to include both projects and play in any early childhood curriculum, because of the diversity that exists among children's learning styles and prior experience with any given topic. Any curriculum plan needs to be flexible enough to account for the individual differences that exist among children in the same classroom.

One of the best demonstrations of the ideas central to the project approach has evolved over the past thirty years in the community of Reggio Emilia in northern Italy. In schools in this region, each child's intellectual, emotional, social, and moral potential is carefully cultivated and guided by involving the children in long-term engrossing projects. Teachers and people from the community collaborate to provide students with a rich supportive environment and time and opportunities to develop their creative as well as verbal and intellectual abilities (Edwards, Gandini, & Forman, 1993; Hendrick, 1997).

When developed and presented in their most idealistic forms, these three models provide opportunities to embed curriculum with play and playful learning. Emergent curriculum is generally play centered. Many ideas for study emerge from children's play, and the mode of learning is cycled back into children's play. Thematic instruction is embedded with opportunities to play, and the children have many choices of modes of learning. The project approach utilizes play as a way to represent what is known or what has been learned, but does not focus on the idea that all learning comes through play.

As discussed in Chapter 2, it is important that educators design curriculum models that provide each child options to learn in ways that are personally meaningful. In other words, it is important that teachers have "wiggle room" when developing or modifying curriculum to fit the children in a particular classroom. This wiggle room allows teachers to be flexible and trust their ability to improvise learning opportunities that fit the needs of the children in their classroom and to be playful in the development of meaningful learning activities. By combining elements of these three models, educators can develop themes that emerge from children's developmental needs and interests while satisfying learning goals of parents and school officials. Adding projects to theme studies creates the possibility of extending play into more focused and sustained learning activities.

Combining Elements of Emergent Curriculum, Thematic Instruction, and Projects to Create Opportunities for Playful Learning

There is certainly no single right way to develop content studies and the projects that flow from them. The process of planning and implementing is both recursive and dynamic and will be influenced by the themes and topics chosen, the children's prior knowledge of the theme and topics, the teacher's experience and comfort level with improvisational curriculum development, and the children's experience with sharing ownership of curriculum and responsibility for learning. Even though there is no one right way to plan for content studies and projects, there are some logical checkpoints along the way. These checkpoints need to be visualized not in a linear way—first do this, then do this—but as dynamic points at which the process of planning considers new options and possibilities and develops new dimensions. Our purpose here is to describe these dynamic checkpoints.

Selecting a Theme

There are many sources for themes. They may emerge from children's interest and can be discovered by listening carefully to children's questions. Themes may be observed in the pattern of children's play. They may emanate from the developmental needs of the children. A good theme may come from an idea or goal supported in mandated curriculum. It also may come from surprises or unexpected events such as natural disasters or personal tragedies. In any case, to find themes that are appropriate for any one class, teachers need to be observant and open to possibilities.

An important skill in developing and improvising curriculum is to begin to see all the possibilities, or to think in terms of possibilities. One way to discover good topics is to keep ongoing lists and refer to those lists often. The following lists may be helpful in developing ideas for themes. Keep lists of children's interests, play themes, questions, and books that particularly spark conversation, discussion, or drama. Also keep lists of your own interests, such as things you enjoy doing with children; things you would like to learn about; previous themes you have studied with other classes, including ideas that emerged during previous work but were never actualized; children's books that intrigue you; and developmental tasks relevant to the children in your classroom.

Another way to discover possible themes that are appropriate for your class is to engage in multiple sessions of brainstorming. When you brainstorm, you write down every idea that you can think of in a rapid-fire manner. The main rule of brainstorming is that you do not judge your ideas as you put them down. To start the process of brainstorming, set the timer for five minutes and begin to list ideas for themes. The more traditional ideas generally come to mind first, so sticking with the task of listing possibilities for the full five minutes will allow more creative ideas to emerge.

After at least five minutes of listing, stop and review your list. Add any lingering ideas. When you are satisfied and feel finished, begin to consider the feasibility of each category or set of ideas, but do not be too quick to eliminate an idea because you cannot instantly see how you could develop its theme. There are many issues to consider when choosing a theme or topic for study. Katz and Chard (1989)suggest the following criteria for selecting a theme: relevance, the opportunity for application of skills, the availability of resources, teacher interest, and the time of year. Table 3.2 outlines a checklist which can be used to facilitate the selection of themes.

Webbing the Possibilities

Webbing is the process of creating a semantic map—a mental relationship of concepts and relationships (Huck, Hepler, & Hickman, 1987). In the process of webbing, you become able to extend and connect ideas, allowing exploration of all possibilities. Webs represent preliminary plans, or first drafts; they are places to begin. The process of webbing uncovers connections between concepts and provides ideas for activities and events that will get theme studies started, extend them in meaningful ways, and provide closure and summation. "Putting all the activities on a web gives you a road map full of possible journeys" (Jones & Nimmo, 1994, p. 129). The process of webbing will undoubtedly uncover more ideas than you will be able to use. Therefore, webs provide a sense of security, a back-up system to the planning process. When one idea does not seem to work, you can review your web and easily discover an alternative.

When developing a semantic web, brainstorm all the possible concepts related to a particular theme. It is important to be true to the brainstorming process by working steadily for five minutes without evaluating your ideas as you list them. If you begin to think, "Oh no. That concept would be too hard to teach" or "We don't cover that concept at this grade level," you are underestimating yourself and your students, and you may be eliminating an idea that fits one or more of you students. Figure 3.1 shows the initial brainstorm list generated by Ms. Gonzales and her class as they embarked on their theme study of wildflowers.

When you have developed a list of concepts related to your theme, create categories by grouping similar concepts together. You will discover the natural connections that exist

TABLE 3.2   Checklist for Choosing a Theme

Before finalizing your theme choice, ask yourself the following questions.

1. Is the topic *relevant* to this group of students?

   How does it relate to their daily lives?
   What will it add to their daily lives?
   How will it help them connect the information and skills they have today to create new
      information that is immediately useful?

2. Is there *intellectual content* in this theme?

   Is the informational content of the theme worth knowing?
   Is the informational content of the theme worth spending extended periods of time?
   Does the content of the theme move beyond entertainment?

3. Are there sufficient *resources available* to carry out an in-depth study of this theme?

   Are there primary resources (experts, field sites, computer simulations, community resources,
      etc.) available?
   Are there secondary resources (reading material, videos, other print materials, technology,
      etc.) available?
   Does the current season of the year support the theme study?

4. Is there a broad *range of topics* that can be included in the theme study?

   Is it likely that all students will find some topic of interest?
   Will there be many opportunities to practice emerging skills (literacy, language, math, social,
      thinking, and problem solving)?
   Will there be opportunities to study topics in-depth?
   Can the topics within the study be linked to content areas required in the school, district, or
      state curriculum?
   Am I interested in the theme and the topics?

5. Does the theme present children with opportunities to *develop understanding and
   appreciation* for each other?

   Are there possibilities for children to encounter different perspectives among themselves or
      among adults in their environment?
   Are there possibilities for children to encounter, confront, and resolve stereotypes (gender,
      racial, ethnic, age, ability, etc.)?
   Does the theme offer opportunities for family members and members of the local community
      to become involved in the study?

6. Does the theme present children with multiple opportunities to *learn through play?*

   Are there possibilities for children to construct models?
   Are there possibilities for children to develop dramatic productions to represent their learning?

---

between these categories and begin to think of activities and experiences that would engage
students in developing their understanding of the concepts and subtopics. Keep a list of these
experiences and activities to refer to as you begin to plan the course this study will take.

As you web, remember that you are drafting possibilities. You are not committing yourself to anything at this point. You are just playing with ideas. It is important to keep webbing

What do we Know (or want to Know) about the flowers in our field?

Where did they come from?
Somebody planted them.
No, they are wild.
Wild, they are not mean. They are pretty.
Weeds.
flowers smell good.
Some flowers stink.
Who planted them?
The principal.
God.
No, Johnny Appleseed.
Will they die when we step on them?
They are magic. They came by magic. They weren't there
     yesterday.
Can we pick them?
Pretty colors.
One is a Blue Bonnet.
flowers have names? That is silly.
Of course they have names. How would we call them?
Who names them?
I have flowers in my garden at home. My grandpa doesn't like it
     when we step on them.

FIGURE 3.1 Initial Brainstorm List for Wildflower Study. Items in a brainstorm list developed with children take many forms. Some children in Mrs. Gonzales's class contributed single concepts. Some had questions. Many had misconceptions about wildflowers. When children's ideas are allowed to flow onto the list, the teacher has a true picture of children's interests, prior knowledge, and misconceptions.

open-ended and flexible. Do not let yourself be led back to traditional thinking and organization ("This is how it was done when I was in school" or "We have always done it this way").

Children can and should be part of the brainstorming and webbing process. When adults put young children's ideas into writing, they help children understand what written language is all about. Developing categories with children models organizational techniques and strategies for considering possibilities. When children develop the ability to think about multiple possibilities at an early age, they will be able to extend this thinking as they grow and transfer this ability to other contexts. Figure 3.2 shows the initial semantic web that initiated the study.

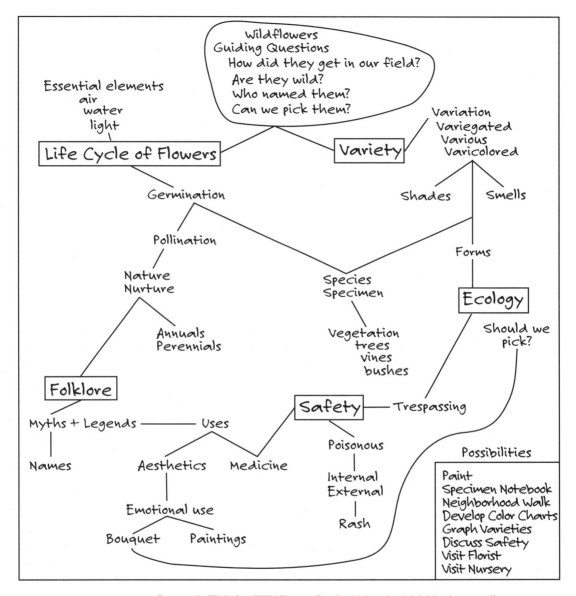

FIGURE 3.2 Semantic Web for Wildflower Study. Using the initial brainstorm list, Mrs. Gonzales created an initial semantic web to guide the theme study. Notice that she has already started to generate a list of activities and experiences to engage children in developing these concepts.

Creating the Connection

At this point, if students have not been directly involved in choosing the theme or planning the theme study, it is important to begin building interest and connections and developing a community of learners. This can be done by conducting several preliminary activities focused on the study of the theme or its subtopics. The purpose of preliminary activities is to

- discover students' understanding of concepts related to the theme
- develop interest among the students
- develop relevant connections between students and their need to know and understand concepts included in the theme
- discover students' ideas and incorporate them into theme planning

Preliminary activities could include any of following ideas:

- Read a book that raises issues about the topic.
- Take a field trip to a relevant site.
- Observe children playing with objects or artifacts relevant to the study.
- Work with small groups to elicit students' understanding of and questions about concepts involved in the theme study.
- Have children represent, through art, music, or drama, their prior knowledge and experience with concepts relevant to the theme study.

It is important to conduct several preliminary activities to give children many ways to express their feelings, understanding, and questions regarding the concepts relevant to the theme. Children have different ways of knowing and therefore need different outlets for expressing what they know. It is also important to reflect continuously on the information received from the children as they engage in these activities and modify the original webs to include the children's ideas and interests.

Organizing the Environment

While children are engaged in these preliminary activities, begin to organize the classroom and prepare for the implementation of the theme. The initial step in organizing the classroom is to draft an agenda for the study. Begin by asking these questions: (1) What will be the major experiences or activities needed to develop concepts? (2) What format will these experiences and activities take (learning center, as a part of daily routines and transitions, whole group, small group, individual, etc.)? (3) What needs to be done before we can undertake this activity? and (4) Who could do this? List each activity or experience and state its basic format (learning centers, routines, and transitions will be discussed in detail in Chapter 4). Under the activity or experience, list the tasks that need to be accomplished to provide this opportunity. Remember the children in your class who have special needs and develop a plan for modifying this activity so that all members of the class can participate. Beside each task, jot down the name or names of people who could perform it.

An important issue involved in thematic instruction is delegation. Delegation helps develop a sense of shared ownership and supports a community of learners. Tasks can be delegated to members of student's families, classroom volunteers, members of other classrooms, and to the students themselves. Teachers who enjoy and feel successful in thematic instruction are good at delegating. Teachers who feel that they have to do everything themselves will give up on this approach to teaching. Shared ownership means shared responsibility. Table 3.3 shows Ms. Gonzales' initial agenda for delegation.

TABLE 3.3   Agenda for Wildflower Study

The following is an excerpt from Mrs. Gonzales's initial agenda for the wildflower study. Notice that she has identified activities and experiences, decided on a format for these experiences, developed a list of actions she needs to take and resources she needs to gather, and in some cases delegated tasks to others. The agenda is a dynamic document and will change as the study develops. Both initial and ongoing organization is necessary for successful theme studies.

Activity: Create a Field Specimen Notebook

Format: Individual or group project. Choice. Work to be done during learning centers.
Materials and equipment housed in discovery center

To Do:	**Delegated to:**
■ Find examples of specimen notebook	Librarian
■ Create center activity card inviting students to create a notebook and giving initial instructions	Me
■ Borrow flower press from science lab	Mrs. Adams (parent volunteer)
■ Gather supplies needed for pressing	Mrs. Adams
■ Schedule volunteers for days when students will press	Me
■ Gather bookbinding material	Me
■ Schedule children to go to the bookbinding lab (in school)	Me
■	
■	
■	

Activity: Neighborhood Walk: Wildflower Search

Format: Excursion. Small Groups. Choice during center time (if everyone wants to go we can schedule it during a whole group time).

To Do:	**Delegated to:**
■ Take preliminary walks in neighborhood to discover the best routes to take. Talk with neighbors along the way to get permission to enter their yards (if necessary)	Me
■ Outline plans and get permission from principal	Me
■ Discuss plans with students and get their ideas about structure of excursion	Me
■ Write FYI (For Your Information) letter to families, enclose permission slip, ask for volunteers	Me
■ Get disposable cameras to capture wildflowers	Mrs. Adams
■ Schedule volunteers to accompany us	Mrs. Adams
■ Hold class meeting to discuss and agree on guidelines for excursion	Me
■	
■	
■	

A second organizational activity that can be accomplished while students are engaged in preliminary activities is to gather the necessary resources. A third organizational activity is to decide on a preliminary sequence of major events and activities. Then schedule field trips and guest speakers and collect equipment and materials needed. As you finish these preliminary organizational activities, you will probably find that the theme study is underway.

Extending the Study

There are many ways to keep a study going. Foremost is constant and consistent observation, interaction, and problem-solving together with students. Help students maintain interest and engagement by (1) continually modifying plans by adding, canceling, restructuring, or rescheduling events and activities; (2) teaching individuals the skills they need to be successful while engaged in activities and events; and (3) developing a format so that students can share their learning with each other on a daily basis.

Adding Projects

As stated earlier, a project is an in-depth study of a topic by an individual child, a group of children, or a whole class. During the course of theme study, the teacher may notice that certain children or a certain group of children shows a remarkable interest in one aspect of the study. Teachers need to look closely for signs of focused interest because children cannot always tell you what intrigues them. They show their interest through their play, their persistence, and their questions, but they cannot always verbalize interest. With help from adults, children's focused energy and interest can be channeled into projects.

To illustrate how projects fit into theme studies, we offer the following example.

A kindergarten classroom was developing a theme study related to domesticated animals. In the course of the study, the class visited a veterinary office. While there, the children saw many things and learned many interesting facts. One of the patients in the office that day was a parrot. In the days following the field trip, the class created a veterinary clinic in their classroom and played out many different scenarios through dramatic play.

As the children talked, played, and drew pictures representing their growing understanding of domesticated animals, the teacher noticed that Randy consistently drew pictures and asked questions about "big, bright, birds that squawk." The teacher helped Randy formalize her questions in a list. Together they discussed how Randy might learn more about exotic birds. They checked out books from the library and discovered that a video was also available. Randy's parents became aware of her interest through her drawings and conversations. They were able to take her to the local zoo, where they arranged to meet with the bird specialist. During the concluding presentation of the class's theme study, Randy not only drew a parrot for the mural, but also gave a short talk describing the characteristics of this exotic bird.

While Randy was busy pursuing her interest in parrots, the teacher noticed that a group of children, Adrian, Paulo, and Robert, were curious about their classmate's pets. A classroom volunteer assisted these children in developing a survey. The children conducted the survey and with help from the volunteer compiled the results and developed a graph. This graph was also presented in the presentation that concluded the entire theme study.

This example shows how projects *float* within a theme study. Here we saw three. The first was a whole-class study, probably instigated by the teacher, of the veterinarian's office. Then there was one individual's study of exotic birds and, finally, a small group's investigation of pet ownership among classmates. The latter two projects were recognized and supported by the teacher, but probably not on any preliminary web. They grew out of the theme. There may have been more projects within this theme. It may be that Randy did not pursue an individual project during the next theme study. What is important is that Randy and the others had the opportunity to lead their own learning and realized the satisfaction that comes with self-directed learning.

Wrapping It Up

When the interest in a theme begins to fade or cycle into another major theme, it is time to draw things together and bring closure to the study. In coming to closure, children need the opportunity to reflect on what they have learned, consolidate it in some way, represent it in ways that can be documented, and celebrate both the individual and communal learning that has taken place. Helm, Beneke, and Steinheimer (1998) state, "Documenting children's learning may be one of the most valuable skills a teacher can develop today. A teacher who perceives how children learn and can then help others to see the learning can contribute significantly to the child's development" (p. 13). In writing about her experiences at Reggio Emilia, Gandini (1997) points out that documentation serves several functions.

> Among these are to make parents aware of their children's experiences and maintain their involvement; to allow teachers to understand children better and to evaluate the teachers' own work, thus promoting their professional growth; to facilitate communication and exchange of ideas among educators; to make children aware that their effort is valued; and to create an archive that traces the history of the school and the pleasure of learning by many children and their teachers. (p. 21)

A common way to conclude a theme or project is for children and teachers to plan a presentation. Presentations can be simple or elaborate. They can involve only class members, or invitations can be sent to families, administrators, community members who have been involved, or to another class. Presentations should not be confused with performances. When children preform, teachers make most of the decisions and direct children's actions and dialogue. Presentations are more informal and student-directed. Examples of ways to conclude a theme include

- a class-made book that depicts the activities and learning that took place in the course of the theme study. This book could stay in the classroom or make its way to each child's home.
- a display of group and individual work in which children act as guides for invited guests.
- a skit, or group of skits, that children have composed to explain their study.
- a videotape, edited to show the life history of the project.

The process of planning and carrying out the activities associated with the theme study, the projects, and the concluding presentation provides children with many opportunities to develop knowledge, skills, and dispositions while engaged in play or playful activities.

Developing Advocacy Skills

Children learn when they have many opportunities to engage in meaningful, playful activities. Developing new curriculum and modifying existing curriculum in ways that provide children these opportunities are essential skills for early childhood educators. To preserve the opportunities for playful learning provided by integrated theme studies and the projects that flow from them, teachers may need to become advocates of thematic instruction and the project approach. Administrators, parents, or even colleagues may not fully appreciate the value of this approach to curriculum organization.

One way to help parents and others understand the benefits of thematic instruction and projects is by providing frequent information. This information can be made available in newsletters or FYI (For Your Information) bulletins. The classroom newsletter can contain student-generated articles about ongoing themes and projects. Pictures, drawings, transcripts of interviews, and sketches can also be included in the newsletter. The newsletter is also a good place to discuss upcoming themes and elicit cooperation and support from parents. FYI bulletins are single-sheet summaries about a particular theme or project. Students summarize the questions they are investigating and the information they are gathering periodically and distribute these bulletins to their families, other classrooms, their principals and curriculum specialists, and to interested community members. It is important to note that FYI bulletins do not necessarily need to be printed material. Kieff and Wellhousen (in press) discuss the need to take into consideration family communication styles when developing strategies for family involvement. Audio- and videotapes, along with voice mail messages, also serve to keep everyone updated, maintain focus and interest in the theme or project, and enlist collaboration from others. They also allow children to show what knowledge, skills, and dispositions they are developing.

Another way to advocate for theme studies and projects is to create displays that showcase what children are learning as they pursue the goals of their project. There is no need to confine these displays to the classroom or even to the school. Find places in the community to exhibit displays; business offices, courthouses and government buildings, stores, and public libraries are all possibilities. Invite newspaper reporters along on field trips. Invite community personnel to culminating events. In short, let the children's work/play speak for itself. It will become your strongest resource when developing advocacy activities.

Successful advocates think positively and generate many ideas for showcasing their cause. Good advocates make positive thinking look easy and natural. For many, generating multiple positive solutions to problems is neither easy nor is it a natural way of thinking. It is a skill that is learned and develops into the disposition of "looking on the bright side" and "finding another alternative."

One way to develop your own power to think in terms of multiple, positive options is to utilize the brainstorming technique discussed in this chapter. Brainstorming helps you break out of traditional ways of thinking, because you are giving yourself permission to be playful, idealistic, and even wrong, if only for the moment. While brainstorming, you disengage that critical voice inside that is always telling you, "You can't do that!" "That's not possible!" Then you are able to visualize what might be possible. And when you can see what

TABLE 3.4 Advocacy Activities: Informing and Involving Families and Administrators

	Think Positively	
Becoming Aware	*Furthering Your Understanding*	*Taking Action*
1. Review several curriculum guides used in early childhood classrooms. Take notes and count the kinds of goals suggested within the lessons. What are the main strategies used to organize the curriculum?	1. Review several early childhood journals and collect ideas that relate to thematic studies.	1. Observe one classroom over several days. Develop lists that document children's interests. From these lists, choose a topic and develop a semantic web for further study.
2. Observe a children's play group and list on a minute-to-minute basis everything that happens within a 30-minute period. Review your notes and try to separate these activities on the basis of learning goals, knowledge, skills, and dispositions. Discuss the efficiency of using play as a strategy for learning.	2. Read and study accounts of the Reggio Emilia approach to teaching. Develop a collection of articles, interviews, and stories written about this approach to educating young children.	2. Develop a theme studies project using the strategies described in this chapter.
3. Repeat activity 2 with an older or younger group of children. Compare your findings.	3. Observe a classroom in which the curriculum is organized around themes. Take note of the schedule. Take note of how individual needs regarding skill development are handled within the theme organization. Also take note of how mandated curriculum goals are incorporated into the theme.	3. Write a letter to a parent. Explain the value of projects in early childhood classrooms.
4. Interview a teacher regarding his or her approach to mandated curriculum. How is this teacher's approach similar to or different from the approach offered in the text?	4. Repeat activity 3 in another classroom. Compare the similarities and differences. Discuss strategies that make the most sense to you.	4. Volunteer in a classroom and help children develop and work through a project.

might be possible, you can see ways to make it happen. Table 3.4 provides examples of activities and experiences that will help you develop advocacy skills.

Summary

Curriculum is everything that is learned in the classroom. This includes learning that is planned, learning that occurs incidentally, and learning that occurs spontaneously. Learning goals common to early childhood classrooms include knowledge goals, skill goals, and disposition goals. Play is certainly not the only way children learn. However, play does form a context for meaningful learning. Combining elements of emergent curriculum, theme studies, and the project approach when planning curriculum allows the teacher to create a framework that is flexible and will meet the learning needs of most children.

R E V I S I T I N G   F I R S T   I M P R E S S I O N S

You were asked to visualize your ideal classroom. How were the ideas you expressed similar to or different from Mrs. Gonzales's classroom? How did play figure into your original vision? Have you changed your idea of the role of play in a classroom? If so, how has it changed?

Q U E S T I O N S   F O R   D I S C U S S I O N

1. In this chapter there is an example of how projects fit into a theme study of domesticated animals. Notice that there is no mention of skill development. Is this because no skills were taught? If you were the teacher of this class, how would you respond to a parent's concern regarding lack of skill development?

2. Describe three dispositions and develop an example showing how they foster the development of reading and writing skills.

3. Develop an example that illustrates how children in preschool and kindergarten learn cognitive, motor, and social skills through play.

S U G G E S T E D   R E A D I N G S

Edwards, C., Gandini, L., & Forman, G. (1993). *The hundred languages of children: The Reggio Emilia approach to early childhood education.* Norwood, NJ: Ablex.

Helm, J. H., Beneke, S., & Steinheimer, K. (1998). *Windows on learning: Documenting young children's work.* New York: Teachers College Press.

Hendrick, J. (Ed.). (1997). *First steps toward teaching the Reggio way.* Upper Saddle River, NJ: Merrill.

Jones, E., & Nimmo, J. (1994). *Emergent curriculum.* Washington, DC: National Association for the Education of Young Children.

4 Fostering Playful Learning throughout the Day

Prereading Guide

First Impressions.   Discuss in your journal your impressions of the concept of *learning centers*. It might be that you have had direct experience with centers as a student or as a teacher. It might be that you have only come across the term in textbooks. Given what you know about learning centers, discuss what you think would be their greatest strength. List some issues or questions you would have about setting up a learning center system.

Revisit
Categories of Play (Chapter 2)

Stories from the Field

The following story was developed from anecdotal notes taken during five days of observation in four public kindergarten classrooms in the Pacific northwestern region of the United States. The observations occurred midyear.

> 8:15 A.M., February 25
>
> Five children are brought to the classroom door by a teacher's aide who had assisted the children with their school-sponsored breakfast. At the door, they say good-bye to the aide and enter the classroom to find their teacher, Mr. Farber, sitting with three boys at a low table. The boys are connecting blocks together to make a "long-long-long" road. There are several other children, already engaged in center activities, in various places in the classroom.
>
> "Good Morning!" calls Mr. Farber to the entering group. "How was your breakfast?"
>
> "Fine. We had oatmeal again!" calls Susan, answering for the whole group. "Oatmeal, oatmeal, oatmeal. It's a good thing we like oatmeal!" All the children laugh and run to Mr. Farber for a group hug, then scatter to their cubbyholes to put away their coats and sweaters. Mr. Farber stands and moves away from the boys building with blocks, who do not seem to notice that he is leaving.
>
> "Can you find your name tags?" he calls to the group.
>
> "Yes. They are right here. Where they always are, on the big table," Robert laughs. The group moves from their cubbies to a table in the middle of the classroom where a group of name tags are scattered about. There are five large circles drawn on each name tag. The children have learned, through the course of the year, that they are to write the name, or the abbreviation, of each

learning center they attend in one of the circles. They may go to any center they choose, choose from a variety of activities at that center, and change centers several times during the morning, but they must keep a record on their name tag. Each day, they receive a new name tag with the current date stamped under their name. Mr. Farber keeps the name tags as a record of each child's activities. Each child finds his or her own name tag and looks about the room, making decisions about what to do first.

Susan heads straight for the classroom library center, talking to herself as she goes. "I am already tired. I just want to read a good book." When she gets to the library center she stops and studies the center sign. On the sign there are pictures of books, the word *Library* with the abbreviation (LIB) circled, and the number 8. Beside the sign is a tray, and in the tray there are already four name tags. Susan picks the name tags up and counts them, "One, two, three, four. That means I am number five. Good. The center is not full yet." Susan slowly and carefully writes "LIB" in one of the circles on her name tag and leaves the name tag in the tray. She then looks around to find Albert and Tracy reading a class favorite. "Can I read with you?" she asks Tracy.

"Yes, but we're not going to start over," replied Tracy.

"That's O. K. I know what happened till now," Susan says as she sits close to Albert.

In the meantime, Germaine has joined the boys building the block road. This activity is a part of the block center. Like Susan, Germaine had approached the center, read the center sign, counted the name tags to make sure there was room for him, copied the word *Block* from the sign into one of the circles on his name tag, deposited the name tag in the tray, and sat at the table close to the boys building the road. After just a few minutes, Germaine, without saying a word, has managed to capture most of the blocks within his outstretched arms and is now handing them to the boys, one by one.

It is now 8:45. Children have been coming into the room in a steady stream. Some are alone, some are with family members. All are personally greeted by Mr. Farber. Many have special stories to tell him. They all eventually put their belongings away, retrieve their name tags, and choose an activity. Some children display independence in making their choices, some need support from Mr. Farber. The classroom is active and alive with voices, movement, and laughter. There are only two name tags, left on the table. Mr Farber gathers them and looks carefully around the room. He seems to be counting. Then he marks two children absent and places the roll call slip on the outside of his classroom door. Kindergarten has begun for the day. In fact it is well under way. Through the use of a learning center system and established routines, Mr. Farber has ensured that each child will have positive experiences, not only at the beginning, but throughout their day.

Recognizing Diversity among Learners

If we had stayed in Mr. Farber's classroom for the entire morning, we would have seen children engaged in multiple activities that revealed each child's unique style of learning. Some children, like Susan, seem to learn best when engaged with others, talking, reading, and writing. Germaine and the others at the block table chose to learn by engaging in building and constructing. To most adults, the children in Mr. Farber's classroom are all *just playing,* and, of course, they are. But Mr. Farber has found a way, through the use of learning centers and classroom routines, to capture the natural playfulness of children and channel this energy into individual and group learning activities that support each child's individual pattern of intelligence while fulfilling the overall goals of the classroom. To create the kind of classroom culture that supports each child, teachers and care providers like Mr. Farber recognize and appreciate the many different patterns of intelligence and play children display as they learn about their world.

Multiple intelligence theory, first proposed by Gardner (1983), suggests, first, that intelligence is not fixed at birth but develops throughout one's life, and, second, that there is no one single pattern of human intelligence, but many ways in which intelligence is demonstrated and developed. Each child has unique potential and strives to develop and express his or her potential and intelligence in unique ways. Therefore, it is important that teachers not only recognize the different ways children have of knowing, but also that they accept and foster all ways of knowing through procedures and activities in the classroom. Gardner first identified seven intelligences (1983) and later added the eighth, naturalist intelligence (Checkley, 1997). Table 4.1

TABLE 4.1 Play and Multiple Intelligence

Children demonstrating *verbal/linguistic intelligence* have a great vocabulary and communicate effectively. They learn easily through reading, writing, and discussing issues and ideas. Therefore they *play with words.* They like to tell stories, make up plays, and "play" at reading and writing.

Children demonstrating *logico-mathematical intelligence* think clearly and analytically and appeal to logic to learn and to solve problems. They think in numbers, patterns, and algorithms. They use numbers easily, sequence, analyze, evaluate, synthesize, and apply. Therefore they *play with numbers and patterns.* They like to count, sort, sequence, and categorize math manipulatives. They also like to conduct experiments, make graphs, and analyze data.

Children demonstrating *visual/spatial intelligence* show an eye for detail, color, and spatial awareness. They think in pictures and "see solutions to problems" through visualization and imagination. Therefore, they *play with images.* They like to paint, draw, make mobiles, watch films and videos, and play with puzzles and mazes.

Children demonstrating *musical/rhythmic intelligence* are sensitive to pitch, timbre, timing, tone, and the rhythm of sound. They have a good sense of rhythm and melody. Therefore, they like to *play with music and sound.* They like to sing, play instruments, listen to music from different cultures, and hum, clap, and snap a tune.

Children demonstrating *bodily/kinesthetic intelligence* are highly coordinated and use their body to communicate. They enjoy dancing, athletics, and acting. They think in terms of music and gestures and body language. Therefore, they *play with movement.* They like to tinker with things, touch and feel things, build, dance, move, explore, and pantomime.

Children demonstrating *naturalist intelligence* have a keen awareness of their natural surroundings and have keen observational skills. Therefore, they *play with plants and animals and other natural phenomena.* They like to learn about nature, care for classroom pets, collect specimens, grow flowers and vegetables, and record changes.

Children demonstrating *interpersonal intelligence* make and maintain friends easily. They are sensitive and can understand the perspective of others easily. They like to lead and organize and resolve conflicts. Therefore, they *play around with people.* They like to work with a partner, role-play, plan events, and solve real or simulated conflicts.

Children demonstrating *intrapersonal intelligence* are introspective and aware of their own feelings and ideas. They enjoy private time to reflect and think. Therefore, they *play with their own thoughts and feelings.* They like having quiet time to reflect on their learning. They also like working independently, reading silently, keeping a journal, and planning ahead.

Adapted from Checkley, 1997; Gardner, 1983, 1993.

gives a brief summary of each intelligence and examples of what forms play might take for a child demonstrating that intelligence.

It is important to understand that young children are in the process of developing multiple intelligences to express their ideas and learn new concepts. However, to do this, children need to have multiple learning options available from which to choose ways to play, learn, and express their understanding. One way for teachers to provide these options is to establish a learning center system and develop classroom routines that promote playful learning. In this chapter we will describe such systems and routines and also discuss the relationship between technology and the play of young children.

Using a Learning Center System to Provide Opportunities for Playful Learning

Learning centers, sometimes called stations, interest centers, zones, or activity areas, are multipurpose areas within a classroom where equipment and materials are organized to promote active, child-centered learning. Although some criticize the use of the term because it may give the impression that the learning center is the only place in a classroom that learning happens, we choose to use this term to connote a systematic way to utilize classroom materials, space, and time that is both versatile and efficient for teachers and students alike. In centers, children have the opportunity to engage in activities that are both self-chosen and self-directed. These activities differ from a traditional lesson in two ways. First, an activity does not have a definitive beginning, middle, or end. Second, the activity is not prescribed by the teacher. Rather, activities flow and take shape as a child or group of children direct their own learning by following interests and building to conclusions (Spodek, 1985). The following example illustrates the concepts of flow and self-direction.

> In the block area of a preschool classroom, three children decide to build *something*. As they begin to put blocks together, they talk about what they are building. At first, the building seems very generic, but within the time allowed for this play episode, about an hour, the building becomes a hospital with roads leading to and from an emergency entry, which is marked by a sign. At one point, an ambulance carries a toy figure to the emergency room to see the doctor.

Neither the children nor the teacher knew at the outset of the activity, where this activity would lead nor how complex the learning opportunities would become.

This building project began spontaneously but developed as the children utilized their prior knowledge about blocks, balance, buildings, and hospital emergency rooms. During the course of the activity, the children made many decisions, solved many logistical problems, and negotiated with each other to come to consensus of ideas. The teacher could not have designed a lesson that would have accomplished, in the same time frame and with the same level of engagement, the goals this activity accomplished. Furthermore, at the same time these three children were engaged in such complex and integrated learning, other individuals and groups of children were likewise engaged in self-chosen and self-directed activity throughout the classroom. Learning center systems prove to be a very efficient use of teacher and student time and energy.

In this text, we will define *learning centers* as places where the schedule, floor space, equipment, and materials are organized in such a way to facilitate learning through exploration and play. In centers children have the opportunity to work and play individually or in small groups, choose materials and activities, and establish the pace and direction of their play and learning. The concept of a learning center system refers to all of the centers in a given classroom and the management system that facilitates children's use of them.

After their initial development and organization, learning center systems are versatile and provide an efficient way for children to learn and for teachers to utilize both time and space to meet the overall goals of the curriculum. For children, learning centers facilitate the integration of knowledge, skills, dispositions, facts, and information in an authentic learning context. They also provide children opportunities to develop multiple ways of knowing and expressing their understanding. A quick look back into Mr. Farber's classroom illustrates this point. Susan was demonstrating both interpersonal intelligence and verbal/linguistic intelligence as she moved through the learning centers and chose activities to foster her understanding. At the same time, Germaine, who during our brief observation seemed much less verbal, managed to become engaged in block building activities, which tend to foster both logico-mathematical intelligence and visual/spatial intelligence. During learning center times, children are able to choose situations that are comfortable, but at the same time encounter situations and other children that challenge their way of knowing and therefore foster further development.

For teachers, learning centers provide an efficient way to

- develop and implement curriculum that fits needs of individuals
- balance instructional modes between teacher-directed and child-directed activities and between quiet time and active time
- increase intrinsic motivation and encourage engagement
- balance opportunities to develop both a sense of interdependence (working together) or independence(working alone)
- create a forum for developing understanding and cooperation among children with differing abilities
- provide authentic contexts for practicing literacy and numeracy skills
- create an authentic context for evaluation

Designing a Learning Center System

Within any classroom, the centers and the system for managing them will change over the course of the year as the children's needs and interests change and as they acquire new skills and abilities. Therefore, the learning center systems in preschool, kindergarten, and primary grades will look and function differently. When developing a system of centers for the classroom, the teacher should consider the number of children in the classroom, the range of children's ages and developmental needs, the range of children's prior knowledge and experiences, the learning goals of the program, children's cultural heritage, children's prior experience with centers, the space available, the number of adults or older children available to supervise, and the resources available.

Determining Number and Type of Centers.   One way to determine how many centers are needed in any given classroom is to determine how many *spaces* will be needed for children to have ample choice when selecting centers. A space simply means the place and materials needed for one child to work or to play at a center. For example, at a sand table you may have room and materials for six children to play safely and comfortably, therefore there are six spaces in the sand center. Isbell (1995) recommends that there be twice as many spaces available in the centers as children in the classroom. For example, in a preschool classroom with eighteen children there would need to be thirty-six play spaces available among all centers. If each center were designed to accommodate, through space and materials, six children, then at least six centers would be needed in this classroom. It is important to understand that not all centers need to be created to accommodate the same number of children. Some centers, for example, the library center, may have space for eight or nine children. Other centers, for example, the block center, may accommodate only four children. The important issue is the number of play spaces that are available throughout the classroom.

If we use the concept of spaces to determine the number of centers needed in a kindergarten class of twenty-five children, we would find that we need nine or ten centers, assuming each could accommodate five children ($25 \times 2 = 50$; $50/5 = 10$). In preschool and kindergarten, a majority of the classroom space is dedicated to centers, because most learning will take place in these areas. However, as children get older, the equipment and materials needed to sustain their play and learning generally become less cumbersome. For example, the block center in a preschool should contain both large hollow blocks and several sets of smaller unit blocks. In a first-grade classroom, blocks are still very important, but one or two sets of unit blocks can generally be included in the math and manipulative center. Therefore, as children grow older, the physical size of many centers will decrease.

In many classrooms, there is limited space available for centers. There are a number of ways to address this issue. When designing center space, include outdoor areas as centers, particularly if they are adjacent to the classroom. Also, find ways to use nooks, crannies, lofts, hallways, and libraries. It may also be possible to share space with another teacher. Of course, careful consideration must be given to how children will be supervised when they choose a center outside the classroom area.

In any classroom, a variety of centers will be needed to account for the diversity in interests and abilities that naturally exists among the students. Not only will a variety of centers be needed to fulfill the needs of all students, but the materials and activities available to the children will necessarily need to span a wide range. Most centers in any classroom should be permanent and always available to children. Within these centers the materials may change from time to time, but the centers themselves should always be available. There can also be centers that are available only on special occasions. These centers might be coordinated with a theme study, or they might represent a way to engage students in projects. Special occasion centers could provide children with the opportunity to engage in activities that require special equipment and special supervision and therefore cannot be offered on a daily basis. Examples of such centers are cooking and woodworking. Table 4.2 lists both permanent and special occasion centers for preschool, kindergarten, and primary classrooms. Detailed descriptions, or prototypes, of many of the centers listed above are included within this text.

If the classroom is simply not large enough for all the centers suggested, teachers may need to limit the number of permanent centers and choose them based on the developmental needs of the students in a particular classroom. It is also possible to rotate centers every few weeks so that within a three-month period children have access to all centers. For example, in a kindergarten classroom, the sand and water center could be available for two weeks, be replaced by an indoor fitness center for two weeks, and then return. Another alternative is to share space with other teachers. For example, if adjacent classrooms scheduled a joint center time, students could move between classrooms. Then the cooking center or the dramatic play area would need to be available in only one classroom.

TABLE 4.2   Permanent and Special Occassion Centers

The permanent centers typically included in preschools and kindergartens are:

Blocks (both unit blocks and hollow blocks)
Discovery
Dramatic play
Fine arts
Library/literacy/writing/listening
Math/manipulatives/table games
Music and movement
Outdoor fitness (indoor if room is available)
Private spaces
Sensory exploration, sand and water play

Special Occasion Centers

Carpentry
Cooking
Theme/project studies

In primary classrooms, the following permanent centers should be available:

Construction
Expression (dramatic play)
Fitness
Investigation/exploration/discovery
    (science and math)
Library/literacy/writing/listening
Theme/Project Studies

Special Occasion Centers

Carpentry
Cooking

Notice in Table 4.2 that none of the lists of centers contains a computer center, even though computers are an integral part of early childhood education. Technology should support all learning. Therefore, the use of computers should be integrated into the learning that takes place in each center. Since few classrooms have the luxury of a computer in every center, activity cards could be placed in each center to remind children of choices available to them at the computer. For example, while working in the manipulative center, a second grader decides he wants to practice his addition facts. He goes to the computer, runs a math software program that he has enjoyed before, and plays the games designed to help him memorize math facts. At the same time, another child, who is playing with friends in the dramatic play center, has decided he needs a sign for his front door. He too goes to the computer, starts a software program, and prints a sign. In this way technology is integrated into all learning activities that happen in a classroom and is not seen as an end in itself. We will discuss the relationship between play and technology later in this chapter.

Developing a Floor Plan.   Once you have decided which centers you will need, it is time to take the next step in planning a learning center system, which is determining where each center will be located. A workable traffic pattern for your classroom is essential to a playful and cooperative atmosphere. Just as you would not design a home where visitors had to go through the bedroom to get to the living room or kitchen, you should not design a classroom where children have to walk through one center to get to another. Here are general guidelines to use when planning the use of space within your classroom.

- Create space in the classroom for large-group work, small-group work, and individual work.
- Create a space where the whole class can gather together. This space could double as the music and movement center.

- Create spaces for children to store their individual belongings.
- Be sure children are able to move freely from one area of the classroom to another.
- Avoid having one long traffic lane. This would encourage running.
- Place noisy, active centers (e.g., blocks, dramatic play, music, and indoor fitness) next to each other.
- Place quieter centers (e.g., literacy, listening, and private spaces) next to each other.
- Place neutral centers (e.g., manipulative and science and discovery) between noisy, active centers and quiet centers.
- Place messy centers (e.g., art, sand, and water) close to a water source.
- Place dramatic play and blocks next to each other to foster possible collaboration between children playing in these centers.
- Utilize all possible space. Consider the hallway, outdoor entry area, school library, and cafeteria.
- Do not limit the use of outdoor space to large motor activities. Design some outdoor space for science (a garden), reading (a tree), or drama (a tent).

Creating Individual Centers.   It is important for each center to have a clearly defined visual boundary so that children will understand and adhere to behavioral expectations related to the center system in general and to each specific center. These boundaries should be at the child's eye level, because this gives the children a clear understanding of the space available while allowing teachers to oversee all center activity easily. Good center dividers include furniture such as couches and chairs, shelves, and room dividers. Fabric can also be used as room dividers, as can heavy corrugated paper. Rugs also help mark spaces, as do signs.

Within each center there should be a work space for the children. This work space will vary according to the purpose of the center. For example, in the block center, the main work space could be simply the floor. In the art center, the work space would include easels for painting and table space for working with collage or clay. In the literacy center, the work space might include rocking chairs, pillows, a couch, a few individual desks for writing, and a table with a listening station. In the dramatic play area, the work space might be housekeeping furniture, or a puppet stage, or a grocery store framed with PVC pipe, or a large refrigerator box that becomes, in the minds of the children, a cave.

In addition to work space, each center should also include ample storage for the materials used in this center. These items should be stored on low shelves or in cupboards so that children can be independent in their selection of materials. Marking shelves and cupboards with pictures of their contents helps children care for materials and keep centers organized. It is also important that each center has an area to display children's work. A bulletin board should be included in the art center for paintings, in the library center to display writing, and in the block center to display pictures of constructions. This will increase the children's sense of ownership of the work they do in each center. It also makes them feel that the time spent in the centers is valued by the teacher and other adults. These displays also send a subliminal message to parents, administrators, and other teachers regarding the value of play. Tables 4.3 and 4.4 suggest equipment, materials, activities, and safety considerations for a block center and one sensory exploration area, the sand and water center. Teachers and care providers will select specific equipment and materials to match the learning needs of the children in their care.

TABLE 4.3   Prototype: Block Center

Space Requirements
Large floor area
Storage shelves for unit blocks and accessories

Basic Materials
Unit blocks—several sets, enough for several children to build large structures simultaneously
Hollow blocks—either in this center or an adjoining center or an outside center
Block accessories
■ people
■ vehicles (cars, trucks, boats, planes, fire engines, helicopters, tractors etc.)
■ signs
Pulleys and inclines
Smooth rug (to cut down on the noise without disturbing balancing ability)

Safety Considerations
Consistently check blocks for splinters.
Predetermine a safe building height and post a demonstration picture in the center area.
Instruct children to keep feet on the floor when building (so they do not climb on chairs or tables).

Examples of Basic Learning Opportunities
Understand basic concepts: balance, size, weight, height, length, etc.
Counting and categorizing skills
Architectural concepts: arch, bridge, stories, columns, etc.
Problem solving while constructing structures
Cooperation and collaboration during planning and construction
Language and concept development
Respect space and efforts of others
Develop small muscle strength and coordination
Designing and carrying though

Examples of Extensions
Literacy
■ develop labels for constructions
■ include books about architecture in center
■ include blueprints in center
■ develop and write stories about constructions

Numeracy
■ develop counting and sorting routines for clean up
■ have students draw blueprints
■ measure structures and keep an ongoing record (name, date, dimensions of structure, and
   number of blocks used)

Arranging Space and Materials to Include Children with Special Needs.   To determine the modifications required for children with special needs in your classroom, it is first necessary to understand the specific nature of the child's disability and how the disability affects the way the child learns and interacts with others. An initial conference with the

TABLE 4.4   Prototype: Sand and Water Center

Space Requirements
Area large enough for sand or water table near sink
Storage shelves and containers for accessories

Basic Materials
Combination sand and water table
Plastic sheeting for floor
Broom, dust pan, and mop
Sterilized play sand, beans, rice, and cornmeal
Water, coloring agent, scenting agent, and bubbles
Accessories (examples)
■ plastic tubing, sponges, straws, medicine droppers, whisks, egg beaters, and tongs
■ funnels, strainers, measuring cups and spoons, buckets and shovels, and spray bottles
■ turkey-basting syringe, small plastic wheel toys, styrofoam pieces, and snow

Safety Considerations
Take steps to prevent children slipping on floor.
Provide goggles for both sand and water play.

Examples of Basic Learning Opportunities
Understand basic concepts: wet, dry, heavy, rough, smooth, full, empty, packed, etc.
Exploration of materials, textures, designs
Problem solving while building 3-dimensional structures with wet sand
Cooperation and collaboration on designs or building projects
Language and concept development
Respect space and efforts of others
Making predictions
Develop small muscle strength and coordination
Develop hand–eye coordination
Observing changes: wet/dry, clear/soapy, quantity, size, shape
Developing an understanding of more and less
Use of tools to solve problem

Examples of Extensions
Literacy
■ labels for storage
■ include books about sand and water in center
■ develop and write stories about changes that occur
■ chart children's predictions concerning floating and sinking
■ make books depicting tools used at centers

Numeracy
■ develop counting and sorting routines for clean up
■ make patterns in sand
■ chart and graph measured amounts

Dramatic Play
■ add small figures
■ wash doll clothes and washable dolls
■ wash dishes

child's family and with specialists familiar with the child will help determine the specific modifications necessary. Here are some guidelines useful in planning for inclusion.

Children with Visual Impairments

- Establish a predictable environment where materials and equipment can be located easily.
- Mark entry to areas with raised symbols. Also mark shelves and storage containers so that children can identify materials they want to play with and return those materials when finished.
- Use sound to identify areas in the room and the playground. For example, hang a wind chime in the reading area.
- Eliminate sharp and pointed objects and remove area rugs.

Children with Hearing Impairments

- Place mirrors around the room so that children are reminded of activities that are happening behind them.
- Use pictures and words together on posters and signs that mark centers and give guidelines for working in the centers.

Children with Communication Problems

- If children use a communication board made up of pictures, make sure that all the items on the board are easily matched to items in the classroom.

Children with Physical Disabilities

- Make room for adaptive equipment in every center. For example, make sure a prone stander can fit next to the sand and water table. Allow space for a corner chair in the dramatic play area.
- Create space for privacy and rest, because disabilities often cause children to need special attention when toileting and also cause them to fatigue easily.

(Cook, Tessier, & Armbruster, 1987; Deiner, 1983; Fewell & Kaminski, 1988; Morris & Schultz, 1989; Wesley, 1992.)

Creating Safe Environments. One of the most critical factors of any classroom design is safety. Therefore, it is important to consider carefully the overall arrangement of the centers and condition of equipment and materials used in each center. Teachers should begin each day with a safety check of the classroom and each individual center. When conducting a safety check, ask yourself the following questions.

- Are floor coverings smooth and unbroken?
- Are traffic paths between areas clear?
- Are heaters, pipes, and vents covered and sectioned off?
- Are electric cords, wires, and plugs out of children's reach?
- Are electric outlets covered?
- Can children quickly exit each center area if necessary? Or do they have to wait for others to get through a small opening between dividers?
- Are smoke detectors in appropriate locations?

- Are fire extinguishers accessible?
- Has peeling paint been removed and surfaces repainted?
- Have broken furniture and toys been removed or repaired?
- Are blocks sanded and free from splinters?
- Are sharp corners of room dividers padded?
- Are emergency procedures and phone numbers clearly posted?
- Are all hazardous materials eliminated or stored in locked cupboards?
- Have all houseplants been studied to determine that they are nontoxic?

It is important not to make any assumptions regarding safety. For example, electric outlets should be covered in all early childhood classrooms; this includes first- and second-grade rooms. We cannot assume that all children, even six- and seven-year-old children, know not to put objects into outlets. Even if children understand this rule, when they are concentrating on something and get an idea, their actions are often impulsive and illogical. Also, remember to reevaluate the room arrangement and safety factors each time a new student enters your classroom.

Choosing Materials and Activities

It is interesting to speculate about the relationship between the toys and materials in a center and the activities that take place in that center. Do the materials in a center suggest the activities that will take place? Do signs, directions or activity cards placed in a center determine activities? Or do the activities determine the materials? To put this question another way, does a child enter a center, see painting materials, and then choose to paint a picture? Or does the child think, "I want to paint today," and then proceed to the art center? Of course, there is no single answer. Therefore, it is important that a center is equipped with materials that both suggest activities and provide the materials needed for activities invented or initiated by children.

As we have stated earlier, learning centers are multipurpose areas within a classroom where equipment and materials are organized to promote active, child-centered learning. Therefore, the materials in any one center will reflect the purpose for which the center was designed. For example, in the construction center, you must first put materials for building, and in the dramatic play center, you must first put materials that spark imagination and pretense. What specific materials you put in the center will depend on both the age of the children and the range of abilities represented by all the children who will normally use the center. Therefore, it is important to review the concept of developmentally appropriate practice discussed in Chapter 2. Remember, decisions about materials and activities appropriate to any group of children must be based on three types of knowledge:

1. *Age appropriateness*—knowledge of age-related characteristics that permit predictions within an age range about what will be safe, interesting, achievable, and challenging,
2. *Individual appropriateness*—knowledge about the strengths, interests, and needs of each individual child in the group, so teacher can adapt materials to be both responsive and safe for all, and
3. *Cultural appropriateness*—knowledge of social and cultural contexts in which children live. This ensures that learning experiences will be meaningful, relevant, and respectful of participating children and their families (Bredekamp & Copple, 1997).

Therefore, two basic criteria for the selection of toys and materials emerge from the concept of developmental appropriateness. First, any toy or material used in a classroom must be safe for all children in the classroom, and, second, all materials used must be chosen and used with sensitivity to the cultural backgrounds of children and families participating in the program. Here are guidelines to use when choosing toys that are both safe and display sensitivity toward all cultural backgrounds.

1. Choose toys and materials appropriate for children's stages of development.

2. Read labels on packaging carefully to determine the age range for which the toy or material is recommended and the suggested care and use of the material or toy. Also, discard packaging that could be dangerous.

3. Select only toys and materials made from nontoxic and flame retardant substances.

4. Inspect toys daily. Discard broken or cracked toys. Keep all toys and materials clean.

5. Carefully supervise the play of all children to ensure that toys and materials are used in appropriate and safe ways.

6. Include in centers authentic objects that represent the different cultural groups of children in the classroom. For example, include a wok and a tortilla press in the housekeeping area of the classroom.

7. Include adaptive equipment, such as braces and a wheelchair in dramatic play centers. Make sure that this is extra equipment, not belonging to any child.

8. Carefully inspect all toys, materials, pictures, and books and remove any that promote stereotypes of cultural or ethnic groups or gender bias.

9. Label centers and materials in multilingual ways. Use all languages relevant to your classroom, including sign language.

10. Avoid referring to any center, activity, or material as a place for "the boys" or "the girls" to play.

Specific suggestions for selection of materials are included throughout this text.

Facilitating Learning within Centers

Scheduling. As mentioned in Chapter 3, two roles teachers have regarding play are those of planner and protector. Teachers must plan children's play environments, and they must also protect children's right to play by scheduling ample time in the daily schedule for play. As we have seen, play supports learning in many ways, and therefore it is important to create environments where children's play can develop into rich and complex episodes involving imagination and social interactions. Christie and Wardle (1992) suggest that free-play periods of thirty minutes or longer facilitate elaborate group dramatizations and complex construction projects. Blocks of time less than thirty minutes seem to produce less complex varieties of play, such as nonsocial forms of dramatic play, building and tearing down simple constructions, and parallel play in sand or water centers. However, because time is so essential to the richness of play, and because time in centers can involve children in a mix of work and play activities, we suggest that blocks of at least sixty minutes be scheduled for center time. Table 4.5 suggests time blocks to be used in determining a daily schedule for preschool and kindergarten classrooms.

In selecting a time frame for play, it is important to reflect on everything a child must do to initiate and sustain play. For example, the steps involved in initiating a sociodramatic play episode include recruiting other players, negotiating the roles, agreeing on story line,

TABLE 4.5   Time Blocks for Preschool and Kindergarten Classrooms

Half-Day Preschool Program	**Full-Day Kindergarten Program**
Morning learning center block	Greeting and planning time
Circle	Morning learning center block (1½ hour)
Outdoor time	Snack
Snack time	Outdoor play (or time with curriculum specialist)
Story	Story
Music and movement	Lunch
Review and dismissal	Rest
	Group time
Full-Day Preschool Program	Afternoon learning center block (1 hour)
Morning learning center block	Outdoor play (or time with curriculum specialist)
Circle	Daily reflections and dismissal
Outdoor time	
Snack time	
Music and movement	
Story	
Lunch	
Rest or quiet time	
Afternoon center block	
Outdoor time	
Daily reflections and dismissal	

designating the make-believe identities of the objects, and determining the area of the room to be used (Christie & Wardle, 1992). And this is only what happens before the actual play begins.

In addition to allowing ample time for work and play in centers, teachers and care providers should maintain a consistent daily schedule. Consistency provides children with structure and security and relieves them from the stress of not knowing what is coming next or when they will *get to play*. Creating a chart that outlines the daily schedule in a way children can read helps them learn to predict and anticipate the events of the day. One way to do this is to arrange, on a large piece of poster board, photographs of children engaged in different activities, together with drawings of clocks that show the time these activities occur.

Notice that we did not include opening activities in either of the daily blocks for preschool programs. Mr. Farber began the kindergarten day with learning centers and included the traditional morning activities (e.g., role, lunch count, and determining the date) within the routines of choosing centers. This gave the children an authentic purpose for activities such as writing their name and determining the day of the week. It also provided Mr. Farber with the opportunity to greet each child individually. Young children and their parents need individual attention and greetings each day. By starting the day with learning center time, teachers have the opportunity to greet children and parents and help children start their day successfully.

Kindergartners are able to sustain attention for longer periods of time in group discussions and activities. It is also more common for kindergarten classrooms to be served by curriculum specialists such as librarians, art teachers, music teachers, and physical education teachers. However, it is still critical that kindergarten children have secure blocks of time to work and play in centers.

Primary students do spend more time in teacher-directed learning activities and subject oriented activities. However, they too need time to choose their own activities and play and work in centers. Many of the activities available in primary centers focus on theme studies or on supporting skill development in literacy and numeracy areas. Therefore, it is important that primary students have access to centers for at least one hour each day. If curriculum pressures prohibit lengthy play periods for primary-age children, Christie and Wardle (1992) suggest that teachers schedule several long periods per week. This is preferred over devoting short periods of time to center work and play or limiting access to centers to before school only or when a child's "work is done."

Developing a System for Choice and Movement. Consistency in scheduling center time is important and so is consistency in how much freedom to allow children for choosing activities within centers and moving among centers during center time. A good management plan that minimizes the time children spend waiting to go to centers and maximizes the time they actually spend in centers will help students develop self-direction skills. The basic element of any management system is the amount of freedom children have to choose and move among centers during center time. In other words, do children get to choose where they work and play and what activities they pursue? Or do teachers choose? Of course, the answer will vary from classroom to classroom and even within a classroom. Levels of freedom to choose activities can be illustrated by the use of the following continuum.

Free Choice —————— Collaborative Decisions ————— Assigned Activities

When children have free choice, they are able to choose among all centers that are open and among all activities available in that center. Teachers who use a free-choice method, like Mr. Farber, create signs for each center that display the number of spaces available. When children come to the center they leave their name tag, or other token, to show that they are choosing to play in the area. This sign shows other children whether there is room for them to play; therefore, children are responsible for themselves. Free choice generally provides children with the richest, most meaningful work and play experiences because they have determined their own activities and are the able to sustain their play longer.

Not every child in any given classroom is able to make choices at the beginning of the year. Indeed, at the beginning of the year, teachers are not always willing to let everyone have complete freedom to choose until rules are established. By using collaborative decision making, the teacher and the child plan together which centers the child will go to and maybe even which activities he or she will initiate while there. This system can be helpful to children who have not had much experience in decision making. It provides the child with some structure and security. It provides the teacher with a way to guide the child into new areas of play and to new groups of playmates.

Assigning centers, or assigning activities within a center, is the most restrictive form of center management. Rotating groups of children through centers is one method of assigning centers. In this method, children are organized into small groups. Each group is assigned a center, and the group plays at that center with the various materials for a certain amount of time, say at least twenty minutes. When the time has elapsed, everyone in the group moves on to another center. This continues until all children have had the opportunity to play and work in all centers. Again, this is certainly not an ideal use of the concepts of centers, but it could introduce children to the idea of centers, the guidelines and responsibilities of center behavior, and the idea of making choices. Or this system could be used to help a particular child who is overwhelmed by the idea of choice. In any case, assigning centers, either to the whole class or to individual children, should be seen as a temporary measure, a stepping stone to help children develop the ability to make decisions about their use of time.

As we mentioned earlier, learning centers and learning center systems are dynamic and change as the needs of the children in a classroom change. No one category of freedom will be right for all children in a classroom. Various levels of freedom of choice will be needed to help move individual children toward greater degrees of self-direction.

Maintaining the Learning Center System.   There are several strategies that help teachers maintain learning center systems that facilitate rich work and play episodes among young children. First, provide children with initial training and practice regarding the use of centers. You may not want to start the year with every center operating at its full capacity. Therefore, in the beginning you may want to limit the number of play spaces available and the materials in each center until children develop an understanding of what is expected of them as they work and play in centers.

It is also very important to develop with children, over the first few weeks of the school year, a routine for choosing centers, working or playing in centers, and cleaning and restoring centers to their original form when center time is over. For example, in Mr. Farber's kindergarten, the children had an established routine for entering into center activities. It is interesting to note that Mr. Farber chose to incorporate the development of many literacy and numeracy skills into the routines of managing the learning center system. This is certainly appropriate for kindergarten and primary-age children. However, the routines developed by teachers of three- and four-year-old children will necessarily be less formal and structured. For example, three-year-old children generally are allowed to enter into center activities without counting spaces or signing their names on cards. They are, however, expected to respect those already playing in a center, enter play appropriately, and do some basic cleaning up before they move on to another center.

Since all children, regardless of age, come to school with differing abilities regarding self-direction and choice making, teachers need to carefully observe individual children and provide individual coaching and support when indicated. Also, they must be sure to provide families with information concerning the importance of center time and how it relates to children's learning and development. When a new student enters the classroom, it is important that the teacher spend the time needed to acquaint this student with the center system, even providing him or her with a well-seasoned buddy. As children grow and develop responsibility and self-direction in their use of centers, teachers will add additional centers or additional play spaces to existing centers.

Another strategy useful in maintaining a learning center system is to build guidelines for student behavior collaboratively with children. For the youngest children (threes and young fours), teachers set the basic safety guidelines, model and reinforce safe and fair play. For older children (older fours, kindergarten, and primary-school children), teachers and care providers should conduct small-group discussions and develop consensus regarding safe practice and fair play. Collaborative formation of guidelines does not give children control of class conduct but provides a learning experience that promotes discussion and problem solving. The teacher is using his or her knowledge of the children's interests and development to enlist their cooperation and appeal to their sense of empathy and fair play.

It is also important to post guidelines for working and playing together. Pair posters of written rules with picture illustrations. Let children do the illustrating. Change the posters from time to time. Post polaroid pictures of children playing safely and fairly near the written guidelines. For example, Beaty (1992) suggests posting pictures in the block center to help children understand how high they can safely stack blocks. Use a picture of children who are building structures that are within safety guidelines.

Teacher's Activities During Centers. What do teachers and other adults do while children are in centers? First let us explain what they do not do. They do not do paper work. They do not plan lessons. They do not prepare materials. They do not visit with each other. All of the above activities may distract teachers from center activities from time to time, but to facilitate the optimal value of learning center systems, and the optimal value of play, teachers and other adults in the classroom must remain engaged and attentive to everything that is happening in the room. In other words, they must be "with-it." "With-itness" is a concept, derived from the work of Jacob Kounin, that describes the ability of a teacher to see and know everything that is going on (Charles & Barr, 1989). It is somewhat intuitive. It informs decision making. Some teachers simply know when to intervene between students or groups of students, when to bring an activity to a close, or when to introduce dissonance, a surprise. With-itness may be partly intuitive, but it certainly can be improved through practice.

A teacher who has a high degree of with-itness consistently circulates among centers. She may pause in the dramatic center to "pet the dog." She may then move on to the art center and refill the paint cups. From there she may pause to enjoy an impromptu puppet performance. She may suggest alternative activities in the block center when the block pile begins to topple. She may help one child enter a new activity and stay long enough for him to feel secure. Most of the time this teacher is relaxed and clearly enjoying her interactions with the children, who are willing to invite her into their play. She is consistently taking mental, if not literal, notes of the activities in which children are engaged. It would be impossible to make a definitive list of the actions of a teacher during center time. Table 4.6 provides examples of different roles and interventions teachers use during learning center time.

Supporting Students with Special Needs. It is important that children with special needs have many opportunities to work and play with their peers. These opportunities not

TABLE 4.6   Roles and Interventions during Learning Center Time

During learning center time, teachers play many roles and must constantly make decisions about whether to intervene and which intervention strategies to use. Decisions are based on the teacher's general knowledge of child development and specific knowledge of the individual children in his or her care. Here are some examples.

Observer
Mrs. Morris observes as three-year-old Nathan stands at an easel and covers an entire page with red paint. Although it seems like a perfect opportunity to engage Nathan in a discussion about color, Mrs. Morris resists because this is the very first time that Nathan has come to the art center and his face display both a sense of accomplishment and concentration.

Safety Inspector
Mr. Trent, a kindergarten teacher, observes three children building tall buildings with large hollow wooden blocks. The buildings are beginning to become taller than the children. Mr. Trent approaches the center and intervenes in the play by saying, "Boy, those are tall buildings, and so shaky! I am really concerned about your safety." The children reevaluate the situation and decide to adjust the height of the buildings.

Learner, Resource Person, Peacemaker, Consultant
A first-grade child has brought an abandoned bird's nest to school and placed it in the discovery center. During the course of the morning several children become interested in the nest and speculate about the kind of bird that built it. In fact, an argument is about to break out. The teacher sits with the children and they ask her what kind of bird built the nest. The teacher responds to the children by telling them the truth, that is, she really doesn't know. She then asks them how they could find out. The children suggest reading a book and calling the zoo. The teacher helps the children write a note to the school librarian asking for resource books on birds. The children go off to the library and bring back the books. In one of the books, there is a reference to a web site that has information about birds. The teacher and children together log onto the web and find much information including pictures of different kinds of nests. The children concluded that this was as good as calling the zoo.

Spectator
A group of five second-grade children have been playing in the music center. They spontaneously form a band and begin to play and sing. An audience gathers to watch the performance. Their teacher joins the audience and demonstrates his enjoyment by clapping along.

Matchmaker
Serenoa is interested in puzzles and often works alone completing complex models. John is very outgoing and is interested in puzzles but gets frustrated easily and quits. Their teacher brings the two children together and facilitates the development of a friendship that fosters each child's strengths.

Other roles teachers play during learning centers include alternative-seeker, communicator, consultant, encourager, parallel player, participant, play tutor, and record keeper.

only support their cognitive, language, and social development, but also provide unique and valuable opportunities for all children in the classroom to interact and develop values of acceptance, helpfulness, and tolerance. Therefore, teachers will need to be protective of the schedules of children with special needs, not allowing one-on-one tutoring or therapy to replace all of the child's learning center time.

Teachers should also develop a system for incorporating the specific learning goals of children with special needs into learning center activities. When reviewing each child's Individual Educational Plan (IEP), the teacher can determine the goal-related activities that most naturally occur in each learning center. Then he or she writes the goal on index cards and lists specific play activities and materials that lead to development of the goal. Then, when observing children's center activities, the teacher can record, in writing or with video recorder, anecdotes that document the child's development. The teacher could also place special materials in appropriate centers to foster children's spontaneous play. The teacher's actions serve two functions. First, they provide children with special needs the same opportunities to choose activities as all the other children in the class. Second, creating IEP activity cards reminds teachers, teacher's assistants, volunteers, or therapists of playful ways to engage children in activities designed to foster learning and development.

Embedding Transitions and Routines with Playful Activities

Learning center systems are excellent ways of embedding classroom culture with play and playful learning. Another way to instill playfulness into culture of the classroom is to incorporate playful activities into the transitions and routines that occur in the classroom. Transitions are the times in the school day when children are changing activities. For example, when children move from center time to circle time, they are making a transition. Routines are established patterns of activity or behavior that are consistently expected to occur at set times or in certain situations. In Mr. Farber's kindergarten classroom, there was a set routine for entering the classroom in the morning—children entered the classroom, greeted the teacher, put their belongings away, retrieved their name tags, chose a learning center, and began working or playing. There was also a set routine for leaving one learning center and entering another. Established transitions and routines help make the school day easy, enjoyable, and as close to stress free as possible for children, teachers, and others who may be working or volunteering in a classroom because they give everyone the ability to predict what will happen during the course of the day and an understanding of what behaviors are expected. Therefore, routines and transitions are very important in early childhood classrooms; when children are able to predict what is going to happen and know what is expected, their mental energy is freed and focussed on learning. Table 4.7 outlines common routines and transitions.

The use of playful activities during routines and transitions can not only increase children's enjoyment but can also potentially provide many opportunities for learning. Reifel

TABLE 4.7 Common Routines and Transitions in Early Childhood Programs

arrival time	hygiene activities
taking roll	going to and from the classroom
lunch count	lunch time
choosing centers	rest time
clean up activities	departure time
snack time	

and Yeatman (1993) describe play as a family of simulations that include pretense, dramatic play, storytelling, games, arts and crafts, rough-and-tumble play, and motor exploration. These categories are all natural play activities for children and are useful in planning because they can easily be incorporated into the center activities, transitions, and routines that typically define early childhood classrooms. For example, engaging children in motor exploration is an easy way to get young children from one place to another without prolonged directions or tedious lines in which children have to wait for a turn, and for everyone to comply. The direction, "move to the door like a camel, without touching anything or anyone," becomes a mental as well as a physical challenge to children. When children's mental energy is challenged, then their physical energy is channeled into positive behaviors. Many examples of ways to incorporate playful activities into routines and transitions are included in the remaining chapters of this text.

Levels of Teachers' Direction for Play Activities

When planning for classroom play or planning to embed the classroom culture with playful activities, teachers are necessarily concerned about the amount of structure and direction they need. Bergen (1988) describes a continuum of play in the classroom that includes the following categories: free play, guided play, directed play, and work disguised as play. Three features distinguish each of these categories: the amount of direction given by the teacher regarding the content and outcome of the play episode, the degree of conformity to rules or freedom to experiment with rules allowed within the play episode, and the amount of choice or selection the teacher allows the children to have regarding a specific play activity.

In *free play,* children choose activities or materials, determine the way the materials will be used, and direct the general outcome of the play episode. Many free-play activities occur during center time or during outdoor play time. Typical activities during free play invoke the discovery and exploratory mode of playing and learning. For example, children use art materials to create original products, or they play with sand and water for the sheer pleasure it brings. In free play of a sociodramatic nature, children may use the props provided in either traditional or innovating ways, as long as they remain sensitive and respectful to others. In other words, we would not allow children to engage in dramatic play that would encourage or support negative images of specific ethnic groups. Teachers supervise all free play that occurs during the school day, but only step in and redirect play that is becoming dangerous either physically or psychologically.

In *guided play,* the teacher selects material for specific children to use in their play. By selecting material for play, the adult guides children toward learning certain concepts. The children still have some freedom in how they play with the objects, but the adult intervenes by questioning and modeling to lead the children to discover certain properties or to refine certain skills. For example, a teacher may assign a certain child or group of children to play at the sand table. While the children are at the sand table, they may choose how to go about playing with the sand, but the teacher may intervene with specific questions that guide the children's learning about the properties of the sand, or how heavy wet sand is compared to dry sand. Guided play often occurs during center time. It may be that at certain times, some children are engaged in free play and some children are being guided in their play activities.

Directed play is typified by teachers instructing children how to accomplish a specific task. Songs, finger plays, circle games, and games with rules are examples of directed play. Most children will enter into these activities freely and will be rewarded by the act of singing and playing, but the teacher's purpose for the activity is to provide children with opportunities to develop, practice, or demonstrate a skill. Directed play activities can occur during center time. For example, children may choose to play a particular board game or computer-generated game in which the specific rules have been previously learned, or they may choose to follow direction cards in the snack center to create a peanut butter sandwich. Other directed play activities can occur during transitions or in small or large groups. Examples include singing and movement games, thinking games such as "Twenty Questions," and craft-making activities.

Work disguised as play is a category describing highly structured activities that are assigned to children. Often teachers create an activity they feel will be fun and present it to the children as a required activity. For example, a teacher may decide that all children are to make a model of a turtle. She provides each child with a portion of an egg carton and proceeds to give step by step instructions on how to make the turtle. The teacher intends to provide a playful learning experience for her class, and for some children it certainly is playful and fun. However, other children may not see this activity as either playful or fun because it may not be intrinsically interesting or challenging or because it requires the child to understand concepts or rules that he or she has not yet mastered. The important point here is for teachers to remember that play is different for different children. Therefore, what might be a playful learning activity for one child may turn into a frustrating experience for another.

To provide positive learning experiences for all children in early childhood classrooms, teachers need to include a variety of free-, guided-, and directed-play activities during center time and as a basis for classroom transitions and routines. They also need to guard against thinking that they are providing playful activities just because these activities seem playful from the teacher's perspective. Teachers should observe each child's activities carefully and intervene, with support and guidance, when an intended play activity turns into work disguised as play.

Technology and Play

Today, technology plays an important role in the daily lives of young children. Children as young as three or four regularly operate televisions, videocassette recorders, audiocassette recorders, and compact disk players, often using remote control devices. Many young children have daily access to computers in their homes, and those that do not certainly need access in schools if they are to successfully adapt to life in a technology-driven society. The use of computers and appropriate software in early childhood classrooms has been shown to enhance socioemotional and cognitive development (Clements, 1987) and offer children another way to play. Therefore, the appropriate question for early childhood educators is no longer whether computers should be used, but how to use computers effectively to support the development of the whole child.

To incorporate computer technology effectively into a classroom culture that promotes playful exploration and learning, early childhood educators first need to understand and appreciate the learning process as children begin to interact with computers and software programs. Davidson and Wright (1994) outline four stages of this process. These stages are

- *Discovery*—a growing awareness that what appears on the screen is what I created or selected
- *Involvement*—motivation to achieve mastery of basic commands and sequences

- *Self-confidence*—ability to execute a plan and to predict outcomes
- *Creativity*—invention of solutions, design of challenges for others, and original creation (p. 78)

It is true that most children are drawn to computers, but it is also true that each child will need individualized support and encouragement, based on prior knowledge and experience, when learning to use the computer in personally meaningful ways.

Even though young children like to work with computers, they are not mature enough to be discriminating users (Haugland & Shade, 1990). Therefore, it is important that teachers not only select software that is generally appropriate for their classroom, but also carefully observe how each child works with these programs and therefore determine individual appropriateness.

Open-ended, discovery-oriented programs, frequently called micro-worlds (Haugland & Shade 1990; Papert, 1980) or simulations, are generally the most appropriate for early childhood classrooms. These programs provide young children with opportunities to work collaboratively with other children, explore new environments, make choices, and then discover how their choices impact the micro-world created by the program. Software programs that promote learning through drill and practice activities, often called electronic worksheets, will be appropriate only to children who have mastered the concepts and therefore must be used exclusively on an individual basis and not as a generalized learning activity.

Criteria for selecting software that fosters playful learning in early childhood programs include the following.

- Does the software promote collaborative work or play among pairs or small groups of children?
- Does the software allow children to make decisions they understand?
- Does the software allow children to decide together what will happen in the course of the program?
- Does the software elicit excitement, noticeable in children's language, from the children?
- Does the software generate pretend play?
- Does the software present concepts and skills at the children's learning level?
- Does the software reflect the children's interests?
- Does the complexity of the software expand? In other words, can children continue to use and be challenged by the software as their knowledge and experience with the software increase?
- Does the software promote a process orientation to learning? Or is the software outcome-driven?
- Can children easily recognize and relate to the images and situations presented in the software?
- Can children use a trial-and-error approach, and therefore develop independence when learning to work with the software?
- Do the images presented in the software program promote antibias values? In other words, does the software present concepts of role and gender equity, concepts of diverse family styles, and concepts of equitable treatment of people of color and people of differing ages and abilities?

Computers and accompanying software are one of many materials in a developmentally appropriate classroom. They can offer valuable learning opportunities because they provide children with experiences that lead to exploration, experimentation, and problem solving. When the use of technology is conceived as a social activity and its use is initiated and directed in child-centered and developmentally appropriate ways, computers become an important part of the playful classroom.

Developing Advocacy Skills

Helping families understand the relationship between children's play and their learning and development is not only a formidable task but also a long-term advocacy goal of all early childhood educators. When taking on such a large goal or task, it is helpful to envision the small steps that will ultimately lead steadily toward ultimate success. By starting small and building success one step at a time, teachers establish credibility, which ultimately results in empowerment by administrators and trust by parents and families.

When administrators perceive a teacher's track record as being successful, they generally give more decision-making power to that teacher. Therefore, the teacher is better able to impact the learning environment of his or her classroom. Likewise, when families perceive their child's teacher as credible, or "a good teacher," they trust the teacher and the school and are better able to build a collaborative relationship with the school and become involved in their child's education. This involvement benefits everyone: the child, the family, the community, the teacher, and the school.

In this chapter we have discussed developing learning center systems that promote playful learning. One step toward the goal of helping family members understand the relationship between play and learning is to keep them informed about the purpose of learning centers and the difference between children's play at home and their play at school. Brewer and Kieff (1997) point out that parents and teachers often have different visions and different expectations of the role of play in educational programs. Newsletters and family night discussions can feature the learning potential of learning center systems. Photographs of children learning while engaged in center activities can be included in newsletters or in children's learning portfolios. Videotaped segments of children involved in learning centers are interesting not only to parents but also to other teachers and to administrators.

Informing parents of the educational value of center and play activities is one step toward fostering an appreciation for the role of play in the learning and development of young children. Another step is to involve family members in the development of centers. Many families have resources they can donate as center materials. Lists of needed or desired materials can be posted in the classroom or included in newsletters. Some family members, maybe retired grandparents or even interested neighbors, have time to donate to supervise centers or to make important materials. Evening, weekend, or holiday work parties provide opportunities for interested individuals to volunteer time and energy while learning first-hand about the important relationship between children's play and their learning. Table 4.8 suggests many different experiences and activities that will help you develop advocacy skills.

TABLE 4.8   Advocacy Activities: Informing and Involving Families and Administrators

Build Success One Step at a Time		
Becoming Aware	*Furthering Your Understanding*	*Taking Action*
1. Visit a developmentally appropriate preschool or kindergarten classroom when no children are present. Make a diagram of the physical arrangement of the classroom. Examine learning centers and compare equipment with equipment suggested in the text. Note the schedule used. Interview the teacher and discuss his or her goals for the children.	1. Review several articles describing appropriate use of computer technology in early childhood classrooms. According to these articles, what are the advantages of using computers in preschool and kindergarten classrooms? What are the drawbacks?	1. Develop a learning center that is based on a theme study or project.
2. Revisit the same classroom when children are present. Observe the children working and playing in centers. Describe how they work and play together. Observe transitions and describe how they are handled by the teachers and the children. List all the routines you observe during the course of your visit. Describe how your expectations for what would happen in this classroom (based on your previous visit and reading and discussing the text) were met or not met.	2. Review five or more software programs intended for use with young children. Critique these programs based on the criteria suggested in this chapter.	2. Develop a newsletter that explains to parents the goals of learning centers.
	3. Observe three-, four- and five-year-old children who are using a computer and appropriate software. Find out how much experience each child has had working with the computer or software program. Describe the children's actions and activities. Describe how experience affects children's actions and learning potential when using a computer.	3. Volunteer in a preschool classroom and facilitate the activities in one learning center.
		4. Volunteer in a kindergarten classroom and facilitate activities in one learning center.
		5. Volunteer in a primary classroom and facilitate activities in one learning center.
3. Visit several primary classrooms and note how learning centers are used. Describe similarities and differences in the way learning centers are scheduled and used in preschool and primary classrooms.	4. Observe children using a computer in a primary classroom. Observe a computer lab when primary-age children are present. From your observations, describe the advantages and disadvantages of each system.	6. Develop a one-hour workshop that explains the relationship between learning and play to parents.

Summary

Learning centers are multipurpose areas within a classroom where equipment and materials are organized to promote active, child-centered learning. A learning center system provides a systematic way to utilize classroom materials, space, and time. Learning center systems are dynamic and change as the needs of the children in a classroom change. Children's involvement in determining which centers they will use may vary depending on their individual needs. Decisions about materials and activities appropriate to any group of children must be based on age appropriateness, individual appropriateness, and cultural appropriateness. Routines are established patterns of activity or behavior that are consistently expected to occur at set times or in certain situations. Routines and transitions are very important in early childhood classrooms because when children are able to predict what is going to happen and know what is expected, their mental energy is freed and focused on learning.

REVISITING FIRST IMPRESSIONS

Review your first impressions of learning centers. Compare your initial impression and your current impression regarding the value and development of learning centers. Which of your initial questions or concerns have been satisfied? How can you resolve your remaining questions or concerns?

QUESTIONS FOR DISCUSSION

1. Discuss the advantages of using learning center systems in early childhood classrooms. First take the teacher's perspective. Next, take a young child's perspective.

2. As a kindergarten teacher, you have developed a learning center system similar to Mr. Farber's. Until now, your classroom has not included any children with physical disabilities. Brandon, a five-year-old with cerebral palsy and confined to a wheelchair, is entering your kindergarten midyear. You learn from an interview with his father that he enjoys playing with other children during center time and particularly enjoys blocks and the sand and water center. Describe the modifications you will make to your learning center environment and procedure.

3. Develop an example that describes how a teacher's idea of play becomes work disguised as play to a child. What are the possible consequences of this event?

SUGGESTED READINGS

Beaty, J., & Tucker, W. (1987). *The computer as a paint brush: Creative Uses for the personal computer in the preschool classroom.* Columbus, OH: Merrill.

Isbell, R. (1995). *The complete learning center book.* Beltsville, MD: Gryphon House.

Wright, J., & Shade, D. (1994). *Young children: Active learners in a technological age.* Washington, DC: National Association for the Education of Young Children.

5 Fostering Playful Learning through Pretense

Prereading Guide

First Impressions.   How do pretense and drama figure in your life today? Do you enjoy it passively or actively? What has influenced the way you perceive drama and incorporate it into your life?

Revisit
Levels of Teachers' Direction for Play Activities (Chapter 4)

Stories from the Field

The following narrative is a description of a theme study about the maritime industry and a project that focused on fire boats. The study was conducted in a preschool classroom in Louisiana, and the voice you hear is that of the teacher, Pat Roig (1997).

I often watched groups of children playing in an old boat we had "docked" in our play yard and wondered how I should react when inevitably, their play would become rowdy and aggressive. I did not want to inhibit their creativity and imagination, but I didn't want them to get so far out of control that someone would get hurt. I remember one particular day when the children had transformed the boat, in their imaginations, into some fantastic space ship and had developed a war play theme. Their play became very intense and some children got their feelings hurt. It was also difficult to get them settled down and engaged in other activities. This certainly was not the first time this had happened. In fact, once we had put fishing poles in the boat thinking that it would stimulate more realistic boat play. However, the children had other ideas. They turned the fishing poles into swords and thus added a new dimension to their war play. The staff had, on several occasions, talked about removing the boat from the play yard because, after all, it was not used as a boat but seemed to facilitate rough, rowdy, nonimaginative, even aggressive play.

While it was tempting to think that by simply getting rid of the boat, we would get rid of the aggressive play, I knew that it wasn't that easy. I also knew that dramatic play fostered cognitive, language, and social development, and what I needed to do was to find a way to make the context of the play meaningful and channel children's energy and imagination into positive learning experiences. Watching the children play gave me the idea for developing a theme study related to the ships and boats in our harbors. We live in a community surrounded by water, and many of the families of the children in the class had direct or indirect ties with maritime industries. More information about boats, ships, and this industry would provide the children a meaningful context for their fantasy and creative play and at the same time enrich their learning opportunities in all disciplines.

I began by asking the children to study the boat on the playground and tell me everything they could about it. Their ideas were amazing. Some children discussed the physical description of the boat and some discussed what they thought was the history of the boat and how it got into the play yard. All children had some misconceptions regarding the boat. For example, one child thought it was made of concrete. Another child thought it was "two thousand hundred feet long." Together, we generated questions about our boat and then about boats in general. I asked the children how we should go about finding the answers. I didn't think they would have any ideas. After all, they were just four years old. Wrong! They had many good ideas. I realized that I had underestimated the children. Our study was off to a great start.

Over the next few weeks we read books about boats, ships, and life aboard ships. We learned the difference between boats, ships, tankers, and vessels. Many parents dropped in with stories and materials that supported our investigation. We interviewed captains and crew members of several boats and ships. Adults were always amazed at the depth of the children's questions. I am sure they thought that I had made them up and the children had memorized them. However, the children's spontaneous follow-up questions proved that the thinking was all their own.

While the class studied the general theme of boats and water transportation, one group of children became particularly interested in the fireboats that worked along the docks of the Mississippi, here in New Orleans. This interest developed into a project and during the course of their project, the whole class was invited to tour a fireboat.

What was amazing to me about the development of the theme and project was that our day-to-day activities and schedules did not change. We still had our center time, snack time, and our circle time. The real change was in the dynamics of the interactions between the children and the adults and among the children. The sociodramatic play of the children became much more complex. Their conversations were richer and deeper and many times revolved around solving problems. After our field trip the children created all kinds of props that turned the play yard boat into a fireboat, and they negotiated authentic roles and themes for their dramatic play.

This experience of developing themes and projects with four-year-old children has changed my understanding of both the role of sociodramatic play and the role of investigation in the intellectual and social development of young children. The play and the investigation went hand in hand. There was a reciprocal relationship between them, each enriching the other. I saw children develop and solve complex problems while engaged in dramatic play. We truly became a community of learners. It was through the play that children "worked out" not only their understanding of boats and those who work on boats, but also their understanding of their relationships with each other. I wasn't the only one who came to these conclusions. Parents who were involved with the project developed a new understanding and appreciation for dramatic play, and saw firsthand how time spent playing enhances children's learning and social development.

Dramatic and sociodramatic play opportunities provide powerful learning opportunities for young children because through pretend play children have the opportunity to assume roles; see others' points of view; develop knowledge about appropriate roles, actions, and behaviors; explore the forms and functions of language by creating dialogue; use their bodies and their words to express emotions; and use past and present experiences to make decisions and solve problems (Shaftel & Shaftel, 1983). Therefore, a developmentally appropriate curriculum for early childhood programs must be rich with opportunities for children to dramatize familiar experiences, try out the roles of others (role-play), and share enactments with both peers and adults (Bredekamp & Copple, 1997: McCaslin, 1996; Nelson, 1986).

We can learn from Mrs. Roig's experience the importance of developing a meaningful context for dramatic play by providing children with information that can be acted on. Initially, the children in Mrs. Roig's school did not have an interest in meaningful boat play because they were not engaged in learning about boats. This often led to the misuse of props and the emergence of aggressive play themes. When she began to create a meaningful context for the children's play through discussions, books, project work, and use of community resources, the children began to engage in rich, meaningful creative drama. They gained a sense of ownership that fostered a deeper commitment to their play. Their play actually became "more serious," and through their play they were able to work out many concepts and role responsibilities related to the theme of their play. Therefore, their creativity and their learning were not suppressed but enhanced.

There are many ways to create a meaningful context for children's dramatic and sociodramatic play. The purpose of this chapter is to explore playful teaching strategies that foster children's development and learning through pretense and dramatic play. We will begin by looking at the benefits of fantasy play and development of pretense.

The Role of Pretense in Development and Learning

Throughout childhood, children will engage in countless episodes of creative and imaginative fantasy play. Fromberg (1998) states,

> Imagination is central to play and to the content of education. When children move between "what if" plans and "as if" execution of those plans, they are employing significant imaginative skills. It is imagination, after all, that makes progress possible in all disciplines of knowledge. (p. 194)

Engagement in dramatic play facilitates the development of children's imagination, thinking, reasoning, problem-solving skills (Fox, 1987; McCaslin, 1996; Vygotsky, 1978), their language and conversation skills (Engle, 1995; Isenberg & Jalongo, 1997; Tompkins & Hoskisson, 1995), their ability to understand the perspective of others (Donoghue, 1990; Tompkins, 1997), their ability to express inner feelings (Erikson, 1988; Mayesky, 1998), and the growth of confidence and a positive self-concept (McCaslin, 1996). Therefore, providing multiple opportunities for preschool, kindergarten, and primary-school children to engage in dramatic and sociodramatic play enables children to develop cognitive, language, and social competency.

The Development of Pretense

Daria, a toddler, is sitting with her mother at the dinner table. The meal is over. The dishes are all empty, but Daria picks up her tippy cup, puts it to her mouth, makes a loud sipping noise, smiles, and proclaims, "Mm-mm ood (good)!" Daria's mother, at first taken by surprise because she knows the cup is empty, realizes that this is the first time she has seen Daria pretend.

"You like your juice!" Daria's mother responds, smiling broadly.

"Mm mm!" says Daria, as she takes another loud pretend sip.

Daria has entered the world of symbolic thought and dramatic play. She can now make mental transformations, altering objects, time, situations, and roles mentally, through pretend play (Kostelnik, Whiren, & Stein, 1986).

When children pretend, they are using a nonliteral, or "as if," modality of thought and action (Fein, 1981). Daria has demonstrated the first aspect of pretense, acting in a nonliteral way. She knows there is no more juice in the cup but is acting as if there is. Over the next few years, Daria's play will become increasingly complex and will begin to involve others. In the beginning, children's pretend acts center on their own actions—pretending to drink or eat, pretending to sleep, or pretending to hide. Soon children will begin to act on some other person or object. For example, Daria might pretend to feed a doll, stuffed animal, or even her mother.

When children first begin to use pretense in their interactions with objects, the objects they use are either real or very realistic toys. With age and experience, children come to rely less on real or realistic objects for pretend play and use one object to represent another. Eventually, children just pretend to have the object in their hand. For example, Daria used her real, but empty, tippy cup to represent a tippy cup full of juice. Soon she may pick up a cylindrically shaped item, maybe a cardboard or plastic tube, hold it to her lips, and begin to sip as if it were her cup. Then one day, she may pretend to hold the handle of a cup to her lips, and sip her pretend juice from her pretend cup.

As children develop their ability to pretend and fantasize, they also develop the ability to comprehend the nonliteral or pretend acts of others (Kavenaugh & Engle, 1998). So, when Daria's mother pretends to eat an imaginary cookie, Daria laughs and takes one from an imaginary plate. During this or a similar play scenario, Daria's mother may initiate a dialogue with Daria, " Mmm, these cookies are so good. Would you like one?" She may then hold out one hand, suggesting that it is a plate of cookies and, with her other hand, pick up an imaginary cookie and bite into it. "Come on, you can have another!" During this play episode, the mother has demonstrated action and dialogue, responded to Daria's attempts to pretend with prompts and props, and therefore sustained and extended the play. These interactions serve as an invitation to Daria to play along. At first, Daria may just imitate her mother's actions, but soon she will be improvising original actions, creating dialogue, and even developing her own pretend scenarios. Therefore, Daria is not only having fun while engaged in this drama, but also she is developing a supportive bond with her mother and learning language, taking turns, and other conversation skills. It is this kind of interaction between the child and an adult or older sibling that fosters the further development of symbolic thought and dramatic play (Dunn, 1988; Vygotsky, 1978).

The young child's ability to carry on pretend play episodes with peers grows from positive interactions with parents, older siblings, or care providers. Sociodramatic play is pretend play that develops from spontaneous and collaborative planning and involves two or more children (Smilansky, 1968). During the preschool years, ages 3 to 5, children develop increasingly complex sociodramatic play scenarios. During these scenarios children often talk about a pretend past and make reference to a pretend future. They collaborate in building

their scenarios by creating roles in which they simulate the attitudes and behaviors of others. They also assign roles to each other, monitor each other's role portrayal, and even negotiate more interesting roles (Kavanaugh & Engle, 1998).

Initially, the themes of children's pretense play center around events with which they have had personal experience. For example, two- and three-year-old children often play "house." As they play house, they generally portray scenes and events that happen in their own homes, for example, cooking, cleaning, reading to the baby, and preparing for bed. They also may portray events that happen not at home but with their care providers, for example, going shopping, going to the park, going to child care or a neighbor's home, and saying good-bye to mommy or daddy. Although these scenes provide valuable windows into the child's world and the child's way of thinking, it is important that teachers and care providers not interpret them too literally because children are only beginning to develop the ability to put their thoughts into actions and words.

The sociodramatic play of four- and five-year-old children, such as those in Mrs. Roig's class, is still centered around their immediate experience, however, it generally becomes more imaginative and may even contain elements of fantasy. This is because children at this age are actively learning to distinguish between fantasy and reality (Piaget, 1962). For example, as a group of kindergarten children play out a cooking scene in the home center, there may be a fairy princess among them. As with the play of two- and three-year-old children, it is also important that teachers not interpret the dramatic play of preschool and kindergarten children too literally, not only because they are learning to distinguish between fantasy and reality, but also because children this age are strongly influenced by television and movies. Often, what is acted out during a play scenario is a complex combination of reality, make-believe, and modeling of the attitudes and behaviors of characters portrayed in television shows and movies.

Children in the primary grades will incorporate their growing knowledge of the world into their sociodramatic play and begin to transform make-believe and fantasy into possibilities. They often imagine themselves in future real-life situations. For example, they may pretend to be a doctor in a hospital room, a firefighter rescuing a child from a burning building, or an astronaut controlling a space shuttle. As parents and teachers watch these play scenarios unfold, they have an opportunity to discover what knowledge or misconceptions the children have about their world, what social skills they have mastered or need help with, and what thoughts and feelings they have about their own competencies.

Fostering Dramatic Play in Early Childhood Classrooms

You will recall how Daria's mother used props and toys to model pretense and then interacted with Daria, guiding her through a sequence of pretend activities. This guidance fostered a more sophisticated use of pretense and therefore facilitated optimal development of cognitive, language, and social skills. Children in preschool, kindergarten, and primary grades also benefit from the scaffolding provided when adults guide the use of pretense and the dramatic play of children. The informal dramatic play of children is spontaneous, exploratory, and experimental. There is no beginning, no end, and no attempt to develop a story. For example, a young child may take on the role or behavior of someone else, use one object to represent another, or act out various events that are familiar to him or her.

There are many opportunities within the school day to provide guided play experiences that lead to dramatic play and creative expression. Some guided activities can be planned for and included in small-group learning activities, outdoor play, and circle time. Other opportunities may develop spontaneously as the day progresses. Guided play is important to the development of pretense and dramatic play because it provides an opportunity for teachers to simulate the same scaffolding interaction that often exists between toddlers and their care providers (remember Daria and her mother). During guided play activities teachers can model, prompt, and suggest fantasy experiences as they interact with children.

Many times, actions that occur first in guided situations will later appear in a free-play situation. For example, if Mrs. Roig had used guided fantasy to help children imagine what might happen if they were caught in a boat during a storm, we would expect to see children pretending that they were in a storm during their free-play sociodramatic activities. Children often transfer what they learn or experience through guided activities to free-play activities and then expand on this new knowledge.

When planning guided experiences it is important to consider space. Young children enjoy moving about during these activities and should be encouraged to do so. However, too much space often encourages them to run and distracts them from the ongoing activity. A large space in a room, free from tables and chairs, is preferable over a stage, because a stage suggests that a product or a performance is expected and may inhibit experimentation with movement or expression (McCaslin, 1996).

Creative movement activities, described in detail in Chapter 8, are guided experiences that often lead children into pretense and drama and therefore are important activities to include when planning for creative dramatics. Other guided dramatic and creative dramatic activities include guided fantasy, pantomime, fingerplays, puppet play, storytelling, story reenactment, story play, choral reading, and reader's theater. These activities will be described in the following sections.

Guided Fantasy

Guided fantasies, also known as guided imageries, are planned experiences, read or spoken by an individual and centered on a particular subject or idea (Edwards, 1990). Guided fantasies can be used to create a relaxed, nonthreatening environment, conducive to increased awareness (Anderson, 1980). In his classic work, *Put Your Mother on the Ceiling* (1955), DeMille states that the use of fantasy helps children gain a sense of control over what happens to them and suggests that children who are taught to use fantasy will be more creative.

During guided fantasies, participants connect their prior knowledge and their imagination to create a scenario in their minds. The guide (teacher) reads from a script or spontaneously creates a script specifically designed to enhance participants' (children's) concrete experiences. The participants visualize themselves in suggested situations and act out their reactions to certain stimuli.

> Guided fantasy provides adults and children with opportunities to create symbols and images that are flexible and original in thought. Guided fantasies are fluent and ever-changing: In the process of pretending and imagining, people can invent and elaborate on images that are as original and individual to them as their fingerprints. (Edwards, 1990, p. 12)

Guided fantasies can be created to correspond to any theme of study. For example, preschool children can take an imaginary trip to the zoo, both before and after a field trip. Kindergarten children studying firefighters can take an imaginary trip to the fire station and even develop ideas of preventing fires through guided fantasy. In primary classrooms, students can revisit historical events through guided fantasy. Table 5.1 provides guidelines for conducting guided fantasy experiences.

Pantomime

When involved in pantomime, children use only gestures and movements to communicate ideas, feelings, and actions. Pantomime activities help children develop nonverbal communication skills, confidence, concentration, memory, and the ability to combine thoughts and actions (Hennings, 1990; McCaslin, 1996). Young children will be most able to pantomime those actions they have experienced or they can imagine. A teacher can begin pantomime activities by asking children, "Show me how you . . ." Then she or he can give various prompts such as "wave good-bye," "drink your milk," "tie your shoe," "brush your teeth," and "eat an apple."

As children gain experience with pantomime they become able to express information they receive through their senses, imagine how they would feel in certain situations, and express those ideas through actions. For example, the teacher might give the prompt. "Show me how it feels when . . . ," followed by prompts such as "you eat a sour lemon," "you are very hot," "you hear something very, very loud or very very soft," "you smell something awful," and "you taste something sweet." When children are asked to pantomime different moods or states (e.g., happy, sad, lonely, afraid, hungry, grumpy, thirsty, and sleepy), they often watch other children or the teacher, identify the feeling and the action associated with the word, and thereby learn names for their many moods and how to express them in the process of acting on the pantomime.

TABLE 5.1   Guidelines for Conducting Guided Fantasy

1. Develop the guided fantasy thoroughly before using it with children. Read it to a colleague and become aware of how and when the images form. The beginning of the fantasy should be simple and focus on evoking the senses. As you move through the fantasy, adjust the wording to fit the knowledge and experience level of the children you will be working with. If you are working from a script, delete passages that won't make sense to the children you are working with and insert new passages that will foster the creation of images. Practice timing your reading to give children opportunities to fully experience their images.

2. Tell the children what you are going to do and give them suggestions to help them relax. Here is one example.

> We are going to take an imaginary journey to the beach. We will pretend to be at the beach and make pictures in our minds using our imagination. The pictures will be like a movie, and you can use your imagination any way you choose. Now, find a place in the room where you can relax without touching anyone else. Close your eyes, relax your shoulders, and let your hands rest in your lap. Breathe deeply and relax.
>
> Listen to the sounds of waves. Feel the ocean breeze on your face. As you walk along the shore, can you see the seaweed that has washed up on the beach? What else do you see?

The guide may continue the scripted fantasy or may interact with the children and follow their lead. When this happens, each guided fantasy will become a different experience. You may want to play soft music in the background.

3. Conclude the fantasy by preparing the children to return to the "here and now" of the classroom.

> It's time we return to our room. Remember how it looks. Where are you sitting? Who is next to you? What do you hear in the hallway? When you feel ready, wiggle your fingers, stretch out your legs, open your eyes, and look around the room until you see me.

4. After the guided fantasy is over, help children reflect and talk about their images. Let them share what they saw and how their images made them feel. Do not attempt to interpret or evaluate children's expression of their experiences, but take note of their ideas and use this information to plan future learning experiences.

Adapted from Edwards (1990).

Children's ability to use pantomime becomes more complex with experience and with growing knowledge about the world around them. Children in kindergarten and the primary grades enjoy combining moods and characters. For example, they might act like a hungry lion, a tired elephant, or a timid mouse. They also enjoy pantomiming characters from the stories they know. This can become a frequent and spontaneous game among a group of children. One child may act out a character or even a scene from a story. Other children in the group try to guess the subject of the pantomime. This is another playful way to pass the time when groups of children have to wait for a few minutes.

When children first begin to initiate their own pantomime scenarios, the teacher may want to ask the actor to whisper the character or scene in the teacher's ear before starting the pantomime. This is helpful because young children often get caught up in seeking a turn, so when they finally have a turn, they may either forget what they were going to pantomime, or they may have never decided. Therefore, they may need some support getting started. Some children enjoy their turn so much that they do not want to give it up when someone guesses correctly. If the teacher knows what the child had intended, he or she can start the applause when the correct answer is given, signaling to both the actor and the audience that the turn is over. Knowing ahead of time what character or scene is being enacted also enables the teacher to offer supportive prompts and suggestions as the pantomime unfolds.

Fingerplays

Fingerplays are often introduced to children in infancy and combine poetry and gestures. At first, the infant just listens to the poem and shows fascination with how the words and movements come together. Soon, the toddler acts out the movements while the adult repeats the poem or song. Over time, the young child puts words and movements together and even anticipates particular passages of a poem.

Children in preschool and kindergarten still enjoy combining the movement of the fingers and hands with the rhythms and words of the poetry. Such combination of movement and speaking often relaxes children and gives greater control over hand and finger muscles. There are many fingerplays that are appropriate and fun for children from infancy through second or third grade. One traditional fingerplay common to early childhood programs in the United States is "The Eency Weency Spider." As the child uses his or her hands to recreate the spider moving up the water spout, he or she begins to associate words and ideas and use his or her body to express these ideas through movement. Other examples of traditional fingerplays include "Two Little Blackbirds," "There Was a Little Turtle," "Open-Shut Them," and "Where Is Thumbkin?" Fingerplays often evolve into songs and movement activities. For example, "Teddy Bear," "The Wheels on the Bus," and "Jack in the Box" may first be introduced as fingerplays, but later, when children have had more experience with them, they are put to music.

Puppet Play

Puppets are important in early childhood classrooms because they invite children to imagine, and to convey feelings, emotions, values, and ideas in nonthreatening ways. Puppets also invite children to tell their own stories or to enact stories they know (Mayesky, 1998). A puppet stage is not necessary, especially with three- and four-year-old children. In fact, a puppet stage could inhibit free expression among children who have little experience with puppets because the stage may suggest that there is a *product* involved in using puppets. This overshadows the *process* of playing with all the possibilities that puppets represent to children. When a puppet theater is introduced to older children, it is simply another option for playing with puppets.

When children are first introduced to puppets, they should have access to many different kinds: hand puppets, finger puppets, marionettes, elaborate cloth puppets, and simple paper bag puppets. Teachers can engage children and puppets in conversations, therefore modeling how to hold them and how to make them talk and move. Puppets should be available as a choice during center time. If from time to time new puppets appear, old puppets are temporarily removed, and familiar puppets reappear in these centers, the children's imagination and pleasure with puppets will be enhanced and extended.

It is common for children, when they first have the opportunity to play freely with puppets, to engage the puppets in aggressive behaviors. Sometimes, teachers will put the puppets away at this point. However, this is a teachable moment, and children can learn about taking turns and collaborative role-play when teachers patiently demonstrate how to use and care for puppets and encourage children to develop scenarios in which the puppets display cooperative characteristics.

Children in kindergarten and primary school, who probably have had many opportunities to play spontaneously with puppets, will enjoy creating their own puppets and even creating stories and enacting them through their puppets. At this point, puppet stages will provide incentive for children to further develop language, literacy, and social negotiation skills by creating puppet shows and puppet theater. However, the stage can be simply made; a table resting on its edge serves this purpose very well.

Storytelling

Children tell stories all the time. Every day they come to school and report what happened the night before or what happened on the way to school. Good stories are a step beyond mere reporting. If you think about it, most of the best conversations you have with your friends involve stories; they have a beginning, characters, plots, a middle, a climax, and an end. Often there is a moral or lesson to the story. Because of the conversational nature of good stories, both listening to stories and telling stories help children develop imagination and communication skills. Young children should have many opportunities to hear stories told (that is in addition to the stories they are read) and to tell their own stories. Stories entertain, educate, transmit culture, instill values, and nourish the spirit (McCaslin, 1996).

Teachers can introduce storytelling to young children by telling stories, as opposed to reading them. At first, choose simple or familiar stories that the children know, and tell them without the aid of a book. This helps children learn to visualize scenes in their mind. This may be hard for children who are growing up in a visual culture in which television and computers provide instant images of events happening around the world. Teachers can use guided fantasy to help children visualize what is happening in the story. In this way, children will not become dependent on seeing pictures to understand the context described in the story.

Teachers can also tell stories that come from their personal lives. Children always enjoy hearing about the teacher's adventures, children, or pets. This sharing creates a supportive classroom culture. When the teacher tells of her or his own experiences, she or he can use the elements of a good story by describing settings and characters, creating some suspense, and developing a climax. This gives children a good model for telling their own stories.

Farrell (1991) suggests the following seven steps to prepare a story for telling.

1. Select the story you want to tell.
2. Learn the structure and block the story.
3. Visualize the setting and the characters.
4. See the action taking place as if you're watching a silent movie.
5. Tell the story aloud using your voice to project the images you've visualized.
6. Learn the story by heart, not by word.
7. Practice telling the story until it comes naturally. (p. 20)

Two important variations of storytelling are participatory storytelling and story weaving (Rubright, 1996). In participatory storytelling, the teller invites the children to join in by singing, echoing a chant, repeating a phrase, or adding appropriate sound effects. In this variation, the storyteller remains in control of the story. Story weaving, on the other hand, invites collaboration between the teller and the audience during an improvisational story-building exercise (Rubright, 1996). In story weaving, the teacher, or story weaver, asks questions of the audience while telling a story. The weaver blends this new information into the unfolding tale. What results is an original, collaborative tale. Both variations of storytelling provide young children multiple opportunities to develop pretense.

Story Reenactment

Story reenactment refers to the process children use when they recreate, in action and with spontaneous dialogue, stories they know by heart. To begin story reenactment, invite children to act out parts of familiar stories. For example, when telling "Jack and the Bean Stalk," invite all the children to stand and act out the story together while you tell it. There are many stories and folk tales that lend themselves to this kind of reenactment. Choose stories or folk tales that are familiar to you and the children and have a repetitive dialogue or story line, predictable elements, and action that can be portrayed easily. Some examples include *Caps for Sale,* by Esphyr Slobodkina (1941); *Millions and Millions of Cats,* by Wanda Gag (1928); and *The Carrot Seed,* by Ruth Krauss (1945). The use of simple props often helps children tell or reenact stories. Because children control the length and complexity of dialogue and interactions, story reenactment easily adapts to the developmental needs of any group of children (Raines & Isbell, 1994).

Another way to support story reenactment is through the use of flannel boards and felt or fabric cutouts of the characters and scenery from familiar stories. Teachers often tell flannel-board stories during story time, inviting children to participate in the telling. Placing these same flannel cutouts in a center where children have access to them during free play promotes children's spontaneous and imaginative interpretation and reenactment.

Groups of children can reenact familiar stories, poems, fables, and even original stories. Cumulative tales such as *The Doorbell Rang,* by Pat Hutchins (1986), and *Ask Mr. Bear* by Marjorie Flack (1932), as well as familiar folktales such as "Goldilocks and the Three Bears," "The Three Little Pigs," "Henny Penny," "The Gingerbread Man," and "The Three Billy Goats Gruff" lend themselves to impromptu reenactments. When working with three-, four-, and five-year-old children, it is best to keep reenactment activities informal and interactive by

- selecting parts spontaneously and not using gender or ability as criteria for reenactment
- allowing enough time so that the reenactment can be repeated more than once in a time period (this gives more children turns)
- narrating the story line as the children are acting it out
- accepting, even encouraging original dialogue so children do not feel that they must memorize lines
- creating a pace that is interesting to the audience,
- creating a part for the audience
- demonstrating your enjoyment of the process of reenactment

Children in the primary grades may want to reenact scenes from longer stories or chapter books. It is also important to encourage children to reenact the stories they have created.

Story Play

Story play is a form of guided drama that uses children's own stories as the source of enactment (Paley, 1981). Children write or dictate their story, choose the other actors, and dramatize the story as it is read aloud. Story play supports children's language and literacy development and increases their communicative competence because seeing their own stories enacted motivates children to write more stories (Paley, 1981).

Story play provides a valuable observational opportunity for teachers. Teachers learn about children's ideas and feelings from watching them reenact their stories. Then teachers can engage students in discussions or provide other activities that help children clarify their understanding. In *You Can't Say You Can't Play* (1992), Paley extends the idea of story play to include teacher-created stories. As the teacher of a kindergarten class, Paley becomes frustrated with children's "habits of rejection." Therefore, she develops a set of stories, *The Magpie Stories,* that illustrate the feelings of imaginary characters when they are excluded from play activities. As children discuss and reenact these stories, through the guidance of Mrs. Paley, they develop a greater understanding of the dilemmas associated with rejection.

Story play also encourages children to use a write-and-revise cycle when composing. They may write a first version of a story, play it out, and revise it based on their own ideas or ideas supplied by the feedback of others. It might be that as the story is enacted, the players improvise a story element that enriches the story line. This gives the author an incentive to revise the original script. Increased opportunities to write will enable children to elaborate on their ideas and develop a greater understanding of story structure and narrative prose.

Choral Speaking

Choral speaking involves children reading or reciting together a verse or narrative selection under the direction of an older child or adult (McCaslin, 1996). This form of creative dramatics certainly shares many characteristics with singing and provides children with opportunities to practice and improve elements of speech such as pitch, volume, rate, and tonal quality. When children recite poems together, their voices blend, and no one child is singled out because of the quality of his or her speech.

Choral speaking also provides children experience in social cooperation and can be adapted to meet the developmental needs of children in kindergarten and the primary grades (McCaslin, 1996). Choral speaking is developmentally appropriate for young children when the purpose of the activity is centered on the process of learning a poem or narrative piece, practice is informal and playful, and the selection serves to support the curriculum in some way. Choral speaking, or any other form of creative dramatics, is not appropriate for young children when the focus of the activity is preparing the piece for a formal performance.

The major criteria for choosing a selection for choral speaking are that it be enjoyed by the children and that they show a desire to say or read aloud and accompany the reading with actions. Children enjoy selections that have an interesting rhyme or rhythm. The procedures for teaching choral reading selections are much the same as for teaching songs. Children learn parts of the selection over several days or practice sessions and eventually will be able to string the parts together. When choral readings are written on charts, which are used during practice sessions, the act of choral reading supports the use of productive reading strategies.

Scripted Drama

Scripted drama is a highly structured form of drama. Children memorize lines and prepare a production under the formal direction of an adult. The focus is generally on technique, not creative expression (Bolton, 1985). Therefore, it is not considered appropriate for young children unless the children themselves choose the script or choose to create a script and then direct the play (Tompkins & Hoskisson, 1995).

Fostering Creative Dramatics in Early Childhood Classrooms

We have seen how children in preschool, kindergarten, and the primary grades benefit from guided activities developed specifically to foster their use of pretense. As demonstrated through the story of Mrs. Roig's boating project, children also benefit when they have multiple opportunities to engage freely in sociodramatic play with peers, and when teachers enrich sociodramatic play by observing children to determine their interests; provide rich and meaningful context for their play through the use of props, field experiences, and project work; and interact with children to support language, cognitive, and social development.

There are many opportunities to incorporate creative dramatics into the free-play experiences that occur in early childhood classrooms. Free-play experiences include opportunities to choose activities and develop creative dramas in various dramatic play centers, block centers, and even sensory exploration centers such as the sand and water table. Many creative dramatic centers evolve from contexts that are familiar to children, for example, the home center or the grocery store center. An advantage of including dramatic play centers in the learning center system is that doing so automatically sets aside space and a time block in which children can choose to engage in drama or sociodramatic play. Therefore, during center time children are able to choose themes, materials, and playmates for developing play episodes.

The introduction of a new dramatic play center can provide a context for informally pretesting children's knowledge concerning a particular theme. In the story that opened this chapter, Mrs. Roig noticed that the four-year-old children in her class were using the playground boat as anything but a boat. She had even put some fishing gear into the boat one day, only to watch the children use it as swords. Because these children lived in a community where maritime life was an important part of the economy and culture, she decided to develop a theme study and project around boats. During the next few weeks, as children investigated many different kinds of boats, they created their own props and accessories for the boat. Because of their field trip to the fireboat, the playground boat was transformed into a fireboat and became not only a very popular dramatic play center but also a way for children to demonstrate their expanding knowledge of boats. In this case, creative dramatic play led to project work and investigation. During project work, Mrs. Roig took an active role and guided the play by providing information, props, and field experiences. In the end, free and guided play experiences existed simultaneously.

In Mrs. Roig's situation, guided play and project work grew out of spontaneous creative dramatics. However, it can work the other way. Creative dramatic centers sometimes evolve from, and therefore extend, a current theme study or project. For example, if a class is engaged in studying a theme related to nutrition and health, a dietitian's clinic or a fitness center could be created in the classroom. Posters, books, and related materials such as graphs, nutrition charts, scales, anatomy models, and exercise equipment invite students to engage in dramatic play. Materials can be purchased through school supply catalogues, collected on field trips, or solicited from families through lists generated by the children. Again, when theme studies and project work are related to and incorporated into dramatic play centers, the play is sometimes free and sometimes guided by the teacher.

Providing Meaningful Contexts for Creative Dramatics

Teachers can support learning through creative dramatics by providing appropriate space and planning the schedule to include blocks of time devoted to creative dramatics. In addition, meaningful contexts for creative dramatic play can be developed by providing field trips, neighborhood or school-bound excursions, guest speakers, video tours, appropriate materials, and prop boxes.

Space.   Classroom space, both indoors and outdoors, should be clearly designated for so-ciodramatic play centers. To encourage spontaneous interactions among children, centers should be pleasant, roomy, have open and clearly marked pathways for entering and exiting, and provide access to a variety of materials related to a topic familiar and interesting to the children who will use it (Woodward, 1985).

Excursions and Field Trips.   Excursions and field trips, as well as interviews with people children encounter during field trips, expand children's concepts of the world around them (Saul, 1993; Skrupskelis, 1990) and provide a meaningful context for children to extend their learning through creative dramatics. Field trips into the community and excursions within the school and neighborhoods surrounding the school do not need to be all-day or whole-group experiences. With proper supervision, small groups of children can travel within the school, neighborhood, or community, gather information, and share this information with classmates by planning and creating dramatic play centers.

It is important to choose excursion and field trip sites and develop timelines for excursions that fit the interests and age level characteristics of the children. For example, three-year-old children benefit more from several short trips to a fire station than one all-day venture. Each time these children visit the fire station, they can focus on a different aspect of being a firefighter. On the other hand, children in the second grade may gain much information from one all-day excursion to the fire station.

To receive maximum benefit from excursions and field trips, children need to prepared for what they will encounter. Being involved in discussions; gathering information from films, books, computer programs, and other related media; studying maps; generating questions; and hearing from guest speakers help children understand what they will encounter on their trips. When children return from an excursion, they should be given opportunities to review and utilize the information they attained. One way to do this is to help children develop dramatic play centers that replicate the objects, materials, and environments they found on their trip.

To be most effective, excursions and field trips should occur at the midpoint of the theme study or project. In that way, children have the time and opportunity to develop questions and goals before their trip and reflect and extend their learning after the trip. Whenever possible, plan to repeat a trip or follow a trip with a guest speaker. In this way, the questions children generate while preparing a dramatic center and playing out appropriate scenarios can be answered. Table 5.2 provides examples of field trips and excursions that inspire dramatic play centers.

Guest Speakers and Video Tours.   Field trips and excursions provide students with the most direct and concrete information. Guest speakers, especially when they bring props and materials, can also provide children with concrete information. Another alternative is for an adult to take a field trip and videotape the experience. Children can prepare questions in advance and give them to the adult who is taping the field trip. The adult talks to the tour guide on camera and asks the children's questions. When the tour guide answers, he or she

TABLE 5.2   **Field Trips and Excursions that Inspire Dramatic Play Centers**

Walking Excursions within the School	**Community Field Trips**
Bus or bus office	Art gallery
Cafeteria	Auto repair shop
Computer center	Bus terminal, train station, airport, or cruise
Furnace room	ship terminal
Health room	Ceramic shop
Janitor's work area	City Hall
Other classrooms	Department store
Supply room or closet	Doctor or dentist office
Teacher's work area and lounge	Factory
Textbook room or closet	Farms and farmer's market
Volunteer center	Fast-food restaurant
	Gift shop
Neighborhood Excursions	Hospitals and emergency rooms
Community facilities such as fire or police	Humane Society
stations	Museums
Construction site	Parks and Recreation offices
Neighborhood businesses: grocery, repair	Pet store
shops, bakery, cleaners, bank, bookstore	Plant nursery
Neighbors' homes and vegetable or flower	Police horse stable
gardens	Restaurant
Roadwork site	Supermarkets
	Wharfs, docks, and warehouses
	Television and radio stations
	Theater or rehearsal hall
	Veterinarian clinic

can use the actual names of the children who prepared the questions. This will make the experience much more personal for the class. It will be even more effective if the tour guide comes to the classroom to view the video with the children.

Materials for Sociodramatic Play Centers.   When selecting props and materials to be used in sociodramatic play centers, teachers should consider the age and developmental level of the children, the familiarity of the theme to children, issues of health and safety, and issues of culture and gender. Realistic props inspire realistic pretense scenarios among three- and four-year-old children and among children who are not familiar with certain dramatic play contexts or materials. For example, in the home-living center, a discarded toaster (with the electric cord removed) may stimulate more pretense play than a wooden play toaster because children may not know what the wooden play toaster stands for because real toasters are not made of wood. Understanding the use of a wooden toaster, or any toaster, would be particularly difficult for a child whose family does not toast bread at all, but warms pita bread on the top of a gas stove. Therefore, the selection of props for any center must represent the tools used by all the cultures represented in a particular play group.

As children become more familiar with the play theme and the accessories associated with it, they will be able to substitute more abstract objects for the real objects in their play.

They many even be able to "just pretend" they have something they need. For example, primary-age children engaged in a project about automobiles may visit a machine shop and sketch the work area, furniture, tools, instruments, and other accessories and observe how they are used. When they return to their classroom, they will recreate the shop as a dramatic play center. They may collect some of the accessories they need, and they may recreate others using their drawings and materials such as boxes, paper cups, blocks, paper, and paint. However, if they cannot think of a way to recreate a particular piece of equipment, it might become an imaginary object with a designated space in their shop. Therefore, these children have created a mix of real, improvised, and imaginary items to use in their play.

Overalls would facilitate the dramatic play fostered in the machine shop center. Dress-up clothes, uniforms, hats, and other costumes often enhance the development of sociodramatic play. In choosing these accessories, teachers must consider the ability to keep clothing items sanitary and safe. Germs and parasites, such as lice, are sometimes transmitted from child to child via clothing. Dress-up clothes are often castoffs and therefore may have rips and tears that may cause children to trip. Small buttons may be a safety hazard in classrooms where infants or toddlers are present even for short periods of the day. Therefore, play clothes and accessories, such as blankets and tablecloths, must not only be clean, but must also be kept in good repair. Many times a teacher can find a parent or other volunteer who is willing to pick up dress-up clothes and accessories and wash, dry, repair, and return them to the classroom on a monthly basis. All hats used in dramatic play centers should be made of paper, hard plastic, or metal because lice cannot live on these surfaces. Plastic and metal surfaces can be easily cleaned with soap and disinfectant spray, and paper hats can be replaced at little expense.

It is also important that play items and play themes be accessible to both genders, because one purpose of dramatic play is to provide children with the opportunity to try out different roles. When children have this opportunity, they develop the ability to take the perspective of others. This is an important goal for early childhood programs. Therefore, in all early childhood classrooms, boys should feel free to make dinner and feed the baby in the home-living center, and girls should feel free to repair cars in the garage center.

Theme Boxes.   When a particular dramatic play center has run its course and is no longer being used effectively, teachers can create theme boxes or dramatic play kits by putting all of the related accessories and props into a box, labeling the box, and storing it near the dramatic center area. Theme boxes are collections of play accessories, props, books, posters, records, tapes, and other materials related to a particular theme. When these items are stored together in a labeled box near the dramatic play center they become accessible to children and facilitate children's spontaneous dramatic play. For example, a group of children may want to "play astronaut" one day and with the aid of some pregathered props, the context of their play will develop more quickly and therefore will be more meaningful and satisfying to them. Theme boxes can be created for particular themes, such as doctor's office, beach, campground, grocery store, and space station. They can also be created to correspond to favorite children's literature selections such as "Goldilocks and the Three Bears," "Jack and the Beanstalk," and "The Three Little Pigs." These boxes stimulate spontaneous reenactment of favorite stories and therefore encourage collaboration and language development. Children can be involved in making theme boxes by suggesting themes and generating lists of needed materials. Table 5.3 shows the prototype for a dramatic play center based on a restaurant theme.

TABLE 5.3   Restaurant Center

Space Requirements

Floor area

Basic Materials

PVC pipe to construct counter and kitchen area

Tables and chairs

Counter, serving station, cash register, plastic utensils
and tableware, cooking utensils, menus, trays,
food models, napkins, and pitchers

Safety Considerations

If real cooking happens here, check to see that
sanitation procedures are followed.

Examples of Basic Learning Opportunities

Language and concept development

Collaboration and creating scenarios

Collaboration in determining roles

Creating decorations for restaurant

Planning and carrying out the theme

Reading and writing menus

Learning about nutrition

Appreciating diversity among families

Building conversation skills

Caring for materials and tools

Examples of Extensions

Literacy

- making shopping lists
- creating menus
- writing orders on pads
- reading newspapers
- reading cookbooks

Numeracy

- using measuring utensils
- sorting and classifying kitchen items
- figuring bills
- one-to-one correspondence when setting table

Managing Creative Dramatics

The successful management of creative dramatics begins with planning the environment carefully, choosing themes that fit the developmental levels of children, selecting props that allow children to act out their understanding of related concepts, and providing children the information and learning opportunities that help create a meaningful context. In addition, teachers need to know their children well enough to provide each child the appropriate amount of guidance to facilitate individual learning. Thorough planning will prevent most group and individual management difficulties. However, situations will occur that teachers must be prepared to handle. We will now turn our attention to two such situations.

Illicit or Aggressive Play.   Teachers plan and develop dramatic play centers based on certain themes and therefore support and encourage play that evolves from that theme. However, children often make up their own themes, and their themes may be different from what the teacher intended. Play that is not sanctioned by the teacher and may in fact be forbidden in the classroom or on the playground is called *illicit play* (Van Hoorn, Nourot, Scales, & Alward, 1993). Examples of illicit play in preschool, kindergarten, and primary classrooms include "war" play, creating guns from any material available, even fingers, and socially aggressive games that involve bullying, taunting, teasing, or passing notes.

It is clear that when children engage in play that hurts or has the potential to hurt others, either physically or psychologically, such play needs immediate intervention. Teachers have many options for intervention and choose the option or combination of options that fits the situation. Among the options teacher have are

1. clarifying their own expectation of behavior
2. accepting children's negative actions as potential learning experiences, not character or personality flaws
3. giving direct information about how children's actions affect other children's feelings or safety
4. modeling appropriate interactions and language
5. staying close to or involved in the play until the immediate issues are resolved

Here is an example of how one teacher, Mr. Jacobs, intervenes in the play of kindergarten students. Justin and Sandra are playing together in the block area. Mildred enters the center and begins to play with Justin and Sandra. However, both Justin and Sandra react negatively. "You can't play with us! You look funny."

Mildred is stunned and hurt, but the teacher, Mr. Jacob, is near, enters into the situation, and addresses the children. "Those words hurt Mildred's feelings. Look at her face. Can you see that she is hurt? I will not allow children to hurt each other with words or actions. Mildred, I am sorry your feelings were hurt." Turning to Sandra and Justin, Mr. Jacob continued, "How can Mildred help you with your building project?"

Mr. Jacob is clear in this situation. He gives direct information about the result of Sandra and Justin's words and actions. He asks for no explanations because he understands that children this age do not always know why they act in a certain way. They are impulsive and need opportunities to learn how their behavior affects others. Notice that Mr. Jacob does not ask Justin and Sandra to apologize, but models a sincere apology, leaving the door open for Sandra and Justin to apologize also. By responding this way, Mr. Jacob has turned this situation into a learning opportunity for all three children.

In the days that follow, Mr. Jacob will continue his engagement with these three children. He will stay close and interact with Mildred, Justin, and Sandra until he feels that the incident has been completely resolved. During the next few days, he will carefully observe all three children, looking for patterns in their behavior. Does Mildred have a difficult time entering situations with other children? Do Sandra and Justin frequently exclude others from their play? Was this a one-time instance or is there a pattern of behavior forming that needs a structured intervention? Mr. Jacob will also create opportunities to informally involve the class in learning about hurt feelings, alternatives to hurting feelings, and the power of apologies. He may choose to involve children in a puppet play, or he may read an appropriate story and involve children in a discussion.

Mr. Jacob knew exactly what to do about teasing and taunting. However, deciding how to deal with other illicit play, such as making guns and playing war, may not be as clear-cut. Often, teachers forbid play with weapons, only to find that children invent other ways to engage in these activities. Some educators believe that illicit play contributes to a child's developing social skills because it creates opportunities for social learning (Sutton-Smith, 1988). Other educators believe that allowing children to play war or play with guns, real or imaginary, gives children the message that violence is acceptable and an appropriate way to solve problems. Unfortunately, in some communities, guns and violence play a significant role in the lives of young children. Teachers may need to work with parents, administrators, and school counselors to find an intervention strategy appropriate for their class. An initial step in finding this strategy is to carefully observe children's play and note developing patterns of illicit themes.

Superhero and Superheroine Play.   Superhero or superheroine play is another theme that often develops without the teacher's encouragement. Some educators ban this type of play from classrooms; others find that it benefits the children who become involved. Superhero play occurs when one child or a group of children transform their identity and become fictitious characters with superhuman powers. Most of these characters are modeled after current media or cartoon heroes. These superheroes and superheroines are unquestionably good, are in control and know what is right, possess powers children wish they themselves had, solve all problems, overcome all obstacles, and receive accolades and recognition (Kostelnik, Whiren, & Stein, 1986). Whereas some children choose to transform themselves into superheroes or heroines, other children choose to transform themselves into antiheroes or heroines such as Dracula or Cruella De Vil.

Through superhero or superheroine play, children can access power not ordinarily available to them and achieve control over their own lives and the lives of others (Greenberg, 1995; Pulaski, 1976). Superhero fantasy allows children to take on characteristics they admire or fear. In this way, they are able to master their fears, if only for a moment (Carlsson-Paige & Levin, 1990; Peller, 1971). As with all other types of fantasy, superhero or superheroine play provides children opportunities to develop language skills, divergent thinking, and problem-solving skills (Carlsson-Paige & Levin, 1990; Saltz & Brodie, 1982; Saltz & Johnson, 1977).

Superhero or superheroine play is often characterized by running, shouting, wrestling, and karate kicks or chops. In true rough-and-tumble play, the attack movements stop short of hitting, are accompanied by words such as "pow," and are accompanied by a laughing and smiling "play face" (Blurton-Jones, 1976). This rough-and-tumble style of play can easily be interpreted by adults as aggressive play. Indeed, the momentum of the play needs to be carefully monitored so that it does not turn into aggressive play.

Children do benefit from superhero and superheroine play, therefore, banning such play from classrooms may deprive children of important opportunities to develop language and social skills (Bauer & Dettore, 1997). Kostelnik and her colleagues (1986) offer the following suggestions for dealing with superhero and superheroine play in early childhood programs.

- help children recognize humane characteristics of superheroes and heroines
- discuss real heroes and heroines
- talk about the pretend world of acting
- limit the place and time for superhero play
- explore related concepts
- help children develop goals for superheroes and heroines
- help children de-escalate rough and tumble play
- make it clear that aggression is unacceptable
- give children control over their lives
- praise children's attempts at mastery (p. 7)

Including Children With Special Needs in Dramatic and Sociodramatic Play

Dramatic play and creative dramatics have been used successfully to foster confidence and develop language skills among children with special needs. While engaged in dramatic activities, all children have the opportunity to try out new roles and perhaps work through fearful experiences. Therefore, activities that promote creative expression provide powerful teaching strategies and should be incorporated into the daily activities and routines of children with special needs. Encourage pretense among children by becoming involved yourself. Include a traditional home-living area in your classroom because it will foster a sense of security. Adapt props in ways that will allow all children opportunities to express their feelings and ideas. Here are some specific ideas that will help you include children with special needs in pretense and dramatic play activities.

Children with Visual Impairments

- Use verbal descriptions when telling or making up stories.
- Allow children to hold and explore props that give tactile cues about the activity that is going on. For example, a toy teapot, cups, and saucers suggest a tea party in the housekeeping area.
- When children dress up, check to see that there are no dangling scarves, skirts, or belts that could cause a child to trip.
- Set up an optometrist's office and have children test each other's vision with an eye chart.

Children with Hearing Impairments

- Use sign language as needed when telling or enacting stories.
- Provide visual clues and props when telling or enacting stories.

Children with Language and Communication Delays

- Make dramatic play areas resemble familiar places, such as homes and restaurants, so that children will feel comfortable.
- Take advantage of dramatic play to help children rehearse a new experience, for example, going to the doctor, so that they will learn what to expect and what they might want to say.
- Use puppets as a way to help children feel comfortable talking.

Children with Physical Disabilities

- Be alert to the first signs of fantasy or pretend play because a child with physical impairment may not be able to push a toy car or pretend to drink from an imaginary cup. She or he will need you to physically assist and to set the stage verbally.
- Help children adapt different roles to their own special needs. For example, when setting up the home center or the grocery store center, make it accessible to wheelchairs.
- Have peers or teachers act out children's ideas if they are not able to act them out themselves. The experience of seeing their ideas acted out can be very empowering.
- Play hospital with casting tape and have children cast doll's legs or their own fingers.
- Use full-length mirrors to encourage children to explore their individual characteristics.
- Help other children become more aware of the challenges that being in a wheelchair or using a walker creates. Have extra adapted equipment available for other children to try.

Children with Learning Difficulties

- Help children distinguish their feelings through songs, playing with puppets, and pantomime activities.
- Use dramatic play to provide children with opportunities to explore basic concepts such as up, down, in, out, over, under, and around.
- Also use dramatic play activities to reinforce concepts and vocabulary learned during theme study and field trips. For example, after going to the dentist office, set up a dentist

office and help children recount the names of the instruments and the activities that dentists perform.
- Include real objects or realistic props in dramatic play centers.

Children with Socioemotional Difficulties
- Have a telephone available, because it might enable children to talk more freely with others.
- Use puppets as a way for children to talk indirectly about their experiences.
- Encourage children to choose play partners with whom they are most comfortable so that the play will likely be at a higher level.
- Encourage children to try on animal roles or roles of things they are afraid of, such as ghosts, monsters, and snakes. This may help them feel in control.
- Let children see how they fit into the various roles and relationships in a family, school, store, hospital, or fire station.
- Help children by entering an ongoing play situation with them. Stay as long as you are needed.
- If a child is afraid to join in the play when many children are present, arrange some special times when this child and another child he or she likes can do things together.

(Cook, Tessier, & Armbruster, 1987; Deiner, 1983; Fewell & Kaminski, 1988; Morris & Schultz, 1989; Wesley, 1992)

Developing Advocacy Skills

While dramatic play areas have become commonplace components of most preschool classrooms, teachers in elementary schools and kindergarten often find that there is little support for dramatic play once children enter "real" school. Many kindergarten teachers have to expend considerable effort to justify maintaining a housekeeping center in their classrooms. First- and second-grade teachers find almost no support for dramatic play at all.

Given the many benefits of dramatic play for children's developing social competence and cognitive growth, however, it is incumbent upon teachers to become advocates for children's opportunities for this type of play. Their advocacy must take two avenues: convincing others (e.g., administrators, parents, and other teachers) that dramatic play is worth the space and time devoted to it; and actively seeking out the resources needed to provide rich dramatic play centers both in the classroom and outdoors.

It is suggested in this chapter that a variety of dramatic play centers is necessary to elicit a broad array of play themes, each enhancing different aspects of children's socioemotional, language, and general cognitive development. It might be tempting for teachers to take an all-or-nothing approach: "Give me everything I need or I can't do centers at all!" However, this approach may be self-defeating. An effective advocate recognizes the importance of focusing on a few priorities in order to move forward. Rather than taking an all-or-nothing approach, good advocates understand the need to start small, directing their energies toward specific, attainable objectives that they have determined to be the most important.

Thus, a kindergarten teacher with no dramatic play area might begin by advocating for the one dramatic play center he or she believes will be most beneficial to his or her children's development. For many teachers, this might be a block center. For others, it may be more versatile space that could be changed periodically using different prop boxes to foster a greater variety of play themes. The major task for a teacher is to convince supervisors that dramatic play is an important, necessary part of an early childhood program. The best way to do this is by carefully documenting learning that takes place when children are engaged in pretense.

Teachers in primary grades must undertake the same task, although it might seem harder because, generally, there is less administrative support for dramatic play activities as children move from kindergarten into first and second grades. Again, setting clear priorities is important. Choose one particular theme, gather the resources, create the center, facilitate children's learning through play in the center, and document this learning. Then, when there is clear evidence that creative dramatics supports learning, create another center. Table 5.4 suggests activities to help you strengthen your advocacy skills.

TABLE 5.4   Advocacy Activities: Informing and Involving Families and Administrators

Focus on Priorities		
Becoming Aware	*Furthering Your Understanding*	*Taking Action*
1. Visit classrooms in which teachers have well-established dramatic play centers. Observe the different play themes that emerge in these centers. List the different uses of language and symbols you see. Document how language and symbolic representation change from one center to another.	1. Search the professional literature to find articles that address how to set up the particular dramatic play centers you decided will be your top priorities. Determine what materials are needed, and seek out suggestions on how best to introduce children to the centers to pique their interest and facilitate richly interactive play.	1. Prepare a presentation for the parents' association, school business partners, or other school support or civic group. The presentation should briefly explain the benefits of dramatic play for young children (through early primary grades), and spell out how the center(s) you are focusing on are the most important for reaping those benefits.
2. Visit an elementary school that does not have play centers for children beyond kindergarten. Observe first- and second-grade children during free-play times, both in the classroom and outdoors. Do they engage in dramatic play? What forms does this play take? What kinds of props do they use?	2. Investigate the costs of all the props you will need for those dramatic play centers. Using a variety of catalogues of educational resources, prepare a budget that reflects a realistic estimate of what the center will cost. Set up your budget with two sections: one for items that will need to be purchased, and one for items that can be made or otherwise obtained at no cost through donations.	2. Deliver your presentation to as many groups as you can, and solicit donations of the necessary items. Follow up your presentation with letters to the organizations thanking them for the opportunity to address them, and reiterating the ways they can help in your efforts.
3. Using information from the preceding observation, determine what dramatic play areas are most important to include in kindergarten, first grade, and second grade to elicit more complex social interaction, language use, and cognitive growth.	3. Observe children involved in dramatic play centers. As you watch, list all potential problems that could occur. These might be safety issues or issues having to do with how children interact with each other. Step back and take a holistic look at the center system used in this room. List all factors that contributed to the prevention of the potential problems you foresaw.	3. Once you have a clear idea of what materials are available, present your budget for purchasing the remaining items to the school administration. Support your request with a well-written narrative rationale for the materials you are requesting.

Summary

Engagement in dramatic play facilitates the development of children's imagination, thinking, reasoning, and problem-solving skills. Opportunities to provide young children guided experiences in creative dramatics include guided fantasy, pantomime, fingerplays, puppet play, storytelling, story reenactment, story plays, choral speaking, and reader's theater. Free-play experiences include opportunities to choose activities and develop creative dramas in various dramatic play centers, block centers, and even sensory exploration centers such as the sand and water table. Teachers develop meaningful contexts for creative dramatics by planning field trips and excursions, hosting guest speakers, and developing video tours of appropriate sites.

Illicit or aggressive play is not sanctioned by the teacher and may even be forbidden. Superhero or superheroine play occurs when one child or a group of children transform their identity and become fictitious characters with super powers.

REVISITING FIRST IMPRESSIONS

Review your reflection regarding drama in your life. How have you benefitted from drama? How will you encourage children in your classroom to develop a healthy interest in drama?

QUESTIONS FOR DISCUSSION

1. Describe how you would set up a dramatic play center in a first-grade classroom. How would you involve the children in developing this center? How would you justify it to parents? To administrators?

2. Two kindergarten children make guns out of Play-Doh and begin to shoot imaginary bad guys. Describe your feelings concerning this situation and create a plan of action.

3. Mrs. Henry has noticed that Baron, a five-year-old child who has been in play group situations since he was three, has spent the last three center periods working alone at the computer creating pictures with a paint program. Should she be concerned? Why or why not? What, if anything, should she do?

SUGGESTED READINGS

Farrell, C. (1991). *Storytelling: A guide for teachers.* New York: Scholastic Professional Books.
King, N. (1996). *Playing their part: Language and learning in the classroom.* Portsmouth, NH: Heinemann.
Paley, V. (1988). *Bad guys don't have birthdays: Fantasy play at four.* Chicago: University of Chicago Press.
Rubright, L. (1996). *Beyond the beanstalk: Interdisciplinary learning through storytelling.* Portsmouth, NH: Heinemann

6 Fostering Playful Learning through Ongoing Assessment

Prereading Guide

First Impressions. What comes to mind when you hear the word *assessment?* How important do you think it is that teachers assess children as they play? In your journal, discuss your feelings and concerns about assessing children's development as it occurs in the context of playful learning and playful teaching.

Revisit
Categories of Play; Individual Factors That Influence Play (Chapter 2)

Stories from the Field

The following conversation took place between two teachers enrolled in a university summer course on assessment. Ms. Mellis, a preschool teacher, is a strong proponent of informal assessment of young children and is vehemently opposed to any standardized testing before children reach second or third grade. Ms. Dimaggio, a kindergarten teacher, is not convinced that informal assessments provide as much useful information as standardized tests. She believes that it is important for teachers and parents to know how well children are doing in relation to other children their age.

MS. MELLIS: I just don't see why everyone puts so much emphasis on standardized tests. No matter what kinds of information I have about children, all anyone is interested in is test scores. I see this every year when it's time to make decisions about children's kindergarten placement. The local school system most of my children go to tests all the kids entering kindergarten with formal standardized assessments. These are supposed to give the kindergarten teachers information about children's development and identify which ones might need extra help. A child who is one of my most capable is declared "not ready" and recommended for delayed entry or special services, while another child who I know will need lots of support is placed in the regular kindergarten, no questions asked.

MS. DIMAGGIO: But in my experience, those kinds of standardized tests are generally the best predictors of who is going to do well in my class. We're sometimes pressured to take children who don't score well, and I can usually tell from day one that those children just aren't going to be successful. They are just too far behind the other children who test well and are ready for kindergarten. While I do think the tests can sometimes be wrong about some children, at least they offer us some solid criteria on which to base decisions about placement.

MS. MELLIS: Aren't kindergartens supposed to be designed to help children develop from wherever they are? That's not to say that some children won't need more support to complete certain tasks than others do, or that some kids aren't capable of more advanced activities than others. But those differences aren't predicted very well by scores on formal tests, especially when they show that a child might not be ready. Even using informal assessments, all I have to do is watch the children the first two weeks of school, and I can get a pretty good idea of their capabilities. Maybe it would be better if schools could just ask children's preschool teachers about the kids before making decisions about them. I think we have better information in our heads than any psychologist will have in her records after meeting the child once or twice for testing sessions.

MS. DIMAGGIO: It sounds like you don't think there's any need to do assessment at all!

MS. MELLIS: I don't think the idea of assessing young children is necessarily bad. When we store that information in our heads, we *are doing* assessment. It's just not formal. The real problem is what counts—and what doesn't count—as valid assessment. Too often, it doesn't really matter what teachers think. All that matters is what the formal tests say. People—parents, administrators, even some teachers—just don't think assessment is valid unless it results in a score that can be used to judge and label children.

MS. DIMAGGIO: I don't know. You may be right that other kinds of assessment are useful. But I like having those scores to back up the decisions I make about children. Besides, children have to start getting used to taking those kinds of tests. The more experience they get with standardized tests when they are young, the better they'll do on them when they're older and they really count.

MS. MELLIS: I just can't agree with that. Unless assessments are developmentally appropriate for individual children, then they just aren't worth giving. They don't give teachers enough of the kind of information they need. Worse, the whole process of taking formal tests is frustrating for such young children. It's unnatural to them, and often, it frightens them! I've seen young children crying when they have to go out of the classroom to be tested by a specialist. It just doesn't seem right.

Definition of Assessment

The discussion between these two teachers demonstrates Ms. Mellis's concern about one commonly held definition of assessment: that assessment equals testing. Look at your journal entry for the beginning of this chapter. How many of your ideas for assessment involve testing children? If testing plays a prominent role in your description of assessment, you are not unlike many others who are just learning about assessment in early childhood.

Testing, however, represents just one aspect of assessment. Bredekamp and Rosegrant (1995) define assessment much more broadly:

> Assessment is the process of observing, recording, and otherwise documenting the work children do and how they do it, as a basis for a variety of educational decisions that affect the child, including planning for groups and individual children and communicating with parents. (p. 16)

A test is no more than a sample of a child's behavior or knowledge at a specific time. Tests offer only limited information about children's knowledge, abilities, and development. If teachers conduct assessments that document children's growth in a variety of areas, they will have significant information that might be used to flesh out pictures of children's development that only begin to emerge through more formal testing.

Ms. Mellis recognized this when she stated that she knows more about her children after two weeks of watching them in the classroom than any tester can possibly determine through one or two formal testing sessions. Her contention that she has this information "in her head" suggests, however, that she may need to develop further her understanding of what it means to assess children. *Knowing* is not useful unless it is derived from systematic, ongoing documentation of observations of children. It is possible that when teachers' knowledge about children is discounted, as seems to have happened to Ms. Mellis, it is because the teachers have not demonstrated that their evaluations of children are based on systematic assessment. If Ms. Mellis can develop a system for ongoing assessment of her students and find ways to carefully document the results of that assessment, she will be well on the way to participating in developmentally appropriate assessment.

Purpose of Assessment

The primary purpose for assessing young children is for teachers to glean information that will help them do a better job of teaching the children in their classrooms. Developmentally appropriate assessment procedures therefore should be directly based on the goals and objectives of the specific curriculum used in a particular program (Hills, 1993; Pellegrini, 1998).

Teachers are generally concerned with assessing children for the purpose of choosing instructional procedures and materials that will best meet the children's needs. They also assess children for the purpose of documenting progress toward goals that have been set for (or by) the children. One additional purpose of developmentally appropriate assessment is to communicate with parents, other educators, and the children themselves about the children's learning and development. Teachers who conduct appropriate assessments establish a procedure for communicating the results of assessment to parents in meaningful language that helps them understand their children's individual progress (Hills, 1993).

Teachers may also use assessment to begin to identify children who may be in need of special education services. Although programs for children with special needs emphasize early identification and intervention, nevertheless, many children enter preschool and kindergarten with undiagnosed special needs. Testing for placement in special education programs is beyond the purview of most classroom teachers. In most school systems, such placements are usually based on formal assessment procedures conducted by a team comprised of specially certified assessment teachers, educational psychologists, and other professionals including medical doctors and physical therapists.

It *is* the classroom teacher's responsibility, however, to refer children for this type of assessment if she or he suspects that a child might have special needs. Informal assessments like those described in this chapter can help teachers to recognize when a child may require additional testing for the purpose of securing special education services (Lowenthal, 1996). These informal assessments are also useful for monitoring the progress of children with special needs once an Individualized Education Plan (IEP) or Individualized Family Service Plan (IFSP) has been established. Because assessment and curriculum are closely related for children with special needs (as they are for all children), ongoing informal assessment can facilitate planning for instruction and making any necessary changes in children's IEPs or IFSPs (Wolery & Wilbert, 1994).

Scope of the Assessment

Assessments that are appropriate for young children are also those that are broad enough in scope to capture the breadth of children's development. According to Hills (1993), assessment should include "procedures that address all domains of learning and development—social, emotional, physical, and cognitive, as well as children's feelings and dispositions toward learning" (p. 24). Good assessments measure authentic performance, rather than simply testing for isolated skills. Appropriate assessments seek to determine children's strengths and capabilities, rather than focusing exclusively on revealing their weaknesses or what they do not yet know. Finally, developmentally appropriate assessments include procedures that allow and encourage children to reflect on and evaluate their own learning (Hills, 1993).

Context for Assessment

The extent to which assessment is developmentally appropriate is further determined by the contexts in which the assessment occurs. Hills (1993) states that good assessments "will rely on teachers' regular and periodic observations and record keeping of children's everyday activities and performance so that results reflect children's behavior over time" (p. 24). The assessments should be based on children's interactions during normal, ongoing classroom activities, rather than on children's performance in an artificial, contrived context (such as that entailed in formal testing).

Furthermore, appropriate assessments are those that rely on multiple sources of information, derived from observation, collection of children's work, teacher interviews, and dialogue with children across a variety of contexts. Children's interactions in centers, during teacher-directed group activities, and outdoors on the playground all offer teachers opportunities for insight into children's learning and development. In addition, appropriate assessments include information gathered in supportive contexts so teachers can determine what children are capable of with support as well as independently (Hills, 1993).

Play as a Developmentally Appropriate Context for Assessment

Many researchers have suggested that play offers the perfect context for determining children's knowledge and abilities (Garvey, 1990; Howes, 1992; Pellegrini, 1992, 1996, 1998). Pellegrini (1998) summarized the benefits of using children's play as a context for carrying out assessment.

■ Children are not very good test-takers, often because they are not motivated to perform tasks (such as answering test questions) that they see as uninteresting. They *are* motivated to play, and will therefore be more likely to "perform" in ways that better demonstrate their actual capabilities.

■ Formal assessment procedures often require children to engage in activities that are unnatural or unfamiliar. Children cannot demonstrate the full range of their competencies under those conditions. Children's play is most often quite natural, especially when it is a self-selected activity. Children can perform at their highest levels when they are engaged in self-selected play.

■ Unlike most testing situations, play has intrinsic values for children, and they are willing to spend considerable social and cognitive resources on it.

■ Formal assessments, especially tests, often assess a very limited set of competencies, in many cases focusing almost exclusively on cognitive development. As children play, their development in all areas—cognitive, creative, socioemotional, and physical—can be observed.

Pellegrini (1998) concludes that "a particularly fruitful approach to assessing young children involves observing them as they interact with their peers in situations that are simultaneously motivating and demanding high levels of social cognitive processing. . . . Observations of children's 'play' seems to be a context that meets both these criteria" (pp. 223–224).

What to Assess

As stated earlier, a good assessment program will investigate children's development across all domains, from cognitive to creative, socioemotional to physical-motor. In general, teachers should look for developmental hallmarks that are important for specific developmental periods (Pellegrini, 1998). Any time they observe a child behaving in a new way that suggests some form of development, that behavior should be noted.

A teacher might observe, for example, that her preschoolers regularly engage in dramatic play that enacts aspects of their own experiences, such as playing mommies and daddies or doctors and patients. Toward the end of the year, however, she may notice that one or two children are beginning to incorporate more fanciful elements into their pretend play. Knowing that assuming fantasy roles is typically characteristic of the play of five- and six-year-olds, she correctly recognizes this new form of play as a significant developmental hallmark, and documents what she observes.

A kindergarten teacher may have observed one child consistently using randomly chosen letters to write down "phone messages" in the housekeeping area. One day, however, he observes the child carefully sounding out the name of the friend for whom the message is intended, resulting in an invented spelling that includes letters to represent the first and last sounds in the name. Recognizing that this behavior represents a new understanding about the connection between letters and sounds, this play episode is also documented.

For other children in these classrooms, development might be apparent in the changing nature of their social interaction during play. A child who is new to the classroom might spend much of his or her time in solitary play, exploring the materials available, and watching what other children do with them. Gradually, he or she may join other children in centers by engaging in parallel play, not really interacting with them, but taking part in the same or similar activities. Eventually, as the child gains confidence, he or she may become a fully interactive play partner. Each of those changes in his or her approach to classroom play indicates significant developments; each should be documented as evidence of the child's adjustment and increasing experience.

Teachers will also want to assess children's physical-motor development. As they observe children on the playground, for example, they may take note of which structures the children make use of, and how they use different equipment. They may notice that one child is becoming increasingly adept at jumping rope, whereas another is now able to catch a ball tossed into the air more often than not. Again, these new behaviors should be documented for future reference.

The types of play children engage in and the centers they select most often should also be documented. Teachers may want to note how often and for how long children engage in each type of play—functional, constructive, dramatic, rough-and-tumble, and games with rules—and under what conditions such play is chosen. They may also want to keep track of which centers children choose and how much time they spend in those centers. Specific methods for collecting and organizing these kinds of data will be presented later in this chapter.

What Can Be Learned from Play Episodes

The following vignettes are offered to demonstrate the wealth of information that can be derived from careful attention to children's play. As you read each description of a play episode, see how many observations you can make about the children's development.

Play Episode 1

Two three-year-olds, Jeremy and Leslie, are playing on a climbing structure on the playground. Jeremy climbs up a short ladder, placing one foot on each step until he reaches a platform. "I'm a monkey!" he exclaims, raising one arm above his head and hopping around the platform making monkey noises.

Leslie follows him up the ladder, putting two feet on each step until she climbs onto the platform. She sits with her back to Jeremy. "Curious George," she says. "Where are my bananas?" She slides down a slide attached to the platform and picks up twigs that she finds on the ground. She climbs up a ramp to return to the platform, and sits down, pretending to peel and eat her "bananas."

Jeremy continues his monkey imitation, walking with his arms hanging low toward the ground, then swinging from an overhead ladder by one arm while scratching his side with the other. Leslie continues her Curious George role-play, setting aside three twigs and commenting to herself, "These three are for the man in the yellow hat." Jeremy is careful not to step on the "bananas" as he resumes hopping around the platform making his monkey noises.

How many areas of development could you document based on this vignette? Some possibilities are as follows.

■ *Level of social play.* Jeremy and Leslie were essentially engaged in parallel play. They both shaped their play around a common theme—being monkeys—but carried out their role plays independent of each other, while remaining in close proximity.

■ *Social development.* The children exhibited a high degree of social competence within the confines of their parallel play. Jeremy demonstrated a willingness to assume leadership by initiating the play theme, and Leslie exhibited the ability to get along with another child by engaging in related play. Jeremy's social competence was also suggested by his respect for Leslie's play space and materials as he took care not to disturb her bananas.

■ *Symbolic play.* Both children demonstrated the ability to engage in symbolic play as they pretended to be monkeys. Jeremy carried out his pretense by adopting a monkey's movements, walking, swinging, and jumping like a monkey. Leslie's symbolic play was slightly more abstract; she engaged in nonliteral use of props when her twigs became bananas to be peeled, eaten, and reserved for the man in the yellow hat.

■ *Language, literacy, and numeracy development.* Leslie used more language in her pretend play than did Jeremy, as might be expected given the nonliteral nature of her role playing and use of props. More significantly, Leslie's play indicated her attention to stories she has heard and her willingness to relate them to other contexts. Her acknowledgement of both Curious George and the man in the yellow hat suggests that she is aware of her favorite characters and can bring them into her play. Finally, Leslie's setting aside bananas for the man indicates that she recognizes the quantity of three and can label it with the number three.

■ *Physical-motor development.* Both children demonstrated the ability to climb a short ladder, although Leslie did so more carefully by placing both feet on each step before attempting the next, whereas Jeremy climbed more confidently, placing only one foot on each step. Leslie also demonstrated considerable balance as she walked up a ramp while holding twigs in each hand. Jeremy exhibited even more varied physical ability by walking like a monkey, hopping, hanging, and swinging from one arm.

■ *Dispositions.* Leslie showed a disposition toward quiet role-playing, maintaining her own pretend episode while Jeremy engaged in more physical play around her. She also demonstrated resourcefulness as she gathered twigs to serve as bananas. Finally, she exhibited a disposition toward using language and stories to further her play. Jeremy showed a disposition toward active physical play and challenging movement.

Play Episode 2

Two five-year-olds, Stephanie and Lourdes, are in a dramatic play area set up as a shoe store. It is equipped with a floor mat that has sets of footprints, each labeled with the corresponding shoe size. A shelf contains a variety of shoe boxes, each with a label specifying the size and color of the shoes inside. The center also includes a cash register with play money, and a pad of blank receipts.

Lourdes assumes the role of the salesperson by asking Stephanie, "May I help you, miss?"

Stephanie replies, "I need to get some shoes for my wedding. They have to be white."

Lourdes kneels down and unties Stephanie's shoes, then directs her to use the floor mat to find the size she needs. When Stephanie stands on the size 4 footprints, Lourdes declares that she needs a size 4 shoe.

Stephanie disagrees and places her foot on the next set of prints, announcing, "No. See? I need a size 5. This one fits better. The size 4 is too short. It will pinch my toes."

Lourdes replies, "Okay. I'll get you a 5," then turns and scans the boxes on the shelf until she finds a box labeled "SIZE 5." She ignores the part of the label that indicates that the shoes are blue. "These should be just right for you," she says as she opens the box to help Stephanie try on a pair of high heels. Stephanie walks around the area looking down at her feet.

"'But they're blue!" says Stephanie. "I need white for my dress."

"We can polish them white," Lourdes replies, cupping one hand like a bottle and pretending to dip in an applicator and spread polish on the shoes. "Now they're perfect."

"I'll take them. Here's six dollars," Stephanie says, handing Lourdes two five-dollar bills.

"Wait. I'll give you change," Lourdes says, and gives Stephanie two one-dollar bills. "And here's your receipt. It says one pair of white shoes. Six dollars." On the receipt Lourdes has written one line of random letters and the numeral 6.

Again, you should have been able to identify a wealth of developmental information from this play scenario. Some of the most significant include:

■ *Level of social play.* Lourdes and Stephanie engaged in highly interactive pretend play, as opposed to the more parallel play of Jeremy and Leslie.

■ *Social development.* Both children appeared to possess a high level of social competence. They collaborated in their play, and willingly assumed different roles without disagreement. Stephanie demonstrated a willingness to compromise when she accepted the blue shoes (and Lourdes's declaration that they were now white) without argument.

■ *Language development.* Both Lourdes and Stephanie demonstrated competent language use. They each used phrases and terms that were appropriate to the pretend scenario, for example, "May I help you, miss," "This one fits," and "It will pinch my toes." Lourdes also used language to signal a pretend prop—the bottle of shoe polish and its applicator—that extended their play and successfully (and creatively) resolved a problem.

■ *Literacy and numeracy development.* Both girls demonstrated that they could read numbers, both on the floor mat and on the boxes of shoes. That Lourdes ignored the part of the label that said "BLUE" on the shoes she selected may indicate that she cannot read color words. This could also simply mean, however, that she was attending more to size in her search for shoes for Stephanie. Further observation would be needed to determine if Lourdes could indeed read color words. Lourdes's receipt for Stephanie revealed that she knows the difference between letters and numbers, and uses them appropriately. Her use of random letters, however, suggests that she has not yet made the connection between letters and sounds. Stephanie's use of two five-dollar bills to represent six dollars, and Lourdes' selection of two one dollar bills as change indicates that neither child has a conventional understanding of money and the quantities it represents, although they do have the underlying concept of the use of money, and the concept of giving change.

■ *Physical-motor development.* There were many opportunities to observe the children's motor development. Lourdes untied Stephanie's shoes and engaged in writing. Her level of fine motor development is indicated by the fluency with which she carried out each procedure. The manner in which both children handled the paper money offers further evidence of the degree of their fine motor ability. Further, Stephanie's balance could be assessed by watching how well she was able to walk in high heel shoes.

Play Episode 3
Three eight-year-olds are playing jacks. They argue about who should go first until Amanda shows them how she and her neighborhood friends flip the jacks

to see who goes first. She demonstrates how they place all ten jacks in their palms, flip the jacks into the air cupping their hands together palms down to catch the jacks on the backs of their hands, then flipping them again while turning their palms back up to catch as many jacks as they can. "Whoever catches the most jacks goes first," she explains.

Chantal and Olivia like her idea, and ask to practice a few times before they flip "for real." All three girls take turns flipping the jacks, laughing together when they sometimes drop most of them, and complimenting each other when they catch a lot. Amanda consistently catches all ten jacks, whereas Olivia and Chantal never catch more than six. Amanda tells the others that her big sister always flips with one hand, and shows them how. "You two can flip with two hands since you just learned how. I'll flip with just one. That will be fair."

The girls begin to play jacks. When they get to the third round, each child must pick up jacks in sets of threes, picking up the remaining single jack by itself. Amanda tosses out the jacks, then looks at the whole set and says, "I'll pick up this one by itself first, then the three threes."

Olivia objects. "No. You have to pick up the threes first. You always pick up the leftovers last." Chantal agrees with her, so Amanda leaves the single jack for last. On subsequent turns, Amanda always knows without counting how many sets of jacks she can pick up and how many will be leftover to pick up last.

When it is Chantal's turn, she tosses out the jacks, then touches each one while counting, "One, two, three," three times until she decides which jack she will pick up last. Then she picks up the jacks in the groups that she counted out. With each successive turn, Chantal touches and counts the jacks to determine how to pick them up.

Olivia picks up sets of three, four, and five jacks without counting them out, but does point and count when she needs to pick up six and seven jacks. When she eventually gets to eight jacks, she is able to complete that and her next two turns again without counting.

All three girls appear to be relatively experienced jacks players. They know how to toss the ball, pick up a set number of jacks, then catch the ball after one bounce. But they play with different degrees of proficiency. Chantal plays the most fluently, rarely missing the ball and moving through all ten rounds of the game most quickly. Amanda is relatively successful, although she frequently tosses the ball too high, causing it to bounce out of her reach, and forcing her to forfeit her turn. Olivia has no problems throwing and catching the ball, but only does well when her jacks are fairly well spread out. She then picks up the jacks by sweeping her whole hand across the floor to pick up a set of jacks. When the jacks are too close together, she is unable to pick up the ones she needs without disturbing or "tipping" the other jacks.

Were you able to identify significant behaviors that demonstrated the capabilities and development of these three girls? Some possible assessment data include:

- *Level of social play.* These girls engaged in a highly structured interactive form of play—a game with rules.

- *Social development.* Each of the girls was quite competent socially. They were able to follow established rules and compromise on new rules (e.g., flipping the jacks to determine the order of turns and deciding that leftover jacks had to be picked up last). Amanda demonstrated a keen sense of fair play and a willingness to accommodate others when she offered to use only one hand to flip the jacks.

■ *Numeracy development.* Amanda exhibited the ability to divide and determine remainders in her head, without actually counting the jacks or touching them to determine groupings. Olivia showed that she can do that for groups of two, three, four, and five, but must count out groups of six and seven jacks to determine remainders. Chantal's play illustrated that she still needs to manipulate the jacks physically and count out loud to determine how many sets of a given number she must pick up and how many will remain to be picked up separately.

■ *Physical-motor development.* The game of jacks requires sophisticated physical-motor ability. Children must be able to toss and catch a small ball, and rapidly pick up sets of small jacks without moving any from the larger group. The children demonstrated varying abilities with these motor tasks.

■ *Ability to plan and solve problems.* That the girls were quite capable of planning and problem solving is evident in their establishment or rules prior to starting the game and in their decision to use Amanda's suggestion for a fair way to begin when each girl wanted to go first.

From the information derived from these three play episodes, it should be apparent that observing children as they play is a viable means of assessing their learning and development. In addition to the types of information gleaned from these episodes, observations of play may lead teachers to document other aspects of children's learning, including

■ misconceptions children demonstrate (e.g., that some things float because they are small whereas others sink because they are big)

■ dispositions (e.g., the persistence evident when a child continually rebuilds a toppling block structure or the curiosity demonstrated when two children spend considerable time watching a classroom ant farm and poking an anthill in the play yard with a stick and watching the ants swarm to the surface)

■ incorporation of classroom lessons into play (e.g., the use of plot episodes and characters from a shared book in dramatic play and the use of newly taught computational skills to divide play materials evenly among a group of friends)

Techniques for Capturing Observations

Teachers may gain a wealth of knowledge about children's learning and development by observing the children at play. The key to good assessment is to develop a system for regularly documenting observations and for compiling, analyzing, and sharing assessment information with children, parents, and other educators. Two good ways to do this are to use anecdotal notes and to document observations with time-activity sampling.

Using Anecdotal Notes

One of the best ways to conduct observations of children as they are engaged in classroom activities is to collect and analyze anecdotal notes about what the children do, what they say,

and what they produce. An anecdote is a short narrative concerning a particular incident or event of interest. Rhodes & Nathenson-Mejia (1992) note the benefits of using anecdotal records to document children's learning and development.

> The open ended nature of anecdotal records allows teachers to record the rich detail available in most observations of (learning) processes and products. The open-ended nature of anecdotal record taking also allows teachers to determine what details are important to record given the situation in which the student is (performing), previous assessment data, and the instructional goals the teacher and student have established. (p. 502)

The open-ended nature of anecdotal records allows teachers to tailor assessment to suit their own purposes and the needs of their children. When taking anecdotal notes (as with any observational assessment), what to assess depends on the individual curriculum and goals and objectives for any given group of children. Teachers should look for evidence of skills and concepts that are relevant to their own programs (Pellegrini, 1998).

Thorndike and Hagen (1997) suggest the following guidelines for writing anecdotal notes.

1. Describe a specific event or product.
2. Report rather than evaluate or interpret.
3. Relate the material to other facts that are known about the child.

Describing and Reporting Specific Events.   The most useful anecdotal notes are those that avoid general evaluative statements, for example, "Peter got along well with the others today! This is a real change." It is better to record specific detailed information, for example,

"Peter joined Jamal in the sandbox, started digging his own hole, then asked Jamal to help him dig. Gave his shovel to Jamal and used a cup to dig. Tried to take the shovel back, but let Jamal keep it when he protested. Got upset and pushed Jamal when sand got in his hair, but resumed playing calmly after a few minutes."

The more general evaluative note certainly suggests that a new behavior was observed, but it offers no basis for comparison. What does "got along well" mean? Did Peter jump right into playing with others? Who were they? Who initiated the interactive play? Were there any difficulties in the interaction? How were problems handled?

The second, more detailed note includes all of this information. It can be used to chart any further new behaviors that suggest Peter's increasing ability to play successfully with others. The next time Peter's interactive play is documented, perhaps a week, or even a month later, the teacher will not have to try to remember the circumstances that led to his or her earlier evaluation. Instead, he or she will know exactly what happened and be able to see if the next observation illustrates even more advanced "getting along." Perhaps then, Peter will immediately join another child in joint play, rather than beginning with parallel play. Or he might be invited to join in, rather than initiating the contact himself, perhaps indicating that he is being better accepted by his classmates. Maybe the teacher will notice that Peter is able to handle something that upsets him without any physical aggression, suggesting increasing development of interpersonal skills. In any case, the detail provided in the second anecdotal note enables Peter's teacher to evaluate and document his development.

Organizing the Observations.   It will be important to set up a system for recording anecdotal notes about children's development. Without a system, teachers are likely to find that over time, they have many notes about some children, and few or none at all about others. This is only natural, given that some children seem to demand much more attention than others, and that some children are more likely to interact with their teachers. Without a system, many teachers also find that they do not remember to keep up with their note-taking and then have to scramble to take notes on large numbers of children in the week or two before conferences or report cards are due.

Many teachers address these problems by setting up an observation schedule with the goal of observing and recording information about at least three children each day. This ensures that they will get to each child approximately once every two weeks. This does not necessarily mean that they will take notes on only those two or three children on a particular day. Once teachers become proficient at observing children and writing anecdotal notes, they will take the opportunity to document really significant behaviors as they occur, regardless of which children are targeted for observation on a particular day.

One way for teachers to maintain this level of spontaneity in recording observations is by carrying sets of large mailing labels in their pockets, or keeping them on hand near each center. When they observe something they want to document, they write the child's name and the date on the label, followed by a detailed narrative of a specific event. They also keep a binder or notebook with pages labeled with each child's name. At the end of the day, the teachers can affix their notes to the child's page. Teachers may eventually want to transfer these notes into an electronic file on the classroom computer, perhaps by scanning in their handwritten notes. This will facilitate easy transfer of information from the notes into conference reports or report cards.

These procedures also help to ensure that all children are observed regularly. At the start of each day, teachers can look through their collection of notes to see which children are lacking recent documentation, and then target those children for observation.

Analyzing the Notes. Simply writing the notes and organizing them according to individual children is not the end of assessment. Over time, the notes collected for individual children should be analyzed to make inferences, to identify patterns, and to identify strengths and areas that need more development.

As Peter's teacher observes him playing more with other children and sees them willingly join him in his play and invite him into their own, he or she might reasonably infer that Peter is developing significant social skills, and that his classmates like him as a result. He or she may continue to observe that Peter gets upset with the other children fairly regularly, and infer that he is developing a short temper that is rather unpredictable.

As the teacher analyzes notes taken over time, however, focusing on the events surrounding Peter's angry outbursts, he or she begins to see a common element across each incident. Peter's temper does not flare unpredictably; he is most easily upset when something makes him dirty—when a lunch mate drips lemonade on his arm, when another child brushes his shirt with a wet painting, and when he splashes water on his shoes and socks while playing at the water table. This pattern in Peter's behavior might not have been obvious from any one incident. Only when detailed notes taken over time are analyzed does the pattern emerge.

In addition to patterns of behavior, specific areas of strengths and weaknesses can also become apparent through analysis of anecdotal notes. Peter's ability to engage other children in his play and his willingness to share materials might be noted as strengths. His apparent inability to deal calmly with messiness might be defined as an area needing further development.

Using Time-Activity Sampling

At times, teachers may want to make more systematic observations of children, or they may need to gather a large quantity of specific information in a relatively brief time period. For example, a teacher may want to know which centers in the classroom children find most enticing, so that she or he can plan to replace some centers with new ones. A technique called time-activity sampling serves this purpose quite well.

To conduct a time-activity sample, the teacher must first construct a form that lists all of the centers in the classroom across the top, and all of the children's names down the side. She or he then reproduces multiple copies of the form. Then for the entire time that children have free access to centers, the teacher records where each child is every ten, twenty, or thirty minutes, depending on the total length of time allowed in centers. This procedure would then be repeated at least twice more and the data compiled and analyzed to guide decisions about which centers to keep and which ones to change.

Teachers may also use time-sampling techniques to make systematic assessments about individuals or groups of children and their activities over the course of a day. The teacher may believe that the children in his or her class need to get more involved in construction, but he or she is not sure how much time children actually engage in constructive play versus other forms of play. The teacher could construct a time-activity sampling form listing each type of play across the top, and children's names down the side. He or she could set intervals during which information about the nature of children's play is recorded, checking off what each child is engaged in every fifteen or thirty minutes, for example. Collected over a period of a few days, the records may support the teacher's belief that children could benefit from encouragement to engage in construction; or he or she might find that they are spending much more time engaged in this type of play than he or she realized.

Time-sampling procedures may also be used to document development over a longer period of time. Teachers may choose to make day long observations once every nine weeks, for instance, to facilitate evaluation of how children's play changes as they gain experience in the classroom and as they mature.

Validity Considerations
for Observational Assessments

As is true for more formal testing, teachers must be concerned with the validity of their observational assessments. The term *validity* refers to the degree to which the assessment procedures measure what they are intended to measure, and the degree to which inferences drawn from the assessments are meaningful and appropriate. This means that teachers must work to ensure that what they observe and document is actually reflective of a child's true capabilities. Teachers should be aware of a number of factors that influence the validity of their observational assessments.

First, teachers must recognize that the presence of adults, even if they are nonparticipating observers, may inhibit children's play or change the nature of it. This is especially true for dramatic and fantasy play (Pellegrini, 1984). Children may be somewhat embarrassed to fantasize or pretend in front of an adult, particularly in the primary grades. They may therefore play more cautiously, limiting their descriptions of pretend scenarios and using props more conventionally than they might if they were not aware of an adult's presence. When this happens, it is possible to underestimate aspects of children's play such as their symbolic representation or their language use.

Conversely, the presence of peers enhances children's play (Pellegrini & Perlmutter, 1989). In interactive situations with peers, children are more likely to demonstrate higher levels of ability than they might when playing alone. Teachers need to be careful to recognize that some high-level performance might be possible for a child only when his play is scaffolded by other children.

Teachers should also be aware that who a child's playmates are may make a difference in his or her performance. Play with friends is often sustained longer than play with nonfriends (Howes, 1992). The longer play is sustained, the more complex it is likely to become. More complex play is more likely to demand higher levels of cognitive functioning than simpler play of shorter duration, thereby allowing friends to demonstrate higher levels of competence than they might when playing with other peers with whom they are less friendly.

When assessing children in the context of their play, it is also important to recognize the influence of props on play themes and types of play (Rubin, Fein, and Vandenberg, 1983). Literal props are likely to induce literal use, requiring relatively less imagination and less language to further a play scenario. Props used in a nonliteral way, however, require extensive description on the part of the players to let others know, for example, that the tricycle has now become a fire engine and the play structure is now an apartment full of children to be rescued.

Pellegrini and Perlmutter (1989) further found that the use of gender-specific toys influences play. Teachers do need to be sure that children have opportunities to play with all kinds of toys and should avoid even subtly steering children toward toys or games that they perceive as being more appropriate for one or the other gender. Yet it has been noted that play is often sustained longer when children select toys that are more often preferred by their own gender. Given the connection between complexity of play and its duration, whether children are observed while playing with gender-preferred toys might be noted.

Other studies of young children's play have demonstrated that habituation facilitates play; that is, the degree to which children are experienced with certain toys and familiar with particular play situations influences how they play (Pellegrini and Boyd, 1993). When children first play with an object, they must explore it before using it imaginatively. Their focus is on what the object can do, as opposed to what they can do with it. With a novel toy, or in a new center, children might be more likely to engage in exploratory or practice play than they will be once the toy is familiar. Again, teachers need to be aware of whether children are being observed in novel situations or if they are using new materials so that they do not draw faulty inferences about children's capabilities.

Finally, teachers need to recognize that observations of children during periods when they have freely chosen what they will play and where will allow observation of only those aspects of a child's development that he or she chooses to exhibit. Behaviors that might more readily be exhibited in certain centers (e.g., pattern formation in the manipulative or block centers) may not be as easy to observe in other areas of the classroom preferred by children. A teacher needs to be careful not to draw conclusions about a child's development of skills and concepts if the child has not been observed in a context that readily elicits behaviors that demonstrate acquisition of those skills and concepts. It would not be valid, for example, to conclude that a child has not yet developed the ability to form patterns if the child was never observed in centers most likely to engage the child in pattern formation.

How to Address Validity Concerns

There is no way teachers can (or should) try to control each of the factors that influence children's play. To do so would render the play unnatural, which in itself would make the assessment less valid. Teachers do need to interact with children while they are in centers, even if this interaction does influence the nature of children's play. They do need to encourage children to interact with their friends, and to broaden their interactions to include less popular children. They do need to supply children with both literal and nonliteral props, and encourage children to explore all toys and materials without regard for stereotypical gender preferences. They certainly need to introduce new toys and new centers regularly, and allow children plenty of opportunities to choose where and with whom they will play.

Although teachers should not attempt to control children's play, they can still take steps to ensure that their observations are as valid as possible. They can start by being sure to observe children in as many different play situations as possible. Given a variety of different contexts for play, children will be able to demonstrate a broader array of skills development and concept acquisition than they will in any one context. A kindergarten child may spend all of his or her time in the writing center drawing pictures and coloring, perhaps enticed by the bright colored markers available there. He or she may, however, demonstrate considerable writing skill while taking orders and presenting bills to customers in a pretend restaurant in the dramatic play center. Thus, drawing inferences about this child's knowledge of writing based solely on his or her activity in the writing center would underestimate his or her writing ability.

Anecdotal notes that include significant detail about the circumstances surrounding a particular play event will also help teachers avoid drawing invalid conclusions about children's learning and development. Any of the factors noted above should be included in a good anecdotal note. Then, when teachers observe a pattern of practice rather than constructive play, for example, they can asses whether this was perhaps because of the novelty of the play context or the child's first use of new materials for play. When parallel play is observed, or when pretend play episodes are brief and literal, teachers can note whether the players were friends. In each case, careful documentation of the circumstances of the play can influence the conclusions teachers draw about the children based on their observations.

Sharing Assessment Information

One major purpose in conducting assessments should be to share insight about children and their development with parents, other educators, and the children themselves. For this purpose, teachers' observations as recorded in anecdotal notes can also be supported by samples of children's products or visual and auditory evidence of their learning and development. The systematic collection of these products forms the basis of portfolio assessment.

Portfolio Assessment

Paulson, Paulson, and Meyer (1991) state that a portfolio is "a purposeful collection of student work that exhibits the student's efforts, progress, and achievements in one or more areas" (p. 60). The emphasis in on *systematic* and *purposeful* collection. A large box or folder into which a child places every product he or she produces, although a good way to begin collecting artifacts, is not in itself a portfolio and is not likely to be useful for documenting and reporting on children's development. Rather, teachers (and students themselves, beginning in kindergarten and first grade) need to decide what should go into the portfolio to demonstrate children's learning.

Sometimes it is useful to include in the portfolio any products that demonstrate a developmental or cognitive leap in children's understanding. Thus, a child's first work at the easel—with colors running together into one great brown blob—will be included, along with a piece that shows the child's growing ability to paint more deliberately with colors only slightly overlapping, and perhaps even a piece that shows the first signs of representation. Similarly, a second grader's writing sample from the first day of school—a "story" four lines long using mostly invented spellings—might be followed by one of his or her first pieces that used significantly more conventional spelling, and another piece with a more well-developed story with three or four plot events.

Writings and drawings are not the only artifacts that can be included in a portfolio. Some teachers photograph or videotape children in the classroom and on the playground, attempting to capture images that demonstrate the youngsters' skills and abilities. These photographs and videotapes can become part of the children's portfolios. Many teachers also audiotape children, particularly as they read, whether their reading is pretend reading of pictures in a story or informational book, or more conventional reading of a portion of a second-grade-level chapter book.

Regardless of the artifacts included, each piece should be supplemented by a statement that explains the significance of the piece and the reason for its inclusion. This can be done by creating an annotated table of contents, or by attaching a brief statement to each individual artifact. As children are engaged in determining what should be included in their portfolios, they should also be invited to offer their own explanations regarding their selections. It is important to remember, however, that young children may understand criteria for including pieces in their portfolios differently than their teachers. When asked to select his best pieces of writing, for example, one first grader chose two very brief journal entries about his dog rather than writing samples that his teacher recognized as significantly more advanced. When asked to explain why those pieces of writing were his best work, he replied, "Those are the best because I really like my dog. He's the best pet we ever had!" Thus, with young children, it is best to supplement their choices and analyses of artifacts with those selected and explained by the teacher.

Checklists and Rating Scales

Assessment information from both anecdotal notes and portfolios of children's work can be summarized for sharing with others through the use of developmental checklists and rating scales. These are lists of behaviors or skills that children typically display or master during particular developmental periods. Checklists can be constructed by teachers to include behaviors related to those goals and objectives that are determined by the curriculum. As shown in Figure 6.1, for example, a checklist related to goals for fine motor development might include the following behaviors: cutting, pasting, zipping, buttoning, coloring, writing, tying, stringing beads, and stacking small blocks. These skills would be listed across the top of the page, with the children's names listed down the sides. As teachers observe that children engage in these behaviors, they mark the date on the checklist beside the child's name.

Some teachers may want to rate the frequency or quality of observed behaviors. They may note that the behavior occurs rarely, regularly, or always, for example, or that the child's attempts are average or above or below average in quality. Such checklists are considered rating scales. The most appropriate use of rating scales is to compare children's current behavior with previous behaviors so that development can be documented (Brewer, 1998).

Checklists and rating scales can be useful for helping teachers summarize information gathered from their observations and for reminding teachers of behaviors that they should

FIGURE 6.1   Sample Checklist Form

NAMES	cuts	zips	colors	ties	pastes	stacks	sorts	strings	buttons	Comments
David B.										
Alicia D.										
Marcela D.										
Gabriel F.										
Nathan H.										
Roshawn J.										
Ari M.										
Ashley M.										
Virginia P.										
Kibbe R.										
Megan S.										
Chris T.										
Daniel T.										
Isabel V.										
Luis W.										
Kali W.										

look for. They should be used with caution, however. Teachers must be careful not to let the behaviors and skills included on checklists drive their curriculum. This is especially a danger with published checklists or those compiled by a school district for use across multiple schools with a variety of grade levels. There is a temptation for teachers to use checklist items to structure specific activities for children that address skills in isolation rather than simply using the checklists to document behaviors that naturally occur in the context of authentic classroom activities such as children's play (Brewer, 1998).

Checklists can also be problematic if they narrow teachers' focus so that only behaviors related to those on the lists are documented (Pellegrini, 1998). Teachers need to remain open to documenting any observations that suggest development, new insight, or subtle changes in children's understanding of previously learned concepts.

If teachers are able to collect a broad range of observational information, supplemented by artifacts collected in portfolios and summaries of children's behaviors as documented with checklists and rating scales, they will find that they have a wealth of assessment data on which to base instructional decisions. Furthermore, they will be able to use this information to help them gauge the effects of their instructional program and to communicate effectively about children's progress, perhaps even influencing "high-stakes" decisions that are being made about children.

Moving away from more formal testing toward observational assessments also has the potential to change the whole nature of the classroom, as Terri Wide (1998), a first-grade teacher in a New Orleans public school, described in a reflection in response to a series of in-service sessions on emergent literacy and observational assessments. She wrote:

> Recently, I have been using many of the observational assessments in my classroom. They include anecdotal records (of the kinds of play children engage in, or the language and play themes that occur in their dramatic play, for example) and portfolios of children's efforts (including things like running records of their oral reading, my analyses of their retellings of stories they read, and artwork they've done in the art center). These forms of assessment have opened many doors for me. They allow me the freedom to move about the classroom observing more than one student at a time. The strategies used for informally assessing my students have not been complicated nor have they detracted from my normal instructional time. They have actually freed me to work much more readily with the students.
>
> The language acquisition of the students has improved due to me being able to actually sit with the students who are novice readers and writers and demonstrate strategies for improving their oral and written language. Their social skills have also improved because I get to spend so much more time interacting with them, and they get to spend more time interacting with each other. Their creativity is blossoming because they now choose the ways they want to share what they've learned. Often, what they choose to do is much more involved than anything I would have tested them on.
>
> It is interesting to see how the students are becoming more experimental and engaged plus motivated about their own learning. They are learning to assess their needs and ask for responses to their questions. They are learning to ask me—and each other—for help with projects or constructions. It is amazing how many students are capable of moving forward once they feel confident to try new activities without worrying about whether they will be tested. Each day is a new celebra-

tion of what the students are doing. They are now enjoying the class more, and I am even happier being their teacher.

There was so much tension in the room when I was attempting to directly teach to some prescribed list of skills and then measuring children's mastery of them with tests. Boy am I learning a lot about the ways to assess young children without damaging their self-esteem or harming their egos. I'm telling you, children who rarely spoke in my room are calling me over and letting me know they are in the class. It is truly a metamorphosis for the children and for their teacher.

This chapter has presented an overview of assessment techniques that can be used in a classroom that incorporates playful learning and playful teaching. Each of the following chapters is devoted to specific aspects of children's development that are fostered through classrooms infused with play. Each area of development offers teachers fresh opportunities to assess children's learning. As you read these chapters, keep in mind the procedures offered here for carrying out ongoing assessment.

Developing Advocacy Skills

Assessment tends to be a very emotional and highly charged issue for parents, teachers, and administrators alike, as the heated discussion between Ms. Mellis and Ms. Dimaggio that opened this chapter suggests. As might be surmised from their comments, attempts to initiate new assessment procedures are likely to be met with opposition ranging from mild to fierce, depending on the degree of investment in current assessment strategies. This is especially true when new assessments are not adequately and clearly explained in terms that are understandable to everyone involved.

A good advocate therefore needs to learn the value of clear and simple communication. This is especially necessary when advocating for new assessments with groups of parents, legislators, or other noneducators. Too often, a good idea is lost in educational jargon, which clouds what is being proposed and opens educators to criticism, or worse, ridicule. Why use phrases such as "optimizing opportunities for children to interact with manipulatives," when we could say instead, "giving children adequate time to play with educational toys"?

It will be helpful for teachers to remember that the kinds of assessment and reporting procedures they favor are likely to be unfamiliar to parents and even some school administrators. People tend to be most comfortable with (and therefore most accepting of) things that are familiar. For many people, that means tests and test scores. When teachers implement new assessment and reporting procedures, parents are likely to feel shortchanged if information from formal tests is not shared. They may have come to know what scoring at the "90th percentile" refers to, and they certainly understand what it means when their child brings home A's, B's, or C's.

For parents, a report card or parent-teacher conference filled with anecdotal observations about their child's development in a variety of different areas may be confusing. Even as they take in the rich information teachers are sharing, they may be wondering, "So how is my child doing compared to everyone else? Is she an A student? Is she average? Do I need to worry about her progress?"

Administrators may be sensitive to parents' concerns and hesitate to implement new assessment procedures for fear that they will be called on to explain and justify a system that they do not fully understand themselves. They may not have a complete understanding of the issues related to developmentally appropriate assessment for young children, and thus may not really understand the benefits of such assessments over more traditional approaches.

Good advocates for developmentally appropriate assessment need to be aware of the concerns expressed by parents, administrators, and others and recognize their need for clear, simple explanations of assessment procedures and results. They must be sure that they themselves understand the issues surrounding assessment of young children and the specific benefits of informal approaches. Most important, they must learn to communicate their views on assessment in simple, direct language that can be understood by their intended audiences.

The activities outlined in Table 6.1 will help you to understand parents', administrators', and elected officials' concerns about informal assessment and to learn more about issues

TABLE 6.1   Advocacy Activities: Informing and Involving Parents and Administrators

Learning to Communicate Simply		
Becoming Aware	*Furthering Your Understanding*	*Taking Action*
1. Interview parents who have received observational assessment information about their child. Find how the information was shared—through a conference, a narrative report, a checklist, etc. Ask the parents to discuss how they felt about the information they received. Did they understand what the teachers were telling them about their children's learning and development? What did they find easiest to understand? What was the hardest to understand? What other information would they have liked to receive?	1. Find journal articles that describe a variety of observational assessments. Summarize each assessment procedure as concisely and as clearly as possible.	1. Decide which observational assessment procedures you would like to use with your class. Visit a school to experiment with collecting observational data and analyzing it.
	2. Read journal articles that address controversies surrounding the use of formal test with young children. Be sure you can summarize the issues raised in these articles in clear language that can be understood by audiences of noneducators.	2. Write a letter to the editor of your local newspaper clearly and simply stating the benefits of informal, observational assessments for young children.
2. Interview a principal from a school that uses observational assessments as a major vehicle for reporting children's progress, and another principal in a school that still uses formal and teacher-made tests as the basis for reporting children's learning. Find out how the first principal was persuaded to move toward more developmentally appropriate assessments. Find out what concerns the second principal has about using such assessments.	3. Search your local and state newspapers for any articles dealing with testing and assessment in your area. What are the issues raised in these articles? What concerns about testing and assessment can you glean from the educators, elected officials, and parents quoted in these articles?	3. Prepare a presentation for your classmates during which an alternative to formal testing for young children will be described. Be prepared to explain concisely and simply how your teaching and your children's learning will be impacted by the procedures you propose. Also, be prepared to answer any procedural questions from others who would like to try the observational assessments themselves.
	4. Find articles in the professional literature that describe methods of reporting assessment information to parents. What advice is given in these articles? Do they suggest ways to help parents understand the information that is being shared?	

related to changes in assessment procedures across the country. They will also help you develop an action plan to advocate for the use of observational assessment of children's learning in the context of their play.

Summary

In this chapter, we defined assessment as a process of observing and documenting children's learning as it becomes evident in the course of their play. Three purposes for assessment were established: to guide instruction; to monitor progress and report it to parents, administrators, and the children themselves; and to begin to identify children who may be in need of further assessment in order to secure special services. Appropriate assessments for young children are those that are broad enough in scope to capture the breadth of children's development; those that are based on children's interactions during normal, ongoing classroom activities rather than on their performance in artificial, contrived contexts; and those that rely on multiple sources of information drawn from interactions with children across a variety of contexts. It was posited that play offers many fruitful opportunities for assessing children's learning in areas such as level of social play; general social development; literacy, language, and numeracy development; and their physical-motor development.

Techniques for capturing observations of children at play were presented. These include anecdotal notes and time-activity sampling. Concerns regarding the validity of observational assessments and ways that teachers can address these concerns, were described. Methods for reporting and sharing assessment information, including portfolios, checklists, and rating scales, were described. Finally, methods teachers can use to advocate for appropriate assessment of young children were described.

REVISITING FIRST IMPRESSIONS

How have your views about assessment of children in preschool, kindergarten, and the early primary grades changed as a result of reading this chapter? In what ways have your views of the importance and benefits of assessing children as they play changed in response to the information in this chapter? In your journal, discuss any remaining questions and concerns you have about assessing children in the context of their play.

QUESTIONS FOR DISCUSSION

1. Brainstorm as many uses of assessment information that you can. Decide which uses are more important than others and why. Compare your list and your rankings of importance with your classmates' and discuss any differences in your opinions.

2. Think of one play episode you have observed recently. Describe the episode in detail to a group of your classmates. Then determine all of the assessment information that can be derived from that episode.

3. List and discuss all of the validity factors that must be considered if assessment information is to be collected in the following situation:

   During the second week of school, Ms. Green introduced a new student, Kenny, to her first-grade class and asked another child, Michael, to be his "special friend" for the day to help Kenny get acquainted with the classroom. On Kenny's second day, she saw the two children playing together in the block center and decided to observe them to get some preliminary assessment data on the new child. As she approached the center, Michael motioned for her to join them, and eagerly explained to her that he was building a fire station, pointing out the doors for the firetruck and the second floor where the firefighters sleep. She noticed that Kenny was building his own construction rather than collaborating with Michael on his. Although his structure looked rather complex, when she asked him about it, he said it was "just a stack of blocks." Ms. Green made a mental note to herself that Kenny appeared not to engage in symbolic play and preferred parallel play to interactive play with other children.

Why might inferences about Kenny based on this play episode be considered invalid?

SUGGESTED READINGS

Farr, B., & Trumbull, E. (1996). *Assessment alternatives for diverse classrooms.* Norwood, MA: Christopher-Gordon.

Harp, B. (Ed.). (1996). *Assessment and evaluation for student centered learning.* Norwood, MA: Christopher-Gordon.

Hill, B., & Ruptic, C. (1994). *Practical aspects of authentic assessment: Putting the pieces together.* Norwood, MA: Christopher-Gordon.

PART THREE

Connecting Play and Content in Preschool Programs and Primary Classrooms

CHAPTER

7 Fostering Healthy Living through Playful Learning and Playful Teaching

Prereading Guide

First Impressions.   What do you think of when you hear the term *health education?* Reflect back to your own experiences in preschool, kindergarten, and early primary school. What role did your school play in promoting healthy living? What are your beliefs about the role schools should play in developing healthy living for children in preschool, kindergarten, and the early primary grades. Write a summary of your current positions in your journal.

Revisit
Scheduling (Chapter 4)
Checklists and Rating Scales (Chapter 6)

Stories from the Field

Denise Simpson is a kindergarten teacher in a large, urban school district. Until recently, she had taught in a kindergarten center—a school comprised entirely of kindergarten classrooms. She had enjoyed the experience, in part because of the support offered by a faculty with common bonds developed out of their mutual concern for the education of young children.

> It was great to work in a place where everyone understood that things like snack time and rest time are important, because everyone else is teaching five- and six-year-olds too! It was also wonderful to be part of a faculty that could unite pretty easily to resist some central office mandates like standardized tests at the end of kindergarten, or changes in bus schedules that meant some children wouldn't be getting home until almost two hours after school closed. Because there were so many of us in one place, people listened when we argued that certain policies just weren't in the best interest of such young children.
>
> I knew I would miss the camaraderie of working exclusively with teachers and administrators focused on early childhood education when I transferred

to one of three kindergarten classrooms in the elementary school. But the change has been good in many ways. One thing I really love is getting to know the first grade teachers I'll be sending my children to next year—and having them get to know me! We really collaborate a lot, and most of them share my views about developmentally appropriate practice. This has really turned out to be a very supportive place for me and for the young children I teach.

But my move into a school designed primarily to accommodate elementary school children has not been without some sacrifices. I never realized how much I took for granted in the kindergarten center! Thank goodness, sinks with hot and cold running water were installed into each kindergarten classroom here a couple of years before I arrived, but children still must go down the hall to use the bathroom. At the kindergarten center, there were three small kitchen areas that teachers and children could use for cooking activities; here, we can sometimes use the cafeteria equipment, but it's oversized and not really very safe for children to use. The biggest problem has been space. The kindergarten classrooms here are so much smaller—the same size as all the rest of the classrooms. It's been a real struggle to fit in all of the centers I need, and as a result, most of the centers feel cramped. Children have to move pretty carefully around the room so they don't disturb each other. It's hard for kids to build with big blocks if someone else has already started an individual structure using unit blocks. And forget about having a hopscotch laid out on the floor! There's just no room.

What that means is that my children really need to go outside for anything other than fairly quiet play. That would not have been a problem at the kindergarten center, but it sure is here. Because there are so many different grades using the same play yards, it can be hard to find times to take the kindergartners outside other than at their scheduled recess period after lunch. At almost any other time, there are lots of older kids playing too boisterously for my kids to mix in safely. Of course, those kids need time to play too, without worrying about small children underfoot.

Even when I can take the children outside, I have to be on constant guard to make sure that they don't try to use equipment that might be dangerous for them. Some of the climbing structures are too high for five year olds, and they definitely aren't allowed on the eight foot slide that the older kids love so much.

The other kindergarten, first-, and second-grade teachers and I have begun to talk about some of these problems. And we are formulating a plan to make the spaces (and schedules) more developmentally appropriate for young children. What we really need is a space designed specifically to meet the needs of our kindergarten through second grade children, so that they can have more—and more flexible—time for playing outside in an environment that is both safe and challenging. We've identified a space that can be set aside for our use pretty easily. Our biggest problem right now is convincing the rest of the faculty and administration that this will be worth the investment. We'll have to prove to them that outside play needs to be more than just recess after lunch—that it needs to be an integral part of our teaching day.

Fostering Healthy Living through Play

Ms. Simpson and her fellow teachers are wise to invest their time and energies in creating appropriate play spaces for their young children. Even when schools have begun to successfully integrate play into classrooms, there is often little urgency about providing for successful outdoor play. The teachers are also correct in their beliefs that outdoor play—as well as space for gross motor activities and facilities for cooking—are essential for children's learning, health, and fitness and should be viewed as important learning and play centers for young children. The activities in these areas have the greatest potential for developing behaviors and attitudes that will lead to healthy living.

There is evidence that dispositions for healthy living begin in early childhood. In her tenure as U.S. Secretary for Health and Human Services during the Clinton administration, Donna Shalala (1997) stated,

> Health habits established early on are habits that will last a lifetime. What teachers and parents teach and, more important, how they behave will stay with children forever and determine how healthy they'll be in the future. It's a big responsibility—but also a wonderful opportunity. (p. 41)

That responsibility, and opportunities for meeting it, will be the focus of this chapter. The major goals of health education for young children were summarized by Shalala (1997) when she stated, "We must help children get off to a good start by ensuring that they eat healthy foods, develop good dental and personal hygiene habits, build self-esteem, and become active" (p. 39), thereby fostering dispositions toward behaving in ways that promote good health. These goals can be attained through a mix of spontaneous indoor and outdoor play, and playful, but more directed activities designed to foster lifelong healthy habits.

Healthy Living and Self-Esteem

When you reflected on the health education you experienced as a young child, did you include the development of self-esteem as one goal of your health education? If you did not, you are probably not alone. Most people tend to think of health education as including nutrition, hygiene, and exercise. In recent years, however, health educators have begun to recognize that many health problems, from poor eating habits to sedentary lifestyles, can be related directly to self-concepts developed early in life.

Children who develop physical skills and view themselves as agile and coordinated are confident in their bodies' responses and therefore much more likely to engage in physically challenging activities than are those who view themselves as unskilled, clumsy, or uncoordinated. Those children who regularly engage in physical activity are likely to value fit, athletic, healthy bodies, and are less likely to become obsessive about thinness and diet to the detriment of nutrition. Children with healthy self-images are also more likely to have better overall mental health than are children who do not feel good about themselves (Zigler & Finn-Stevenson, 1987).

Thus, it is imperative that early childhood educators begin to support children's development of healthy self-concepts and self-esteem. In preschool and kindergarten, children's self-concepts are to a great degree shaped by the way important adults such as parents and teachers respond to them. As children enter the early primary grades, their self-esteem becomes more heavily dependent on how they believe their peers view them (Marshall, 1989). In either case, it is important for children to perceive themselves as competent and able to achieve their own goals and goals set for them by others, be they parents, teachers, or peers.

The Teacher's Role in Promoting Self-Esteem

If teachers are to ensure that children develop healthy self-concepts, they must carefully select materials and activities in all areas of the curriculum that will allow children to be successful while at the same time providing an appropriate level of challenge. (Bredekamp & Copple, 1997). Repetition of already mastered skills does not build self-esteem; successful attainment of new skills does. While first graders might really enjoy learning to dribble a ball and delight in their growing proficiency as they participate in dribbling games, their sense of accomplishment will diminish unless new challenges are presented. Teachers must avoid falling into the habit of engaging children in the same games day after day simply because the children initially enjoy them. They must keep in mind that enjoyment often stems from trying and succeeding at something new. Once the children master dribbling a ball, for example, they should be encouraged to devise their own games in which that skill can be demonstrated and refined, and new skills can be learned.

Children's self-esteem is also enhanced when they feel that they are in control and that they can influence their own environments (Harter, 1983). Children's need for control, however, is often overlooked as teachers attempt to impose order on children's play. In the interest of using playground space efficiently and keeping tabs on playground equipment, for example, teachers may decide to set up obstacle courses themselves, and instruct children never to move the pieces. Although this procedure might facilitate efficient and orderly use of outdoor play equipment, it leaves children with little control over their own play and little opportunity for improvisation and exploration, each of which enhances children's play and what they learn from it.

That is not to say that a teacher should never set up obstacle courses for children. In the interest of promoting certain types of movement and physical-motor activity, a teacher may certainly give careful consideration to how available materials can be put together to enhance children's development. In addition to teacher structured activities, children need to spend significant time exploring their world in their own ways, setting and achieving their own goals. This means that children must be able to approach all areas of the curriculum playfully. Active engagement in theme studies and projects helps to ensure that children take control of their own learning by generating questions of interest and pursuing answers in their own ways. This type of exploration also extends to outside play. If allowed to organize their own outdoor play, for example, children might arrange the components of an obstacle course to become a trail through the mountains. Children will eagerly try to climb the "boulders" and "cliffs" along the path, learning much about balance, climbing, and jumping and feeling pride in their accomplishments along the way.

Teachers can also build self-esteem by interacting with children in ways that make them feel valued and help them to value themselves. This entails accepting and praising children's *approximations*—attempts that fall somewhat short of correctness or convention, but nonetheless demonstrate development. This can be seen in the response of Miguel's teacher when the three-year-old first attempted to propel himself around the bike path on a tricycle. Rather than pedaling, Miguel moved the tricycle by placing both feet on the ground on either side of it and pulling himself forward. Recognizing Miguel's choice of a tricycle rather than the push toys that he was accustomed to as a first step toward eventual mastery of an important new ability, his teacher praised him by saying, "Miguel, you decided to try a bike today! You were really moving!"

It is not enough, however, for teachers to respond positively to children. They must also work to establish a classroom environment that encourages children to respond positively to each other. All of his teacher's attempts to encourage Miguel to continue exploring the use of a tricycle can be undone if other children are allowed to taunt him and tell him that he rides like a baby. Teachers have to help children accept that everybody does things in their own ways, and that often no one way is best. Levy's teacher did just that when she overheard him taunting Caitlin, another four-year-old, saying that she was just scribbling when they worked together at the art table. During circle time the next morning, the teacher showed the children some new markers and textured paper that she would be placing in the art center. Then she demonstrated that there were many different ways children could use the new materials, holding up samples that included representational drawings, pages filled with random lines of different colors, and pictures made from repetitive use of a few shapes or designs. "What's really nice about all of these is the bright colors," she said. "Aren't they interesting to look at?" Over time, as children see again and again that there are all kinds of ways to use materials and participate in activities, they will begin to be more accepting of each other. At that point they will all become allies in developing each other's self-esteem.

Waiting for occasions to arise that offer opportunities to reinforce acceptance of individual differences, however, falls short of a teacher's responsibility to ensure that all children are valued and accepted by their peers. Peer rejection is a critical issue in the development of self-esteem, and its effects are long lasting. In fact, rejection beyond kindergarten is difficult, if not impossible, to change (Paley, 1992). For this reason, it is imperative that teachers be proactive in their efforts to establish a classroom culture of respect and acceptance. Teachers must make it clear that taunting and teasing are not acceptable and will not be tolerated. When Levy teased Caitlin about her scribbling, his teacher should have stopped him right then by saying, "Caitlin is drawing the way she likes. I like the way she's using so many colors. You need to let her experiment and not try to tell her that she has to draw like you do."

Finally, it is important to recognize that children's self-esteem is often closely tied to their body images. One of the often cited benefits of engaging children in physical activity is that it promotes the development of self-esteem by helping children gain a more accurate perception of themselves (Grineski, 1988). In a society that is obsessed with thinness, it is not unusual for children as young as fourth or fifth grade to say they are dieting. Younger children are not immune to these influences. Even in preschool and kindergarten, children are teased about their weight; many believe themselves to be fat even when they are healthy and developing quite normally. Thus, it is incumbent upon teachers to foster positive body images by helping children value healthy (rather than simply thin) bodies. They can begin to achieve this goal by getting children interested in good nutrition and by engaging them in challenging physical activity. Ways of doing both will be addressed in the sections that follow.

Healthy Living and Nutrition

When asked to discuss young children and health concerns, many adults, both parents and teachers, immediately cite poor nutrition as a major concern. Although it is true that many

children in areas with high levels of poverty often come to school hungry (Kotch & Shackelford, 1989; Reicks, Randall, & Haynes, 1994), it is also true that even children from middle-class homes may come to school undernourished. The problem is not always how much children eat, rather it is what they eat. Regardless of economic status, many parents are unaware of how important an adequate diet is to children's development. In many families, regular mealtimes are no longer a part of the daily routine. Even when families do share meals, they often rely heavily on convenience foods, fast-food, or other take-out options, with the result that there is little emphasis on well-balanced meals that include fresh fruits and vegetables. It has been demonstrated, in fact, that more than half of the calories consumed by children in urban areas come from foods prepared and eaten outside of the home (*Children's Nutrition and Learning,* 1994). The nutrition coordinator for one city's Head Start program summed up the problem succinctly: "Poor dietary habits is our number one problem. Too many children in our programs eat too many high-sugar, high-fat, high-salt foods" (Hereford, 1997, p. 55).

This same lament is often heard with regard to the eating habits of adults. Clearly, the eating patterns adopted during childhood have long term implications for lifelong health and well-being. Teachers need to recognize that dietary patterns are significantly influenced by cultural and ethnic considerations. Not all cultures share the same views regarding appropriate foods. In some Asian cultures, for example, milk and milk products are rarely consumed. Other cultures may place little value on including fresh fruits and vegetables in healthy diets. Teachers must be particularly sensitive to these kinds of cultural factors, especially if they try to educate parents about children's nutritional needs (Robertson, 1998).

Although dietary patterns are shaped by parents, teachers can also have a positive effect by helping children to understand three basic concepts about nutrition (Cherow-O'Leary, 1997):

1. we need to eat more of some foods than others
2. there are "sometimes" foods and "everyday" foods
3. eating a variety of foods makes us feel good and gives us energy (p. 44–45)

Children will best come to understand these concepts when they playfully explore different foods, participate in preparing nutritious meals and snacks, and see good models of healthy eating.

The Teacher's Role in Promoting Good Nutrition

There are many ways teachers can encourage children's playful exploration of different foods. This can be done through center activities, at snack times, and through classroom routines.

Center Activities to Support Nutrition.   There are many ways that teachers can support children's understanding of nutrition in the context of classroom centers. Dramatic play centers, in particular, offer potent opportunities for helping children to recognize the value and importance of a wide variety of foods.

A dramatic play area set up for housekeeping can include a kitchen stocked with different kinds of recycled food containers, including vegetable and fruit cans, boxes from nutritious cereals, milk and fruit juice cartons, and frozen food containers with pictures of healthy cuisine. Teachers can subtly reinforce concepts about healthy eating by excluding containers for products such as sweetened cereals, cookies, and sodas. They can also increase appreciation for different cultures by including containers for healthy ethnic foods that are staples in households of families representing different ethnic or cultural backgrounds.

Setting up a dramatic play center as a grocery store or restaurant (see prototype restaurant center in Chapter 5) will engage children even more directly in the exploration of healthy eating and shopping habits. In a center set up like a cafeteria, for example, teachers can play with the children, pretending to select foods to complete a meal. As they do so, they can make comments such as, "Let's see. I already have meatballs and spaghetti, so now I need a vegetable and some fruit. I'll take the carrots and some peaches for dessert." As they overhear children placing orders, teachers can acknowledge the children's' choices and ask what kind of vegetable (or fruit or bread) they want, thus encouraging them to think about balanced meals.

They can participate in similar ways and offer comparable responses when children play in a dramatic play area set up like a grocery store. They can take the role of a shopper, and make out a shopping list that includes ingredients for a balanced meal. They can also comment on children's "purchases," acknowledging their selections as "sometimes" or "everyday" foods to reinforce the concept that some foods are always healthful, and others are best eaten in moderation.

Dramatic play centers are not the only option for developing and reinforcing concepts about healthful eating. The concept of "sometimes" and "everyday" foods can also be reinforced in a manipulative center focused on sorting and categorizing. Plastic food items, small containers for different kinds of foods, or even pictures of a variety of food items can be placed into a center for children to sort into sometimes and everyday groups. These items could then be combined into sets of four items that together represent balanced meals.

Promoting Nutrition at Snack Time.   Perhaps the best opportunity for teaching children about nutrition and encouraging them to develop healthy dietary habits comes at snack and meal times. Teachers should be sure to serve only nutritious foods and, equally important, should eat them with the children. Discussions about healthy eating are easily ignored when children observe their own teachers regularly snacking on foods such as chips and sodas that they have identified as "sometimes" items.

Children are more likely to try new foods if they have been involved in their preparation. Ms. Simpson recognized this, and sorely missed the child-friendly cooking area in her kindergarten center when she moved to an elementary school. Even though it was difficult to do lots of cooking, she found many ways to engage children in preparing snacks and occasional meals.

One way she engaged children in food preparation was to plan snacks for the coming week during circle time on Fridays. Children were encouraged to discuss snack ideas with their parents ahead of time, and brought their suggestions to the class meeting. Children described the snacks they would like, and the group determined the nutritional value of each, deciding if they are sometimes or everyday items. The goal was to help children balance their snack choices so that few or even no sometimes foods were included in the weekly snack plan.

Teachers can also select snacks with an eye toward how easily they can be prepared by children. Preschool and kindergarten children can be included in making their own finger sandwiches, for instance. Examples of nutritious choices include cheese on whole wheat bread, or peanut butter on raisin bread. These children will also enjoy building their own treats salad bar style. Although salad fixings offer one nutritious option, children as young as preschool will delight in adding their choices of dried fruit, finely chopped nuts, or fresh fruit toppings to small cups of yogurt. They will enjoy spreading cream cheese on celery sticks and adding raisins to create "ants on a log."

Children in kindergarten and primary grades will enjoy many of these same activities, but can be even more involved in the preparation of the food. With close supervision to ensure safety and proper food handling, they will be able to wash and chop fresh vegetables (using plastic knives), and they will be able to follow simple recipes to prepare snacks with more ingredients. With supervision, they can also use hot plates or microwaves to warm or melt ingredients such as grated cheese to prepare sauces or dips for vegetables.

Children will be most engaged when they actually grow some of the food they will eat at school. Engaging children in gardening will support their learning about nutrition and may entice them to try new, healthful foods. An outdoor vegetable garden with small sections for different plants will encourage children to take an active interest in such easily grown and harvested crops as carrots, broccoli, cabbage, and beans. Even the youngest children enjoy checking on the progress of their sprouting plants every day. In kindergarten and the primary grades, children can be invited to measure and take written records of their crops' growth. This daily involvement in growing food for the classroom builds children's anticipation of the day when they can pick and eat their harvest.

Regardless of children's age, their interest in trying new foods can be enhanced while they are eating. Teachers should invite children to talk about the different foods—their colors, textures, smells, and tastes—as well as why they are nutritious (Cherow-O'Leary, 1997). Their interest can also be piqued when parents come in to help children prepare healthy foods typically eaten in their households. While the children are eating, the parents can explain how the particular foods fit into typical meals in their households. Children may be surprised to learn, for example, that tortillas may be served with all meals in a Hispanic household, much as bread is served with breakfast, lunch, and dinner in other homes. They may then be willing to try tortillas fixed in a variety of ways they had never before considered.

Teachers can also use snack time to play simple games that encourage children to try new foods. They can serve each child a plate with samples of five or six different kinds of fruits or vegetables, for example, and then invite children to guess which ones will be crunchiest, juiciest, sweetest, most sour, and so on. Children's predictions can be recorded, and then they can take bites of each item to see if they guessed correctly. Although children may sometimes take only single bites of an item, they may also discover a new taste that is appealing and finish all of that item. If they encounter these foods frequently enough as part of an ongoing game, the foods will become more familiar, and ultimately more appealing.

Snack time also offers an opportunity to teach children hand-washing, a routine that will significantly contribute to maintaining good health. Children should be taught always to wash their hands before eating, since bacteria and viruses that cause many childhood illnesses (and adult ailments as well) are often transferred from hand to mouth. Of course, they should also be taught to wash their hands after using the toilet, after handling pets, and after cleaning pet enclosures.

It is not enough to remind young children to do this. Rather, teachers must provide time during which everyone is expected to wash hands before moving on to the next activity. Where facilities for hand-washing are not easily accessible for frequent use whenever needed, teachers can use any number of antibacterial gels or lotions designed to disinfect without the use of water.

Healthy Living and Physical Development

In addition to developing children's self-esteem and teaching healthy dietary habits, schools must also take on the major responsibility for encouraging children's motor development through activities that challenge children to use their bodies in new ways. Physical fitness, in the adult sense of optimum heart rate, blood oxygen concentration, and ratio of muscle mass to body fat, is not an appropriate goal for young children. Because most physical fitness data are based on older populations, which differ in many ways from populations of young children, not enough is known about the connection between physical fitness and overall health in early childhood (Seefeldt, 1984). As a result, the goals of physical education for young children should focus on promoting their overall motor development and helping them develop dispositions that encourage them to choose to be physically active. The major concepts that children need to learn when they are young are that physical activity helps their bodies grow strong and stay healthy, that some kinds of movement make their hearts work harder, and that it is fun to move (Cherow-O'Leary, 1997).

Although most parents, teachers, and school administrators agree that these are appropriate goals for young children, they may not give physical or motor development the same level of attention they devote to cognitive or even to socioemotional development. In many cases, this lack of urgency is based on the belief that children are naturally prone to running, jumping, and rough-and-tumble play. The assumption is that children will have opportunities for motor development away from school, therefore schools have less responsibility in this than in other areas of the curriculum.

This is often a false assumption. Because of changes in parents' work situations in the past few decades, many children remain in school or in traffic commuting for up to ten hours per day. In the fall and winter, it is often dark when children and parents are finally home together. Typical evening routines often leave little time for active play. For these children, there is little time outside of school for the rough-and-tumble outdoor play that can so significantly contribute to motor development.

Even when children have time to choose free-play activities, they often choose sedentary, quiet play, spending little time engaged in physically challenging activities. Moreover, in recent years solitary technology-driven activities such as video and computer games have begun to consume much of children's free time. It is therefore imperative that children be encouraged to participate in a variety of activities that will foster their motor development, help them develop gross motor skills, help them develop a positive attitude toward active movement experiences, and help them develop fine motor skills (Brewer, 1998).

The Teacher's Role in Promoting Physical Development

Teachers can facilitate children's motor development by providing materials and activities that invite children to engage in vigorous physical activity, and by structuring (and participating in) games that encourage movement and promote the development of physical skills. As is true for all other areas of the curriculum, the teacher's role is also to carefully observe children to determine when it is appropriate to introduce more challenging tasks and when it is better to allow more time for skills development.

Many fine motor skills can be facilitated in regular classroom centers. Painting and drawing in an art center both enhance fine motor development and hand–eye coordination. Many activities in manipulative centers, for example, stretching rubber bands onto geoboards, stacking pattern blocks, and stringing beads into different patterns, serve the same function. Handling artifacts and dismantling small machines in a discovery center also aid fine motor development, particularly as children learn to use screwdrivers and tweezers to take apart small components. Indoor sand and water tables can also promote coordination and fine motor skills as children pour from one container to another.

It is more difficult, however, to fully develop gross motor skills in a classroom, particularly in schools such as Ms. Simpson's, where space is especially limited. Certainly, children who are gathered around a rug for a morning meeting or circle time can be invited to participate in a variety of movements ranging from stretching to hopping in place. Using classroom routines such as these to promote children's health and well-being will be addressed later in this chapter. These activities fall far short of meeting all of children's needs, however. It is therefore imperative that teachers develop a comprehensive plan for promoting healthful play, outdoors as well as in the classroom.

The Outdoors as a Learning Center

Outdoor spaces can serve as an expanded learning center in which children can develop motor abilities. Good outdoor play spaces will provide a variety of play opportunities, including daily opportunities to develop gross motor skills. Outdoor play spaces should include different surfaces, such as grass, sand, pavement, and soil; each surface encourages different kinds of play. Grassy areas are ideal for tumbling, playful wrestling, and dramatic play. Sandy areas, especially a large sandbox, encourage digging, scooping, pouring, and even construction if water is nearby to make the sand more malleable. If appropriate props such as dump trucks and bulldozers are included in the sand area, it may quickly be transformed into a construction site that invites dramatic play. Paved areas invite children to experiment with as many kinds of riding toys as are available. These, too, often foster dramatic play, as tricycles become ice-cream trucks cruising through a neighborhood or fire engines racing to put out fires. Paved areas are also conducive to playing games with bouncing balls. An area with loose soil promotes digging, planting, burying, and perhaps real gardening. In fact, it is recommended that school gardens always have an area of unplanted soil, specifically so that children can have a place to dig and bury treasure just for the fun of it.

Any outdoor play space should be equipped with an apparatus that invites climbing, swinging, sliding, hanging, balancing, and crawling. This apparatus may be simple and designed to support one function, as is the case with a swing set, or it may be more complex, allowing for a variety of different uses. An example of a highly complex apparatus is a play structure that has both metal and rope ladders leading to a platform from which children can move to either a slide or spiral pole to get down. In general, more complex units invite more collaborative play, whereas simple units allow for more solitary play.

Beyond providing both simple and complex play structures, teachers can enhance children's outdoor play by encouraging them to create their own play structures and play spaces outdoors. Every play yard should include items such as boards, boxes, cones, and barrels that children can move around as they find a need for them. These materials often become the walls of impromptu clubhouses built into corners behind bushes, ramps for racing toy cars and trucks, or simple balance beams.

Outdoor play centers should also provide opportunities for water play, particularly in warm weather. When outdoor water tables are provided, children's engagement in water play will take on different qualities than the play at indoor water tables, especially if waterproof smocks or aprons are provided to keep their clothes dry. Because there is no need to worry about splashing and spilling, children can use the water in more creative and boisterous ways than is possible indoors. In addition to measuring and pouring, children can stir the water in an outdoor water table to create whirlpools that rise up and spill the water over the sides of its enclosure. Then the water play becomes both physical exercise and an exercise in elementary physics!

Outdoor play areas should also include opportunities for children to engage in artistic expression. Again because messiness tends to matter less outdoors than it might indoors, children are freer to experiment with paints and other media in different ways than they normally do at an indoor art table or easel. An outdoor art area may also invite children to include things from nature, for example, leaves, pieces of fern, twigs, and feathers, in their creations. Children can also use an outdoor art area for large-scale creations that are simply too big to complete indoors.

The Teacher's Role in Scaffolding Outdoor Activities

As with activities and materials in all other areas of the curriculum, teachers must carefully select those for outdoors that best fit children's developmental needs. Although there are many commonalities in children's physical/motor development needs from preschool through the early primary grades, each group of children has special characteristics that should guide the kinds of outdoor play teachers provide.

Children in Preschool. Three- and four-year-old children particularly enjoy experimenting with different kinds of physical movement using their whole bodies. Movement games with no rules are appealing; children at this age will eagerly participate in pretending to be ducks in a row waddling behind their leader and jumping into a "pond" (perhaps the sandbox or a grassy area) and "swimming." They thoroughly enjoy practicing running, climbing, stepping, and jumping, and therefore need to have appropriately sized climbing structures to scramble onto, climb into, and jump out of (Taylor & Morris, 1996). They also value solitary play, however, and will benefit from the self-discovery and individual practice that a simple play apparatus such as a swingset provides.

It is important for teachers to remember, however, that preschool children often overestimate their physical abilities, and are sometimes overly daring (Aaronson, 1988). This became clear to Scott's teacher when she turned to see the four-year-old scramble onto the picnic table in the play yard and leap off before she could intervene. As she hurried over to him, he stood up and wailed, "I jumped off the big high!" On each of the previous two days, she had observed Scott clambering onto boxes and overturning buckets and leaping off with arms spread wide. Having mastered jumping twelve or fifteen inches to the ground without falling, Scott apparently believed he was capable of jumping safely from any height. It was fortunate that he was only frightened and not injured.

Children in Kindergarten. Five- and six-year-olds enjoy testing and practicing motor skills in more challenging ways than do most three- and four-year-olds. They also tend to be more interested in playing and interacting with peers for the purpose of socialization and establishing role definitions (Aaronson, 1988). Kindergartners also enjoy fantasy play, including taking on the roles of superheroes or superheroines and other characters. The increasing sophistication of their play means that children at this age prefer more complex play spaces and materials that can accommodate shared play. Thus, sandboxes should be equipped with enough buckets, shovels, trucks, and bulldozers to allow at least two children to play together. Enough riding toys, jump ropes, hula hoops, or balls should be provided to ensure that groups of children can join in one game or play scenario at the same time. Clubhouse structures, whether freestanding or part of complex climbing units, should be large enough to house at least three children.

Kindergarten children are also fascinated with their own bodies; they are intensely interested in finding out more about how they work. They delight in any signs that their own bodies are growing bigger, stronger, and more coordinated. Awareness of their own physical development is a source of new levels of self-esteem. Children are acutely aware of their own increasing physical prowess and enjoy learning to use their bodies as tools to open containers, lift large or heavy objects, and to balance themselves and other objects (Church, 1997).

Play spaces should facilitate this new prowess by offering greater levels of physical challenge. More complex play structures that invite experimentation and new means of moving through space (e.g., by swinging forward hand over hand across a suspended ladder structure) are appropriate for most kindergarten children. They will also benefit from more construction materials such as boards, tires, and ropes that fill their need for lifting and pushing to test their prowess. Theme studies and projects that entail building large structures can integrate this kind of play into ongoing learning from other areas of the curriculum. Finally, their skill at running, skipping, and jumping suggests that they will need more physical space to accommodate faster, broader movements.

Children in Primary Grades. Seven- and eight-year-olds continue to benefit from many of the same types of physical play activities as do children in kindergarten, using familiar games, materials, and equipment to solidify and refine previously learned skills. Their developing coordination and increasing physical skill, however, prompt them to become more interested in refining skills such as throwing, batting, kicking, and catching. This interest, coupled with their emerging ability to engage in more structured games, sets them apart from younger children.

Although many seven- and eight-year-old children still enjoy exploring complex outdoor play structures and building their own constructions, their running, jumping, and other explorations with movement are often channeled into organized games governed by complex rules. Many teachers find that primary-grade children are often able to extend a single game of soccer, kickball, or baseball to last an entire recess period, particularly if the sides are well matched and winning is a reasonable possibility for both teams.

Seven- and eight-year-olds' interest in games with rules may also lead some of them to use their play time for more sedentary games that nonetheless require significant coordination. Many children discover games such as marbles and jacks at this age. These games are appealing because primary-grade children are beginning to develop the cognitive and socio-emotional maturity to negotiate and understand complex rules, and because they are beginning to develop the coordination and fine motor control necessary for success. When children begin to play these games, they need to have an appropriately surfaced space where they can play relatively free of interruption.

Teachers can facilitate the play of seven- and eight-year-olds by providing sufficient space and appropriate equipment. They can also help by serving as a referee at the request of the children, who typically need help learning and negotiating rules when playing a new game, and by suggesting a variety of fair methods for choosing teams.

This latter role is especially important given the prominent role good self-esteem plays in children's health and well-being. Syndicated advice columnist Ann Landers frequently runs letters written by adults who vividly recall dreading recess and the humiliation of always being chosen last because they were not athletic enough in the eyes of their classmates. Their pain is clearly evident, sometimes as much as fifty years later, and suggests that allowing children to select their own teams is clearly inappropriate.

Because having evenly matched teams tends to make games more enjoyable and mutually satisfying for everyone involved, there needs to be a way to divide the most skilled players so that they are not all on one team. A good way to do this is simply to assign teams in advance. Doing so allows teachers to balance the teams for fair play without embarrassing any children in the process.

Because a major goal of outdoor play is to engage children in vigorous activity, games should be chosen that have the greatest potential for actively engaging most of the children most of the time. Using this criterion, soccer and basketball, which require both offensive and defensive players to move rapidly with the flow of the game, are highly preferable to baseball, for example, during which eight offensive players sit on the bench waiting their turn at bat, and defensive players stand around while play occurs in other areas of the field.

Organized games for children in primary grades need not be limited to traditional sports competitions. In fact, children can learn many of the prerequisite skills of throwing, kicking, or catching in the context of inviting, often more free-flowing games. An example of one such game is provided in Table 7.1.

Designing Outdoor Play Spaces

Ensuring Safety. When designing outdoor play areas, teachers such as Ms. Simpson must make children's safety a top priority. Any outdoor play area for young children must be

TABLE 7.1   **Example of a Free-Flowing Skills Development Game**

Dr. Bomb Ball

1. Divide the children into two teams, each standing behind a line at the far end of the playing field.

2. Place eight to ten soft rubber or foam balls on a center line between the two teams.

3. Provide each team with two flat, platform scooters pushed by a child who is designated as the "doctor" for a round of play.

4. When a whistle is blown, children run to the center line to try to scoop up balls that they then throw at members of the opposite team.

5. If someone on the other team catches the ball, or if the ball hits someone above the shoulders, the thrower must sit in his place. If the thrower tags someone on the other team with the ball, that person must sit down. Anyone who is seated is out of the game.

6. Seated children can resume playing when they are "rescued" by the doctors, who run to them with the scooters and then push them back to the team's starting point. They are then free to rejoin the team.

7. Doctors must also avoid being tagged by a ball from the other team. If they are tagged, their scooter is out of service for the remainder of the game. The doctor is free to join his or her teammates as a regular player.

8. The game ends as soon as one team has both doctors out of service or when time is up. In the latter instance, a winner is determined by counting which team has the fewest children seated and waiting for rescue by a doctor.

Note: Any number of variations of this game are possible. The specific rules can easily be adapted to fit the developmental needs of the primary-grade players involved. Regardless of how the game is played, children will have opportunities to develop a variety of skills while engaged in vigorous physical activity. They will be able to refine their throwing and catching skills while also engaged in running, dodging, and pushing the scooters—all movements that will increase agility and coordination. More important, all children can remain actively engaged in the game, regardless of how skilled they are, because they can always be rescued and returned to the action.

securely fenced with gates that can be opened only by adults. Fences serve to keep children in supervised areas, as well as keep them away from potential hazards such as air conditioner condensers, electrical transformers, swimming pools, and play structures and areas designed for older children.

Teachers should also check to be sure that the play structures are the *proper size* for their children. In general, children should not be able to climb any higher than the height they can reach when standing erect. Even a fall from two or three feet can result in broken bones or head injuries, if children fall onto tightly compacted surfaces. Therefore, all climbing structures and swings should be surrounded by *resilient surfaces,* which absorb the shock of falls. These include loose gravel or mulch at least twelve to eighteen inches deep, interlocking rubber mats specifically designed for outdoor playground use, and loose aggregate material such as that made from recycled, shredded tires. Mud or grass surfaces are not appropriate for these areas because the ground can be quite compacted and thus as unyielding as concrete.

Even structures of proper size placed on appropriate surfaces need to be further checked for safety. As with any equipment, outdoor play units should be free from *sharp edges and protruding parts.* There should also be *no openings* that might entrap a child's head. Openings between ladder steps or between different adjoining parts of a structure must be either smaller than four or larger than eight inches wide (Frost & Wortham, 1988).

Finally, teachers should check the play yard each day for *unanticipated hazards* such as broken glass or other debris that may have been tossed over the fence or blown into the yard. Other hazards that sometimes appear overnight include anthills, wasp nests, and beehives.

Making Use of Limited Space. Another design consideration that must be faced by many teachers is how best to use limited space. Particularly in older urban schools, there is relatively little outdoor space that can be devoted to young children's play. Yet these children must be provided with opportunities for development through outdoor free play. Although space may be limited, it can be used efficiently to provide all of the functions of larger areas. The key is in creative planning. Table 7.2 offers steps for effective use of small outdoor play spaces. Figure 7.1 shows one design plan for a small outdoor play space.

TABLE 7.2   Effective Use of Small Play Spaces

1. *Install a single complex structure rather than a series of simple units.* A play structure that includes climbing ladders, platforms with attached slides, and a couple of swings will take up much less space than separate monkey bars, slides, and banks of swings. Many structure designs are available that also include large tubes, perhaps crossing under the slide or below a platform, for children to crawl through. These structures conserve playground area by making good use of vertical space.

2. *Make use of vertical space.* Although a traditional garden that can accommodate a variety of plants may consume a large area of a play yard, a smaller area can be used by building a graduated series of low shelves on an outside wall to support potted plants. Although an area of loose soil for planting and digging is still important, adding planters on elevated shelves above the garden can double the number of plants that can be grown without consuming more yard area. The key to successful gardening in pots is to be sure that the shelves are low enough that even small children can see into them. Because some of the plants might not be within easy reach, they should be grown in pots small enough to be lifted down by teachers so that children can participate in weeding, pruning, and harvesting.

3. *Use portable equipment that can be added or removed from the playground as needed.* Rather than having a balance beam extending permanently from a structure, for example, a portable balance beam can be brought out to the yard for a week or two at a time. The novelty of the equipment will spark children's interest in it. Having it available for a week or more will allow children to become familiar with it and develop their skills using it. When the children seem to be losing interest, the balance beam might be replaced with a series of cones, boxes, and other items to form an obstacle course. At other times, this same area might be used for a wading pool, woodworking equipment, or a tent clubhouse. Viewing some outdoor spaces as multi-purpose areas enables teachers to provide a variety of experiences that will enhance children's development, even in relatively small areas.

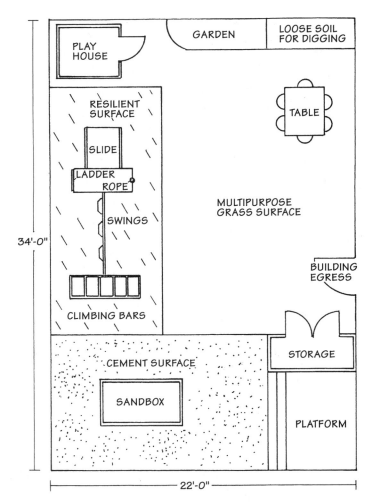

FIGURE 7.1 Design Plan for Outdoor Play Space This is one example of a plan for maximizing use of a relatively small outdoor space. The multipurpose grassy area can be used to accommodate portable obstacle course equipment, a balance beam, or construction materials such as boards, tires, and large spools. Illustration by Michelle M. Verdigets, New Orleans, Louisianna.

Routines and Transitions That Foster Healthy Living

There are many ways to use daily routines to make children aware of different aspects of healthy living. One important routine involves helping children with personal hygiene. As discussed earlier, this includes providing time and encouragement for hand-washing and proper cleanup of areas used for food preparation.

Other routines can focus children's attention on healthy eating. One routine described earlier is engaging children in planning snacks for each week. Another is to preview what is being served for lunch each day, with encouragement for children to try at least some of each food offered for a balanced meal. Teachers may also use part of their morning meeting to invite children to describe any nutritious meals they had the night before, with an emphasis on the healthful foods they liked best and how they were prepared. This routine could culminate in the collection of recipes from each family to create a classroom cookbook.

Transitions can also be used to involve children in movement and discoveries about their own bodies. When it is time for children to come together for circle time between activities, they can be instructed to freeze in place, then hop (or tiptoe, creep on all fours, or waddle like ducks) over to the meeting area. Or once they have gathered together, they can be engaged in vigorous movement activities that burn energy and reduce stress. For example, they may stand in place and begin moving by first wiggling only their fingers, then shaking their hands, then adding their arms, and finally shaking their entire bodies. They can then relax by reversing this process until only their fingers are moving, and then they become completely still.

Transitions can also be used to engage children in movements that are relaxing and develop body awareness. They can lie flat on their backs with all muscles completely relaxed. Then, when instructed to do so, they can tighten their muscles, beginning with the toes, then the feet, then the calves and thighs, and so on until their whole bodies are rigid. Then they can gradually relax each muscle group in reverse order. Other movement activities such as tai chi or yoga can be used effectively with young children, although these are best done under the supervision of a trained instructor who can be sure that children do not move or stretch in ways that might strain muscles or cause other injuries. Inviting a parent who has such expertise will benefit children's motor development and enhance their cultural awareness.

Including Children with Special Needs

Children with special needs will require many adaptations if they are to fully develop dispositions toward healthy living. This is especially true for physically challenged children who may need extra encouragement to participate in physical activities and outdoor play. One way to provide play opportunities that are both challenging and accessible for all children, including those with special needs, is to establish parallel obstacle courses—one that is relatively easy and one that is more difficult. This allows children with special needs to participate alongside their classssmates without being limited to specially adapted equipment. In addition, the following adaptations are offered to enhance the outdoor play of children with specific special needs.

Children with Visual Impairments
- Lead the child through the outdoor play area, orienting him or her to major features (e.g., the climbing structure, the sand box, and the garden) that can be used as points of reference.
- Mark the location of different outdoor areas or structures with audible clues, for example, different types of wind chimes and bells, to help the child find them.
- Describe what is happening in different areas to help the visually impaired child find her or his friends and join in their play. When the child enters the playground, for example, tell her or him which children are playing on the climbing structure, which are in the sandbox, and which are gardening or playing on riding toys.
- Purchase toys specifically designed for blind children to help them participate in a variety of games that other children enjoy, for example, balls that beep so that the child can hear and then kick, catch or bat them.

Children with Hearing Impairments

■ When the child is playing in the sandbox or working in the garden, position him or her so that he or she is facing other children, thus making it easy for them to get his or her attention and communicate.

■ Encourage the child to communicate about what she or he is doing on the playground. Use both sign language and spoken words to acknowledge the child's play and invite interaction. Open-ended questions work best for this, for example, "Tell me what you're building there."

■ Since much of the child's information about his or her environment is visual, be sure that he or she can see most areas of the yard from any given space. Avoid dividing areas by using walls, fences, or hedges that might block the child's view of other children at play, thereby further isolating him or her.

Children with Developmental Delays

■ Children who are developmentally delayed may not have the same balance and coordination as most of their classmates. Encourage them to participate in running, jumping, and climbing activities to stimulate their physical and motor skill development.

■ Be sure that there are physical challenges that they can achieve. This may mean providing a shorter balance beam, or varying the difficulty of different parts of an obstacle course so that all children can test their abilities and feel success.

■ Lead the children in noncompetitive games. This will relieve less coordinated children of peer pressure to perform up to standards that lead to team success. Noncompetitive games allow children to simply compete against their own previous performance and enjoy their individual achievements.

Children with Physical Disabilities

■ Position a child with impaired physical ability so that he or she can achieve the maximum range of motion, muscle control, and visual contact with what he or she is doing. A child may need to lie on his or her side or prone over a bolster, for example, to play successfully with other children in a sandbox or participate in gardening.

■ Be sure that the child is moved or assisted in moving to many different areas during the day. This will enable her or him to attempt all kinds of activities, rather than returning only to those that are the most comfortable.

■ Encourage the children to use their own means of getting around, whether walkers, wheelchairs, or scooters, to participate in the games of those children using riding toys.

■ For children with limited use of or control over their hands or upper bodies, facilitate activities that they can do with their feet. Examples include painting, moving puppets, and splashing in a wading pool.

■ Furnish specifically adapted play and recreation equipment, including large outdoor equipment such as swings and hand-operated tricycles, for physically challenged children. Resources for these toys and equipment are included in Table 7.3.

■ Increase the width of balance beams and modify slick floor surfaces using mats or carpets for children with balance difficulties.

■ Use softer balls or lightweight objects to facilitate throwing and catching for children lacking strength and endurance.

(Cook, Tessier, & Armbruster, 1987; Fewell & Kaminski, 1988; Morris & Schultz, 1989; Wesley, 1992; Wolery & Wilbert, 1994)

TABLE 7.3   Resources for Adapted Play and Recreation Equipment

Able Data

National Rehabilitation Information Center
8455 Colesville Rd., Suite 935
Silver Springs, MD 20910

Able-Child

154 Chambers Street
New York, NY 10007

Lekotek Guide to Good Toys

Lekotek
613 Dempster Street
Evanston, IL 60201

Discovery Toys

400 Ellinwood Way, Suite 300
Pleasant Hill, CA 94523

Flaghouse

18 West 18th Street
New York, NY 10011

Developing Advocacy Skills

As Ms. Simpson and her elementary school colleagues discovered, it is often necessary to advocate for the needs of young children in settings that are not designed for their exclusive use. Like most early childhood teachers, such advocates feel strongly that children need appropriate space, equipment, and flexible time for a variety of indoor and outdoor play activities. The challenge, then, is to find a way to make their needs known and solicit help in meeting their goals.

Under similar circumstances, it may be tempting to pepper administrators with complaints about the inadequacy of available facilities. Operating under the adage that "the squeaky wheel gets the grease," teachers may raise the issue of the facilities' shortcomings at every faculty meeting or informal visit by a school administrator. They may even goad parents into becoming their allies in this effort, adding to the litany of complaints heard by those in charge. These efforts are likely to fail, however, if they put administrators on the defensive and alienate potential allies.

Good advocates recognize that there are appropriate and effective ways to air concerns and generate support for change. They understand the importance of finding an appropriate way to address the issues that matter most. This allows them to clearly focus their message and present it in an organized, professional fashion.

Determining the appropriate vehicle (or means of addressing a problem) takes research and planning. Obviously, before teachers can push for change, they must know what they want and need. They must also be aware of what is possible. Although it might be nice to have a large playground with separate areas for each type of outdoor activity appropriate for young children, that might not be possible if such a yard could be designed only at the expense of the older children, requiring them to sacrifice their needs for outdoor play. Thus, Ms. Simpson and her fellow teachers found the right vehicle when they first identified a portion of the outdoor area that was not getting much use and then tried to figure out how to gain that space and adapt it to meet the needs of their young students.

After deciding what is needed and determining that there is a reasonable way to accommodate those needs, an advocate's next step is deciding on a plan of action. It is helpful to determine what kinds of presentations are most likely to be well received by those with decision-making power. Some administrators prefer informal interactions with their faculty. Scheduling a brief meeting in a principal's office to state problems and discuss proposed solutions might work well in that case. Other administrators prefer to see problems firsthand. A teacher who knows his or her administrator well could then invite the administrator with this preference to visit while the class is using the playground and point out specific instances of children's and teachers' difficulties with current arrangements. Still other administrators are more formal, preferring to take their time to respond thoughtfully to written presentations. Change is most likely to be forthcoming from those administrators when teachers put together concise, well-written, and carefully thought out proposals that both state their concerns and make suggestions for positive change.

Each of these approaches provides an example of teachers who are proactive and therefore find the appropriate vehicle to address issues of concern. When groups with similar concerns agree on a common vehicle and work together to bring about change, success is likely to follow. Table 7.4 contains activities to help you develop skills that will enable you to discover common vehicles and work together with others to bring about change.

TABLE 7.4   Advocacy Activities: Informing and Involving Families and Administrators

Finding Appropriate Vehicles for Addressing Issues		
Becoming Aware	*Furthering Your Understanding*	*Taking Action*
1. Visit a classroom for young children and observe them playing outside. List all the areas that children make use of. Are there any areas that are not used? Based on your reading of this chapter, are there any changes that might be made to enhance children's play experiences?	1. Review several articles that describe specific benefits of different kinds of outdoor play for young children's development. Make note of any suggestions for outdoor activity not included in this chapter. Begin a file of activities that you would like to try with children.	1. Collaborate with another teacher to write a proposal for a specific change that will benefit children's learning and development.
2. Visit the same classroom again, this time focusing your attention on how the teachers interact with the children outdoors. Are they able to safely supervise all areas at once? What do they do to engage children in different kinds of play?	2. Learn to play at least five non-competitive games intended to develop the motor skills of young children.	2. Volunteer in a preschool and lead the children in playing some of the games you have learned.
3. Interview teachers to find out what changes have been made in the past in response to their suggestions. Find out how the teachers made their needs known and how they garnered support for their ideas.	3. Interview two school principals or childcare center directors. Find out how they prefer to receive suggestions from teachers about changes that might be made in their programs or facilities.	3. Volunteer in a kindergarten classroom and lead the children in playing some of the games you have learned.
	4. Ask teachers at different schools to share any successful written proposals they have made for new programs or changes in existing programs.	4. Volunteer in a primary-grade classroom and lead the children in playing some of the games you have learned.
		5. Work with a teacher to develop a plan to make the best use of the outdoor space available.

Summary

In this chapter, we have demonstrated that healthy living begins in early childhood. Self-esteem, healthy dietary habits, and dispositions toward vigorous physical activity are all established early in life and represent the major goals of health education for young children. These goals can be achieved as teachers provide appropriate challenges and opportunities for success and create a culture of acceptance in their classrooms; as they model healthful nutrition in play centers and during snack times; and as they provide materials and activities that invite children to engage in vigorous physical activity.

This chapter also presents outdoor play as a critical component of children's development and suggests that outdoor play areas need to be designed as carefully as any other centers to provide a variety of play opportunities. The chapter stresses the importance of selecting activities and equipment to fit the developmental needs and capabilities of children at different ages, with an emphasis on safety and efficient use of limited space. The chapter concludes with a discussion of ways to accommodate children with special needs, and the importance of advocating for appropriate play spaces for all children.

REVISITING FIRST IMPRESSIONS

How did you describe health education before you read this chapter? In what ways has your perspective about health education changed? How do the activities presented in this chapter differ from your own early experiences with health and physical education? How well did your initial beliefs about the role of outdoor play in children's development fit with that described in this chapter? How have your beliefs changed?

QUESTIONS FOR DISCUSSION

1. Brainstorm five ways teachers can encourage children to take control of their own learning both indoors and outdoors. How will this benefit children's self-esteem?

2. Review the following description of a playground area for kindergarten children in an urban public school:

   The playground is comprised of a narrow grassy area between two wings of the school building. One end of the playground is fronted by a fence to provide security from the street. The area along the fence has been landscaped with a row of hardy shrubs that require little care. Just beyond the grassy area on the other end of the playground is a small paved area that opens onto the larger school yard for older children. At the back of this area stands a small, child-sized basketball hoop.

   Against the wall of one building is a large wooden bin with doors that open outward into the yard. Inside are balls, jump ropes, and hula-hoops that children can use. In the center of the grassy area is a set of three swings and a freestanding slide.

   What activities will this playground promote? What problems can you identify? How might this space be adapted to improve safety and promote more varied play and physical movement?

SUGGESTED READINGS

Bruya, L. (Ed.). (1988). *Play spaces for children: A new beginning.* Reston, VA: American Alliance for Health, Physical Education, Recreation and Dance.

Frost, J. (1996). *Play and playscapes.* Albany, NY: Delmar.

Miller, K. (1989). *The outside play and learning book: Activities for young children.* Mt. Rainier, MD: Gryphon House.

Morris, L., & Schulz, L. (1989). *Creative play activities for children with disabilities.* Champaign, IL: Human Kinetics.

8 Fostering Creative Expression through Playful Learning and Teaching

Prereading Guide

First Impressions.   List all the things that you do in a creative way. Is gardening, writing, playing an instrument, dancing, drawing, cooking, or sewing on your list? Write about your own creativity. What inspires you? How do you feel when you are in the process of being creative? What do others do that supports your creativity? What do others do that inhibits your creativity?

Revisit
Designing a Learning Center System (Chapter 4)

Stories from the Field

The following narrative, written by Jeff Oremland (1997), an experienced early childhood educator, describes how he uses music to set the tone of the classroom and facilitate children's learning.

> From the recordings of Ella Jenkins to *The Lion King,* it is quite easy to find music created specifically for young children. However, music that we often consider to be "just for adults" is also a rich resource of appropriate music for children. When choosing music for my classroom, I let the interests and needs of the children guide my decisions. I start with the curriculum themes we have developed together (like "space") and then choose music that matches the theme (like Gustav Holst's *The Planets*). I find that this music enhances play and stimulates learning. Music playing in the classroom can stir children's imagination and act as a springboard for creative writing and art work. Children can even write their own music by inventing a notation system or using special software programs to visually represent the sounds they imagine.
>
> Young children use music in a variety of ways; the most common one is movement. Barney, Raffi, and other children's artists are excellent for certain types of movement, but for creative movement I prefer "adult" music. For example, the familiar tune and routine of "The Itsy Bitsy Spider" are clearly fun and effective. However, children can create their own interpretive dances to a flowing Tchaikovsky ballet such as *Swan Lake* or a high-energy Duke Ellington tune such as "Take the 'A' Train." It is easy to integrate multicultural understanding

into movement activities when children have the opportunity to interpret an Indian raga or African tribal dance music.

Some teachers feel that cost is a barrier to expanding the musical experiences in the classroom. I feel that "where there is a will there is a way." Teachers and schools do not need to own an extensive or expensive musical collection in order to provide children with opportunities to open ears and minds to new music. Most public libraries have recording collections. Good stereo tape players can be purchased for less than thirty-five dollars. Admittedly, CD players are more expensive. However, they can sometimes be acquired through donations. Who knows, if children decide music is important enough to have around, they could initiate, plan, and carry out their own fund drive! Now that would be an exciting way to integrate all aspects of the curriculum.

I have met teachers who feel that their lack of musical knowledge prohibits them from expanding musical opportunities in their classrooms. Again, where there is a will, there is a way. It is not the extensive musical knowledge that counts, but the desire and willingness to spend the time and energy listening to a great variety of music. I often listen to new or unfamiliar radio stations, especially Public Broadcast stations or non-English stations, to sample new (to me) genres of sounds. I will also visit the library and check out recordings with an attractive cover, just to see what it is. I do, of course, always preview music I play in the classroom, even music that children bring to share. I want to make sure that it is appropriate for all the children, is sensitive to the different values and backgrounds of the families represented in my class, and has potential for stimulating creativity and learning.

Some believe that young children cannot relate to adult music. I believe this stems from the "concert hall mentality." This is the idea that we must sit quietly and listen for long periods of time when formal music is played. This, of course, is appropriate behavior at a performance, or in a concert hall. In the classroom, however, I can let children experience the richness of the world's music by singing, dancing, writing, drawing, painting, sculpting, or playing in other ways while they listen. Of course, some children may enjoy sitting and listening quietly. If they are engaged, they listen, and if they listen, they learn.

Fostering Creative Expression

Young children approach life with a spirit of wonder, an original perspective, curiosity, and a drive to understand their world. They intuitively manipulate, explore, and experiment with objects and ideas in order to make sense of them. In others words, they play in order to learn. When we observe young children as they play with art materials or musical instruments, we are compelled to admire and delight in their spontaneity, imagination, and ability to move freely between a world of fantasy and their own sense of reality.

Holden (1987) describes creative individuals as sensitive to internal and external stimuli, uninhibited, and capable of becoming completely absorbed in an activity or process. Indeed, these characteristics not only describe aspects of creative expression but are also intuitive and natural ways young children approach the task of learning about their world. In this chapter, we will discuss how early childhood educators can foster creative expression through playful exploration of music and art in early childhood classrooms.

Defining Creativity and Creative Expression

When we think of a creative person, we think of someone who has the ability to see things in new ways and to use familiar objects, ideas, or words to make something unique and original. There are many ways to define and describe creativity. For example, the term *creative* can refer to a product, a means of original expression, or a process of development and change (Edwards, 1990). Torrance, a pioneer in the study of creativity, defines *creativity* as the process of sensing problems or gaps in information, forming ideas or hypotheses about such gaps, and communicating the results (1962, 1963). He identified four characteristics of creativity: fluency, flexibility, originality, and elaboration. Although there may be different dimensions and levels of creativity, Torrance believes that everyone has the ability to be creative. Parnes (1967), another pioneer in the study of creativity, describes creativity as a process of thinking and responding to objects, symbols, ideas, people, or situations by making a connection with previous experience and then generating something new or unique.

Several dispositions work together to foster creativity. These dispositions include curiosity, flexibility, insightfulness, optimism, and the ability to blend convergent and divergent thinking. Convergent thinking is required when searching to find the one correct answer, and divergent thinking is required when searching to find many possible solutions or ways of interpreting a problem. Creative thinking requires a skillful blending of both convergent and divergent thinking (De Bono, 1992, Hughes, 1999). Creative expression is demonstrated when children

- think about and invent new ways of doing things
- use language to tell or write stories or poetry
- construct buildings or cities of blocks and wooden tunnels
- develop dramas, pretend, pantomime, or fantasize
- engage in art projects and activities
- explore music through movement, dance, and playing instruments

Therefore, in early childhood classrooms, imagination, creativity, and creative expression are not limited to one part of the curriculum or one area of the classroom but are fostered continually through the playful exploration of objects, language, and ideas.

The Teacher's Role in Fostering Creative Expression

As described in Chapter 3, the teacher's role is not limited to providing the opportunities and materials children need to play but also includes interacting with children to foster optimal development and accounting for the time children spend playing through assessment activities and records. Young children's play and creative expression are often indistinguishable activities. Therefore, the teacher's role in promoting creative expression is identical to the teacher's role in play.

Creative expression will flourish when it is valued by teachers and parents. Teachers show they value creativity when they protect children's schedules and provide daily blocks of time for children to explore materials and develop projects. Teachers also show they value creative expression when they provide children with access to interesting materials. A third way teachers express value for creative endeavors is through the use of available space. When ample space in the classroom and outdoor play area is devoted to art, music, movement, and construction activities, children come to understand that these activities are worthwhile and important. Therefore, their natural attraction to creative endeavors is rewarded and, in turn, the energy and attention they devote to creative activities will be extended and intensified.

Again, in order to foster creative expression among young children, it is not enough to provide materials, time, and space. A vital component of a classroom culture that fosters creativity is psychological safety. In a psychologically safe, or risk-taking environment, children feel free to invent, experiment, pretend, and explore ideas, symbols, and objects. Therefore, children play and express their ideas, fantasies, and understanding without the risk of being corrected or held to a particular, often adult, standard. Children in risk-taking environments do not feel pressured to conform to the ideas of others but can work and play without the risk of being wrong. Their ideas are accepted, valued, and supported by the adults in the environment.

The foundation of a risk-taking environment is found in the ways adults interact with children as children play and work. Actions and interactions of teachers that contribute to a psychologically safe or risk-taking environment include the following.

1. celebrating children's emerging creative talents and resisting the temptation to display their own talent, thereby upstaging the children
2. responding to children's creative process with encouragement and support and resisting the opportunity to make judgments or provide external rewards
3. minimizing competition between children over creative expression or the products that result and supporting each child's unique form of creativity in the way it is presented
4. accepting the movement, mess, noise level, and excitement that come with young children's creativity and creative expression as a functional part of the classroom environment and resisting peer pressure to create quiet and controlled classrooms
5. sharing power with children (Jones, 1986), allowing them to move an activity in a direction that makes sense to them, and resisting the temptation to focus on preconceived outcomes
6. displaying sensitivity to the process children use as they create and suspending the adult need for a product to display
7. accepting the perspective of the child and forgoing the urge to explain an adult perspective to the child
8. observing and respecting a particular technique a child is using and suspending the temptation to teach a new technique before the child truly needs it

Specific examples of the above interactions are included within the discussions of music and art that make up the remaining sections of this chapter.

Another role teachers have in children's play and creative expression is to be accountable to both parents and administrators for the time children spend engaged in activities that foster creative expression. When teachers collect, preserve, and share samples of children's creative endeavors, they are able to provide parents and administrators examples of the developmental progress children are making. Teachers will also be able to use these samples to demonstrate the connections that exist between creative expression and cognitive development. This will provide proof of the integrative nature of children's learning and development and the power of children's play. Specific techniques for documenting children's growth and development were discussed in Chapter 6. We will now turn our attention to how early childhood educators can foster creative thought and expression through playful exploration of music and art in early childhood classrooms.

Fostering Creative Expression through Music

Music, by its very nature, brings energy, life, joy, and playfulness to a curriculum and an environment. It has the ability to ease tension, heighten awareness, and create a mood. Therefore, music is valuable to early childhood programs simply because it is music. There are many developmental benefits associated with musical activities as well. They can enhance a child's physical, social, intellectual, emotional, and aesthetic development. Table 8.1 suggests some

TABLE 8.1   Benefits of Music

Children have many opportunities to learn and develop when they engage in music activities. Here are some examples of how play with music unifies learning and development.

Physical Development

■ Children develop muscular control, coordination, and balance as they sing, dance, clap, and sway to music and rhythm.

■ Children develop control over the muscles in the mouth as they sing and respond to music. Listening also requires muscular control.

■ Children develop an awareness of body movement when they participate in musical games like the "Hokey Pokey."

■ Children develop psychomotor skills as they make their bodies respond to the mood and rhythm of music.

■ Children develop the disposition of self-control.

Social Development

■ Children develop respect for the ideas of others as they listen and respond to musical games.

■ Children develop the disposition of patience and the ability to defer gratification when they wait turns to play a favorite instrument or chant a favorite refrain.

■ Children develop the ability to participate, share, and cooperate as they put the goals of the group to sing songs in unison above their own impulses and desires to sing faster or louder.

Intellectual Development

■ Children develop perceptual skills as they recognize the sounds of specific instruments or request and respond to a favorite action song or game.

■ Children develop the disposition of attention to detail and the ability to focus, sequence, recall, and relate words and actions as they recite fingerplays or sing action songs.

■ Children develop their vocabulary and comprehension skills as they learn the meaning of new lyrics.

Emotional Development

■ Children develop the ability to identify or clarify their own feelings when they listen to music that depicts differing emotions such as happy, sad, humorous, serious, angry, and scary.

■ Children develop the disposition of self-confidence and feelings of success when they engage in musical activities that are pleasurable and do not require precision or correctness.

■ Children develop pride in their cultural heritage when their traditional music is played in their classroom and responded to positively by their classmates.

■ Children develop a feeling of belonging as they learn a repertoire of songs and sing them together throughout the year.

Aesthetic Development

■ Children develop the disposition of sensitivity as they begin to understand the feelings, images, and impressions portrayed by music as they listen to music in the classroom.

■ Children develop an appreciation of many kinds of music when they are exposed to it in classroom situations.

examples of how music fosters both the growth of positive dispositions and the development of young children.

Embedding Musical Activities into the Culture of the Classroom

Children will develop an appreciation for music when relevant and informal musical activities are incorporated throughout the day: during centers, group time, routines, and transitions. Music programs in early childhood classrooms should provide both spontaneous and planned experiences, as well as group and individual experiences. The basic elements of the music program are listening and responding to music, rhythmic movement, playing instruments, singing songs, and playing musical games.

There should be a balance between free, guided, and directed experiences in early childhood programs. (Review Levels of Teachers' Direction for Play Activities in Chapter 4.) Encouraging spontaneity and improvisation through the use of a music center allows children to play freely with the elements of music. Allowing children to choose the songs they sing or the music played during circle time or during transitions is also a way to provide free and spontaneous activities.

Guided activities occur when teachers have definite objectives for an activity or experience but children have choices in the materials they use and freedom in how they play with these materials. For example, a teacher may select several recordings representing different musical genres (e.g., jazz, classical, and rock) and place them, with a cassette player, in the art center. Children may select any recording and use chalk, paint, or crayons to illustrate, on paper, the mood and rhythm of the music. In this example, the teacher has guided the children into an experience that may result in their appreciation or perception of mood in music, and the children have had the choice of both the music and the art materials, as well as having the freedom to interpret the music in their own way.

Directed activities include teaching specific songs, fingerplays, and action games. After these activities are learned, they become a part of the classroom repertoire and are often requested or even enacted spontaneously. Therefore directed activities can evolve into guided and free-play activities.

A teacher might choose to teach vocabulary to a group of children by teaching a song. If the vocabulary is meaningful to the children and learning the song is both fun and purposeful, then this would be an example of a directed experience. However, if the vocabulary was not relevant or geared to the interest or developmental level of the children and the teaching of the song became stressful for either the teacher or the children, then we might conclude that this directed lesson had turned into work disguised as play and is not appropriate to early childhood classrooms.

Developing Appropriate Goals for Music Experiences.   General goals in any music program for young children include providing children with many opportunities to chant and sing, move and dance, listen and respond to a variety of music, discriminate sounds, express emotions through music, create and play musical instruments, and develop self-confidence and an understanding of age-appropriate concepts such as tempo, volume, tone, timbre, rhythm, and harmony. Specific objectives need to be developed using the criteria for developmentally appropriate practice (Bredekamp & Copple, 1997). As discussed in Chapter 2, these criteria require an understanding of age appropriateness, individual appropriateness, and cultural appropriateness. All music activity should be designed to facilitate appropriate developmental tasks, should be intrinsically interesting, and should make meaningful contributions to children's lives at school and at home.

The diversity in developmental levels, cultural background, and general experience that exists among children in any particular group will make it necessary to develop a wide variety of music experiences and activities for use in music centers and in small- and large-group activities. Each child's natural strengths and abilities should be considered when developing individual objectives. It is vital that children's level of development, cultural heritage, and style of participation be not only considered but also accepted and celebrated when formulating classroom activities and experiences. One way to help children understand and appreciate their own unique possibilities is to study the biographies of musicians with disabilities, such as Ray Charles, Stevie Wonder, and Joaquine Rodrigo, as well as musicians representing many different cultures.

Process and Product Goals. As with other aspects of play and learning, the process of doing, experimenting, and exploring the sound and rhythm of music is a vital element in children's general development of musical interest and ability. When children first begin to explore music, the process (e.g., singing, playing an instrument, and moving to a beat) is much more valuable to the child than the product (e.g., the song, the sound, and the dance). With time and experience, children will develop an understanding of sound, movement, and rhythm and gain more confidence in their abilities to produce music or movements that please them. Only then will children become interested in the by-products of their musical endeavors. When adult attention is focussed only on the product of musical experiences (the song or the dance), children get the message that only the product is important. This can create stress for children, a loss of confidence in their own abilities, and even a loss of interest in music and rhythm.

Early childhood teachers are often called upon to involve the children in their classrooms in school performances. They may be asked to have their students sing a song at a parent-teacher meeting or perform a skit or play at an all-school assembly. Generally, people who suggest such performances do not understand the developmental implications of their request. Devoting time to multiple rehearsals disrupts routines, creating stress for children and displacing developmentally appropriate activities. However, early childhood teachers must consider how the request will affect the children in their care and either turn down the offer or devise an alternative that does not compromise the integrity of a developmentally appropriate curriculum. For example, teachers of three- and four-year-old children could record classroom activities and present them on large monitors with a commentary explaining what the children are doing and why it is important. Some kindergarten children, particularly at the end of the year, and most children enrolled in primary classrooms may enjoy performing a short song or skit before an audience. This is especially true if the song or skit is an old standby, something the children have done for a long time, know well, and enjoy doing.

Another way to make a performance appropriate for young children is to approach the performance in an informal manner. Treat it as you would treat an activity in the classroom. Seat the children around you on the stage, just as you would in the classroom, and conduct the song just as you would in the classroom. Make it familiar, fun, and informal. Do not force any child to participate. Start over, if you need to. Parents and older children will enjoy seeing young children's spontaneity and humor. It is up to teachers to take control of performance situations, protect children from stress, and model to parents and other adults appropriate expectations and practices.

Providing Listening Experiences for Young Children

Young children thoroughly enjoy listening and responding to music, and even though listening to music seems easy and natural, it involves much more than simply hearing. Listening involves attending to sound, perceiving and recognizing certain sounds, and mentally organizing sounds in ways that can lead to recall or reproduction. Young children develop listening habits and skills when they have many opportunities to listen to and have fun with music and musical activities. Through a balance of free, guided, and directed play experiences with music, children can develop both an appreciation for a wide variety of music and the ability to perceive and discriminate the individual sounds and rhythms that make up music.

There are many genres of music, and young children need opportunities to hear and respond to a great variety. Genres of music include children's music, classical, country-western, gospel, folk, jazz, soul, rock, rap, patriotic and marching songs, new age, movie and show music, zydeco, and the traditional music of many cultures and ethnic groups. Teachers provide free-play experiences with music when they allow children to choose recordings and listen to them in the music center or during group time. An example of a guided play activity would be asking children to choose a recording and respond to it with movement using scarves, balls, or hoops. Here the teacher's goal is to have children use their bodies to respond to music, but the children are free to choose both the music and the form of response. An example of a directed play experience is a teacher selecting a piece of music and asking children to listen for a certain element in that music, such as the beat, tempo, or the mood.

Music selections enhance and support theme studies. Oremland (1998) created a web of possibilities that support the theme topic of weather (Figure 8.1). The music presented in this web represents many genres: jazz, rock, Latin jazz, classical, folk/rock, contemporary, traditional children's music, and new age. These selections not only provide many opportunities for children to listen to music, but also provide opportunities for children to interpret music through art and movement.

Some directed listening experiences make great transitional activities because they can be done anywhere (even waiting in line to get into the cafeteria), take little advanced planning, and require no special equipment. Directed listening experiences that help children focus their attention and learn to discriminate sounds include listening games, such as guessing environmental sounds, repeating rhythms by clapping, and recognizing voices. Other directed listening activities can be designed to give children experience in identifying elements of music, sound, or rhythm. For example, children can be asked to apply concepts such as loud, soft, fast, slow, high, and low to the clapping, stomping, humming, or singing of one child or the teacher. It is also fun to have one person hum a familiar tune and let others guess what it is. Directed listening activities used during transition times provide important information and valuable experiences for children as well as fun and pleasure during what could otherwise be tedious times of the school day.

Children can benefit greatly from attending live musical performances. These events can be either a great experience in music appreciation for children or a challenging experience in management for the teacher. It all depends on the expectations teachers and event planners have for children, the specific arrangements made for the performance, and the way children are prepared for the experience. Events geared to the developmental needs of three- and four-year-old children are generally informal in nature and provide children multiple opportunities to participate by moving, dancing, experimenting with instruments, and singing. It is always important to have many playful adults accompany children to performances. Adults

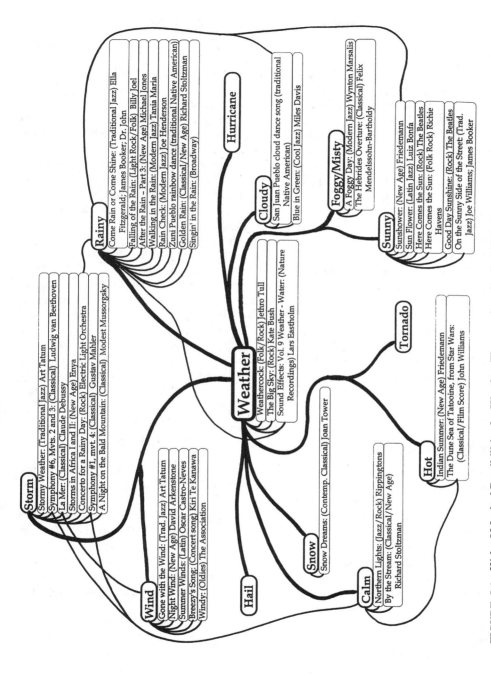

FIGURE 8.1 Web of Musical Possibilities for Weather Theme Oremland's *A Web of Musical Possibilities* provides an example of extending any theme by selecting appropriate music from many genres. Reprinted with permission.

Source: Jeff Oremland (1998), *Weather: A Web of Musical Ideas,* Unpublished class project, University of New Orleans.

can support children's participation by attending to each child individually and modeling ways to respond to the music. Also, having several adults with the class makes it possible to allow a child to leave the performance if the event proves too stimulating.

Kindergarten and primary-age children enjoy the informality of presentations that invite participation. However, they will also find formal events enjoyable if they know what to expect and what they might have the opportunity to learn during the performance. Teachers should prepare children for performances in the same way they prepare them for other field trips. If possible, preview the performance or find out what musical content will be presented. Give children the opportunity to hear the music or learn about the composer, conductor, or musical group in advance. When teachers have advance notice of musical performances, they can involve children in themes and projects that will provide them with relevant background information. Then, when the children attend the event, they will have a much richer experience and come away with a greater depth of knowledge because they had prior knowledge and an understanding of what was going to happen.

An important issue related to providing listening experiences for young children concerns the use of background music. Many teachers feel that playing background music at certain times of the day, for example, at center time, can enhance the environment and relax the children. This may be true. However, it is important to consider the other side of the situation. For many children, background music may be distracting. It may even be perceived as noise and add stress to their environment. It is also true that sound that is constant is tuned out, and the process of tuning out takes energy and concentration away from the task at hand. Therefore, teachers need to make decisions about the use of background music carefully. It may be necessary to search for compromises regarding selections and volume and to provide times when there is no music rather than develop a routine of using music as a background to classroom activities.

Providing Creative Movement Experiences for Young Children

When children hear music, it is natural for them to want to move and they should be encouraged to do so. When young children have many opportunities to experiment and respond expressively to music, they refine fundamental movements such as walking, running, hopping, and skipping and develop balance and coordination. Creative movement activities also support children's growing self concept because through experimenting with movement children can discover their ability and potential for both movement and expression through movement.

As with listening experiences, teachers foster children's enjoyment of and learning potential for creative movement when they provide a balance between experiences in which children can be free and spontaneous and activities in which teachers give children directions or otherwise guide their explorations. It is also important for teachers to remember to show children that they appreciate and enjoy the process they use as they explore movement. The freest experiences children can have result from inviting them to move to different musical selections in any way they wish, provided they not interfere with others and maintain a safe environment for themselves and others. A variation of this free-play experience involves providing children with props, scarves, balls, balloons, hoops, yarn, or ribbons to use as they move to different musical selections. These experiences can take place during group time or during center time. Table 8.2 provides examples of ways to move and vocabulary that can enhance movement exploration.

TABLE 8.2   Ways to Move and Movement Vocabulary

To help children develop awareness of how their body can move, ask them to

bend	leap	soar
contract	march	spread
crawl	plop	stomp
creep	plunge	stretch
expand	pull	sway
explore	push	swirl
fall	shake	tiptoe
float	shimmy	track
fly	shuffle	trip
gallop	skip	turn
hop	slide	twirl
jump	slither	twist

Help children express different qualities of movement by pairing one of the following terms with an action.

Examples: Tiptoe slowly in place.
            Hesitantly track a bear from here to there.

Qualities of Movement	**Related Terms**
Tempo	slowly, quickly, hesitantly, rapidly
Fluidity	softly, flowingly, ridgidly
Dimension	large, small, tiny, huge, gigantic
Direction	in place, from here to there

Adapted from Rubright (1996).

You can guide children's development of movement and expression by asking them questions about their movement. "What, in the music, is making you move so slowly?" Or you can ask them to move in certain way, "Move quickly!" Sometimes you might want to describe how particular children are moving instead of suggesting or telling them how to move. Another way to guide children's development of movement and expression is to ask them to observe movement patterns in nature—leaves, snowflakes, raindrops, different animals, or even different people. It adds interest to any environment when teachers remember to call children's attention to interesting movements that happen naturally. The act of careful and frequent observation can become a useful habit for young children. Guided experiences such as these allow children to explore movement that they might not have thought of on their own. Once children have discovered a new way of moving, they will probably incorporate it into spontaneous movement activities. This is one reason there needs to be a balance between free, guided, and directed activities and experiences.

Directed movement activities require giving children specific suggestions and ideas, for example, to hop like a rabbit or flutter like a butterfly. Many recordings for young children provide directed movement experiences. Some take the form of games, modeled after

"Simon Says," and others take the form of songs or stories that require specific movements at specific times. It is important for teachers to realize that these activities are really exercises in following directions. Learning to follow directions is important, but it is not the same as learning to move and express feelings through music. However, directed activities do provide children with ideas and experiences and should be combined with many opportunities for children to respond freely to instrumental music.

Developing Rhythm.   One goal we have for young children is that they develop, over time, the ability to perceive a rhythm and move to it. To move to the beat or rhythm of music, children must master three skills: (1) they must have control over their own movement, (2) listen to the beat of the music, and (3) combine the two (Seefeldt & Barbour, 1990).

Weikart (1982) suggests that activities designed to help children feel and move to a beat begin with encouraging children to repeat single words as they move—"walk, walk, walk." The next step is for children to match the chant, "walk, walk, walk," with the motion of walking to a beat. The third step is for the children to whisper the chant, "walk, walk, walk," while continuing to keep the beat with walking motions. When they become proficient, music with a clear beat is added to the activity. The last step is to have the children stop whispering and just think the chant while they continue the movement. Varying the music and varying the movement to include clapping, hopping, marching, running, skipping, or galloping will provide children with additional experiences. When introducing new music to children, have them listen to the music first. Ask them to think about what their feet or hands could do to represent the rhythm of the music.

There are many different activities and rhythm games that can facilitate learning to move to a beat. Clapping names and rhythms and echoing rhythms can be done informally while waiting turns or waiting for the group to gather on the rug. Children can be asked to walk, run, hop, skip, or crawl to rhythms played on drums, bells, or a piano. Time, multiple experiences, repetition, and patient accepting adults who support children's first efforts will facilitate the process.

Playing musical instruments stimulates and challenges children to create and recreate rhythm patterns. The rhythm instruments used in early childhood classrooms should be of high quality and produce accurate musical timbres. Homemade or "found" instruments are interesting additions to classroom collections but should be limited because the sounds produced, or the way in which the sounds are produced do not always give children an accurate experience or understanding of the instrument's capabilities.

Children need a variety of experiences with instruments. These experiences should include free exploration during center time and guided play experiences during group time. Children should have experience with all instruments and become familiar with the sounds associated with each. When children are first introduced to instruments, the focus of the experience should be on the sounds instruments make and the way they can be played to produce sounds and rhythms. Teachers can play guessing games with children by recording different instruments and asking children to identify them. As children gain more experience with instruments, they will enjoy playing along with recorded music and moving to recorded music while playing instruments. Children should be allowed to make their own rhythms with the instruments in addition to following the rhythms of others. Only after children have become familiar with instruments by using them extensively for open-ended exploration should they be expected to play melodies and perform as a band. Table 8.3 outlines essential elements needed to create a music center.

TABLE 8.3   Music Center

Space Requirements
Floor space near electrical outlet
Storage for instruments
Away from quiet areas

Basic Materials
Tape recorder and blank tapes
Variety of cassettes (e.g., children's music, folk,
    classical, western, bluegrass, rap, rock, traditional
    music from many cultures, and jazz)
Instruments (e.g., shakers, drums, cymbals, triangles,
    rhythm sticks, sand blocks, xylophone, drums,
    and bells)
Music books
Music paper and writing materials
Song charts
Pictures of famous musicians from many cultures
Keyboard
Software for writing music

Examples of Basic Learning Opportunities
Creating homemade instruments
Singing
Recording original music and rhythms
Collaborating to develop rhythms
Experimenting with sound
Expressing feelings and moods

Examples of Extensions
Literacy
  ■ read from song books or song charts
  ■ write original music or lyrics
Numeracy
  ■ figure costs of instruments from catalogues
  ■ create rhythms and draw the patterns

Providing Singing Experiences for Young Children

Singing and chanting come naturally to children. By the age of two, most children sing spontaneously as they play with language and melody (McDonald, 1979). In preschool programs, many spontaneous songs grow out of playful motor, language, and vocabulary activities. Two- and three-year-old children enjoy listening to familiar songs repeatedly, but generally regard group singing experiences as opportunities to listen and watch others. They join in, first with actions, and then singing only when the words and phrases are familiar or exceptionally fun to say. When children begin to sing in groups, they do not always match pitch or tonality to the singing of others but choose their own. McDonald suggests that teachers introduce young children to group singing by matching the pitch children choose.

Four- and five-year-old children enjoy singing together informally in small groups. They begin singing simple songs, such as "Mary Had A Little Lamb" and "Three Little Ducks." They enjoy repeating the songs they know quite frequently. As children gain more experience singing with a group, they begin to enjoy more complex songs, especially when there are multiple opportunities to match singing with movements and several parts of the song are repeated frequently.

If children in the primary grades have had many opportunities to sing as a part of a group, they will develop the ability to sing in tune and match the pitch of the leader. They can also learn to sing simple rounds. For example, "Row, Row, Row Your Boat" is often sung in a three-part round; three different groups sing the same song, but each group starts at a different time. Primary-age children can also develop the ability to sing songs that call for responses. Such songs are typified by one group of children singing a line or phrase and then another group responding by singing a line or phrase that answers the first group. "Little Sir Echo" is an example of a song that calls for responses. Therefore, with opportunity and experience, young children are able to greatly increase their repertoire of songs and their ability to sing as they grow and develop.

Choosing Songs.   Young children enjoy learning and singing songs that feature a prominent rhythm, suggest movement and actions, have frequent repetitions, use nonsense words or syllables, evoke a particular mood, or tell a story (Bayless & Ramsey, 1991). When choosing songs for children, it is important to keep in mind their previous experience with singing, their interests, and their cultural and ethnic backgrounds. The length and complexity of the song should match the development and experience of the children who will be singing. The youngest children or novice singers enjoy short, simple songs. The tune and rhythm of a selection should also appeal to children. Songs that lead to movement and have a repeated lyric or chorus appeal to three- and four-year-old children and to novice singers.

Another important consideration when selecting songs for group singing is familiarity. The words and concepts portrayed in the song should have meaning for the children, or at least be easily explained. Selecting songs that relate to the theme currently being studied supports vocabulary and concept development. Selecting songs that represent the languages and cultures of children in the classroom enriches the self-concept of all children by providing positive multicultural experiences.

Presenting Songs.   Children learn songs in a predictable pattern. They begin by learning the words, then move to rhythms, phrases, and contours (McDonald & Simons, 1989). New songs should be introduced to children gradually, beginning with rhythmic speech. Chants and rhymes help children move from speech to song (Brewer, 1998). If teachers sing or play a song informally and spontaneously several times before they plan to teach it to the children, they will have created both interest and a sense of familiarity with the song.

When presenting a new song, you many want to ask children questions that will help focus their attention on the meaning of the lyrics. You will also want to break the song into meaningful chunks and support children as they learn one part at a time. You might also use a chart with written lyrics to help children make associations between written and spoken language.

Many teachers are intimidated by the prospect of teaching music in early childhood programs. They have limited confidence in their own ability to carry a tune or play an instrument. Lucky (1990) reminds nonmusicians that early childhood teachers are expected to teach *with* music not to teach music. Isenberg and Jalongo (1997) state that the focus should be on children's musical activity, not the teacher's talent. There are many creative ways for teachers to compensate for their lack of musical talent or confidence. Teachers who are uncomfortable with their own musical abilities could do the following.

1. First, remember that children are not a critical audience and enthusiasm overrides lack of perfect pitch.
2. Use recorded music to introduce songs. Repeat the recordings until both teacher and children feel comfortable singing without accompaniment.
3. Find someone who plays an instrument or sings well and have him or her record music or a song in a style that can be easily used with children.
4. Practice songs before presenting them to children. Just as you read a book out loud only after practice, sing songs with children only after you know them by heart.

5. First teach a song to a small group of children and then let them assist you when you teach the song to the whole class (Isenberg & Jalongo, 1997).
6. Team-teach group music activities with someone who has more confidence in his or her singing ability. Or you might want to swap classes for a short time. Facilitate an art lesson with your coteacher's class while she or he leads a music experience with yours.

Wolf (1994) gives the following suggestions for teachers who want to ensure success when presenting songs.

1. Have an expressive face.
2. Look at the children.
3. Be a participant and get involved.
4. Have fun!
5. Know the song well; learn it from a recording, if necessary.
6. Start the song with "ready, go!"
7. Use visuals and props.
8. Choose success-oriented songs. (p. 24)

Including Children with Special Needs

Music is a joyous way for all children to express themselves and create sounds and rhythms. Through music and musical activities, children have the opportunity to develop physical, social, aesthetic, and intellectual skills and abilities. Teachers need to understand both the strengths and the limitations of children with special needs in order to modify activities and adapt equipment in ways that maximize a child's ability to participate. Specialists and parents can often assist teachers and suggest specific modifications that make musical activities fun and meaningful for each child. Here are some examples of ways to modify musical activities.

Children with Visual Impairments
- Guide the child, either physically or with words, through music or rhythmic activities.
- Play musical or sound games in which no one in the class uses vision. For example, hide a ticking clock and let several children search for it, or play recorded sounds of different environments and let children guess where they are.

Children with Hearing Impairments
- If a child has some residual hearing, let him or her use earphones to listen to recorded music.
- Seat children near speakers and let them touch the speakers or hold the cassette recorder while music is playing so that they can feel the vibrations of the music coming through the speakers.
- When singing songs or chanting, tap the rhythm lightly on the child's arm or knee and help him or her keep the rhythm of the song or chant.
- Use sign language and encourage all children to incorporate it into their singing. Prepare song charts pairing signs and words.
- Accompany songs with visual cues.
- When you sing, use your hands to show when the pitch goes up or down.

Children with Language or Communication Delays

- Use songs that incorporate motion so that all children can participate in more than one way.
- Keep the activity fun and informal and do not focus attention on single children but emphasize group participation. Children may be encouraged to participate if they do not feel pressure.
- Encourage the children to hum along or keep the rhythm of a song with an instrument.
- Help children make musical instruments and encourage them to use them in musical activities.
- Slow the pace of the song or musical activity.

Children with Physical Disabilities

- Plan ahead and develop opportunities for children to participate in an activity in the best way they can, clapping using one hand and a table, slapping their knee, smiling, blinking, waving, or nodding their head. An adult can help a child one-on-one to make appropriate responses. When introducing a song, give different children different actions to do. If everyone is doing something different, no one person stands out.
- Children with physical disabilities often tire easily. You might want to create a small group of children that sings only one part of a song and include a child who tires easily in this group.
- Have the children move their wheelchairs to the beat of the music.
- Adapt instruments so children can hold on to them.
- Slow the pace of the song or musical activity.

Children with Cognitive Difficulties

- Show pictures or use props to set the mood for songs and make the meaning of the song clear. For example, if the song is about falling leaves, have some leaves in the classroom and use them to demonstrate the concept of falling.
- Use visual, verbal, and physical cues to maintain focus on the song or activity.
- Use songs or activities that involve repeated actions or phrases.
- Reduce distractions and background noises.
- Teach songs or activities in small segments over several days and then put them all together.
- Frequently repeat old favorites.
- Use songs and activities that teach basic concepts such as shapes and colors or create body awareness by bringing attention to the names of body parts.
- Slow the pace of the song or musical activity.

Children with Attention Disorders

- Use music to help children release energy in appropriate ways.
- Change the pace of music used in creative dance often during an activity. This gives children the chance to develop control over motor impulses because they will need to change their pace from fast to slow to somber to joyous and so on.

Children with Socioemotional Difficulties

- Use lots of old favorites to provide predictability to the classroom environment and group activities.

- Use musical activities to help children gain social acceptance. For example, the creative dance movements or the lyrics one child contributes to the group activity may allow other children to appreciate his or her strengths.
- Emphasize relationships between feelings and sound so that children can develop the ability to use music to express or release feelings.
- Provide many types of music for children to listen to in the music center.

(Cook, Tessier, & Armbruster, 1987; Deiner, 1983; Fewell & Kaminski, 1988; Morris & Schultz, 1989; Wesley, 1992).

Responding to Children's Musical Expression

Children's expression through music and movement is not merely an imitation of adult expression but is unique and represents the process of learning and developing. Therefore, children's music and movement are to be valued and appreciated for their own sake. The manner in which adults respond to children's singing, dancing, and play with instruments will affect their confidence and motivation. Adults support children's creative development when they appreciate the playfulness of children and respond playfully. Here are some examples of playful responses that encourage children to continue to explore and experiment with music and movement.

- Show genuine interest in what children are doing by moving toward them when they are engaged in spontaneous activities. Stand nearby and smile.
- Sing along with children or join in spontaneous movement activities.
- Follow children's lead. Replicate their movements or verses.
- Respond to original songs or musical improvisations with joy and laughter.
- Write down original songs or use audio- or videotapes to preserve musical creations. Share them with other adults.
- Engage children in authentic conversations about their actions and songs.
- Encourage children's persistence by extending the time period.

Fostering Creative Expression through the Visual Arts

Young children are constantly in the process of creating art—at home, in their backyards and bathtubs; at restaurants, in their plates and on table linens; and on their way to school, in the dirt and on sidewalks. The spontaneous and exploratory nature of children naturally turns play into art and art into play (Szekely, 1991). In fact, art and play are so interconnected in the lives of children that it is difficult, if not impossible, to distinguish between them. The art of young children flourishes in environments in which adults recognize and appreciate the uniqueness of children's artistic expression and, indeed, do not feel the need to distinguish between art and play or channel children's artistic impulses into images of adult art. The goal of art in early childhood programs is to make sure that the enthusiasm and natural artistic talents of young children are not left at the schoolhouse door.

Art can be an individual endeavor or it can be a collaborative effort. A child's art is one means of self-expression and is strongly influenced by his or her culture and prior opportunities to work freely with materials. When children create, they draw from their previous experience, respond to both internal and external stimuli, and express themselves in unique, inventive, and symbolic ways. Through art, children discover both who they are and where they are in the world.

Defining Art

We can define art as a form of open-ended communication that conveys impressions, ideas, perceptions, and feelings (Hendrick, 1992). Children engaged in art activities should have the opportunity to explore materials and experiment with artistic techniques freely in an environment where the process of creating is valued over the product that results (Brewer, 1998). Examples of art experiences include experimenting with crayons, chalk, and paint by drawing, painting, or coloring; exploring fabric, paper, and ribbons by sewing, weaving, or pasting; and using clay, wood, or papier-mâché to mold, build, or sculpt. The only limit to true art is the imagination of the artist.

When defining children's art, it is important to distinguish between true art experiences, such as those described in the preceding paragraph, and other curricular activities that might seem like art to adults but will not feel like art to children and do not meet the definition. Crafts are one example of such activities. Crafts resemble art because children are working with art materials, but the outcome is often predetermined by the teacher, and the focus of the activity is on the product not the process of making it. In many craft activities, children are required to make something in particular; for example, a spider, butterfly, or basket. Often, children's craft products look similar because all children were asked to use the same patterns, materials, to follow the same general directions, or to use exactly the same techniques. When teachers predetermine the outcome of craft activities, children lose the experience of setting their own goals and expressing their own ideas. They also get the message that their ideas are not quite good enough, not quite right (Clemens, 1991).

There are times when making a certain craft supports a theme of study and enhances the development of relevant concepts associated with the study. But teachers should keep in mind that whereas such activities further the goals of curricular areas such as science and social studies, they do not enhance children's artistic development. Nonetheless, craft activities can be appropriate when individual children have a choice about which crafts to make, what materials to use, and what the final product will look like. Teachers should carefully keep track of classroom time devoted to art activities and classroom time devoted to craft activities and strike an appropriate balance, taking care to ensure that crafts do not take away time devoted to art. The appropriate balance will depend on the individual child's age, experience, and style of learning.

Examples of other activities presented to children as art include

- cut-and-paste activities that follow a certain set of directions
- coloring books or dittos in which children are asked to use specific colors or to make sure they are coloring in the lines
- dot-to-dot ditto sheets
- precut shapes that need to be put together in a prescribed way to form a predetermined picture

These activities are neither arts or crafts. Any activity that requires children to follow step-by-step directions and consistently wait to be told what to do next does not involve children in exploration or decision making and cannot be considered as either art or play. Whereas a teacher might decide that these activities are important learning opportunities for specific children, she or he must guard against allowing these activities to completely displace the time allotted to engage in creative art experiences.

Some teachers justify activities such as these by stating that they are designed to teach children to wait, share materials, and follow directions. However, there are many ways to help children develop the ability to work cooperatively, delay gratification, and follow directions by involving their imagination and enlisting their mental attentions. Activities that cause children to become frustrated or bored, doubt their abilities, or displace the time and energy they could be using to be creative are not appropriate and cannot be justified in early childhood programs.

Teachers sometimes justify highly structured "artlike" activities by saying, "Children just love doing this!" When you know young children, you know that they are trusting and appear "to love" doing whatever they feel will please the adults who are significant in their lives. We must not take this trust lightly and should instead strive to select activities that foster optimal learning and development.

The Benefits of Art in the Curriculum.

Children's art mirrors their development. Their painting, drawings, collages, songs, stories and constructions reveal what they see and understand about the world around them. Art not only mirrors children's developmental progress but facilitates further development in all domains as children explore the properties of materials and make connections between their cognitive and expressive abilities. Table 8.4 suggests some examples of how art fosters the growth of positive dispositions and fosters the development of young children.

Developing Appropriate Goals for Art Experiences.

One fundamental goal of art programs in early childhood classrooms is to safeguard children's use of art as a means of self-expression and provide many meaningful opportunities for them to be creative (Read, 1980). Teachers do this by valuing the process children use as they create, providing activities that give children sensory pleasure, encouraging children to explore a wide variety of materials, and allowing children to make discoveries about the elements of art.

Another goal of art programs is to involve children in the work and world of art and artists. When children have the opportunity to talk to, work with, and observe artists and illustrators, they learn that they have much in common with these grown-ups who make a living "playing around with art." These experiences help children value and maintain the artist within themselves. It really is not difficult to get artists involved in classrooms. Most communities have an arts association and maintain a directory of local artists. Many are willing to volunteer time to children's programs. Every newspaper has an art director and many businesses, grocery stores, and shopping centers employ commercial artists. Architects are artists and most communities have at least one architectural firm. Finding art in the world is as easy as finding artists. Children need to view many forms of art from many cultures. Teachers do not have to worry about explaining art to children. They only have to begin a discussion about the elements of art. Children enjoy pointing out different elements and will develop the ability to express their own feelings about the art they view.

TABLE 8.4 **Benefits of Art Activities**

Children have many opportunities to learn and develop when they engage in art activities. Here are some examples of how play with art unifies learning and development.

Physical Development

■ Children develop fine muscle control and hand–eye coordination as they as they paint, cut, sculpt, mold, trace, draw, and color.

■ Children develop an awareness of what their fingers and hands can do when they work with art materials.

■ Children refine their understanding of how their bodies move in space, fill space, and interact with space.

Social Development

■ Children develop respect for the ideas of others as they view and respond to the work of professional artists and classmates.

■ Children develop the disposition to be patient and defer gratification when they reshape a clay structure or add more paint to a work in progress.

■ Children develop the ability to participate, share, and cooperate as they work together on a collaborative project such as a sculpture or mural.

Intellectual Development

■ Children sharpen their observation skills and develop the disposition to attend to details as they draw objects in their environments.

■ Children develop their vocabulary and comprehension skills as they learn about the elements of art (e.g., color, form, line, shape, texture, pattern, volume, mass, and space).

■ Children develop perceptual skills as they recognize the elements they are using in their art work or respond to another's work by describing particularly pleasing elements.

■ Children develop the ability to focus, sequence, persist, and solve problems as they return, day after day, to work on a chosen project.

■ Children construct physical knowledge as they engage in sensory experiences with materials such as sand, water, mud, clay, bubbles, paste, and paint.

■ Children begin to develop awareness of symbolic representation as they attempt to represent movement, feelings, and eventually things in their environment in their drawings and paintings.

Emotional Development

■ Children develop the ability to identify or clarify their own feelings as they express them through art materials and techniques.

■ Children develop dispositions of positive self-confidence and feelings of success when they display the results of their creative activities.

■ Children develop pride in their cultural heritage when they share traditional art from their heritage.

■ Children develop a feeling of belonging when their art is shared with and appreciated by others in their class.

■ Children develop tolerance for others' ways of expressing themselves.

Aesthetic Development

■ Children develop the disposition of sensitivity and develop an understanding of the feelings, images, and impressions portrayed by the art displayed in classroom.

■ Children develop an appreciation of many kinds of art and art materials as they encounter them in classroom situations.

Embedding Art Activities into the Culture of the Classroom

Art supports children's total development. Therefore, the art curriculum is fundamental to early childhood programs and should not be considered a frill or something children "get to do" after they finish their work. Teachers support children's artistic development by creating a time in the daily schedule devoted to art, arranging interesting materials in ways children can access easily, and creating a risk-taking environment that promotes children's willingness to explore and experiment. Opportunities to engage in art activities should be a daily ritual for every young child; not just in preschool and kindergarten, but also in first, second, and third grade.

The schools of Reggio Emilia, Italy, are known for their ability to support the cognitive and creative development of young children. Katz (1993) reports that one lesson that can be learned from these schools is that "preprimary children communicate their ideas, feelings, understandings, imaginings, and observations through visual representation much earlier than most U.S. early childhood educators typically assume" (p. 25). One way this community supports children's artistic development is by providing an *atelier* and an *atelierista* at every school. An *atelier* is a workshop or studio, furnished with a variety of resource materials. This room is available and used by all children and adults in the school. An *atelierista* is an art teacher. She is in charge of the workshop and supports teachers in curriculum development and documentation (Edwards, Gandini, & Forman, 1993).

Most American schools have not yet adopted this practice, and many times art is treated as a whole-group learning activity. However, the advantages of center-based art activities and the workshop atmosphere are great. It is possible for teachers to simulate the workshop atmosphere by developing well-stocked learning centers that emphasize art and by creating a learning center system (see Chapter 4) that facilitates children's use of these centers. There are several centers that specifically support children's artistic development: the block center, the sand and water center (described in Chapter 4), the carpentry center, and, of course, the art center. Table 8.5 provides examples of the essential elements needed in a carpentry center. Table 8.6 provides examples of the kinds of materials needed in the art center.

Choosing Material for Art Activities.   There are three categories of materials needed in centers that promote artistic expression. These are tools, standard art materials, and "found materials." Tools should be selected carefully to match the developmental abilities of the children in the group. Some tools should be stored away from the center so that teachers can provide direct supervision if children ask to use them. It is easy to see how a little imagination can turn tools into materials.

Standard art materials can be found in art stores or ordered from school supply catalogues. Found materials are just that. They are found—by teachers, by parents, and by the children themselves. Some might call these materials junk, but they have the power to inspire. Teachers must use the same caution in providing materials as they use in providing tools. Not all materials are appropriate for all children.

Of course, not all tools, materials, and supplies should be available at once. This would create chaos and would be overwhelming for children and teachers. Rotating tools and materials every two to three weeks allows children ample opportunity to use materials several days in a row. That way they begin to know the item well before it disappears. New tools and materials inspire new techniques. When familiar items reappear, they will probably be used

TABLE 8.5   Carpentry Center

Space Requirements
Large floor area
Away from quiet areas
Shelves for storing materials
Wall area for hanging tools
Floor space that is easy to sweep

Basic Materials
Table for construction
Hard hats and safety goggles
Hand tools, small size (hammers, sandpaper, nails, screwdrivers, screws, saws, wrench, pliers, clamps, measuring tapes, level, etc.)
Building materials (soft wood scraps, styrofoam, bark, cardboard, etc.)
Other materials (wood glue, wire, masking tape, toothpicks, wallpaper scraps, etc.)

Safety Considerations
Provide consistent supervision, maybe by a parent or other volunteer
Consistently check wood for splinters
Use safety goggles and hard hats
Limit the number of children in center (in relation to space and supervision available)
Clearly mark where children are to stand as they watch others work

Examples of Basic Learning Opportunities
Understand basic concepts (balance, force, size, weight, height, length, etc.)
Counting and categorizing skills
Architectural concepts (arch, bridge, stories, columns, etc.)
Problem solving while constructing structures
Cooperation and collaboration during planning and construction
Language and concept development
Respect for space and efforts of others
Develop small muscle strength and coordination
Develop hand–eye coordination
Designing and carrying though
Exploring different dimensions

Examples of Extensions
Literacy
- develop labels for constructions
- include books about carpentry and interior design
- include blueprints in center
- develop and write stories about constructions

Numeracy
- have students draw blueprints
- measure structures
- design

in new and different ways. When teachers rotate materials and supplies regularly, they do not have to spend time thinking up new art activities. The combination of children, tools, and materials will create new possibilities spontaneously.

There are, however, two constants that should be in every center: a poster that displays the images of different elements of art and a poster that states that play is the preferred activity in this center. Some elements of art are color, line, mass, volume, pattern, shape, form, space, and texture. Displaying them in poster form helps everyone, including the teacher, to recognize and discuss these elements in relation to what the children are doing. Children can help make the poster. You can add one or two elements a week, or you can fashion an elements board with spaces labeled for each element. When children produce examples of certain elements, they can be displayed on the board. Children can also make the poster proclaiming that the center is a free-play zone, and they can change it from time to time, altering the wording but keeping the message. The purpose of the poster, of course, is to let everyone who comes into the classroom know that the process any child is engaged in is more valuable than anything else that comes out of the center.

The process of art can often be an individual endeavor. Therefore, children may need to have space to work alone and away from others. However, Hendricks (1992) suggests that art is often highly social and collaborative. Consequently, art centers should be set up to meet

TABLE 8.6 Tools and Materials for Art Center

Common tools include:

scissors	rulers	straight edge
compass	paintbrushes	sponges
glue sticks	water pistols	eyedroppers
staplers	protractors	paper clips
strainers	tweezers	popsicle sticks

pepper shakers (the holes are bigger than salt shakers)
all sizes and kinds of containers

Standard art materials include:

clay	crayons	felt-tip markers
paints	finger paints	glue
paste	pencils	chalk

many weights and sizes of drawing paper, manila paper, construction paper, graph paper,
and fingerpaint paper

Found materials include:

leaves	paper plates	milk cartons
egg cartons	cottage cheese cartons	masks
buttons	receipts	plastic stuff
sticky stuff	gooey stuff	ribbons
shiny stuff	foil	wallpaper samples
wrapping paper	fabrics	

boxes (from refrigerator boxes to paper clip boxes)

the needs of both those who like to work alone and those who like to work together. Children are encouraged to work together when easels are set side by side. If you have room for three easels, you might want to put two together and one set off somewhat by itself. Small, narrow tables facilitate conversation and the sharing of materials. Square tables give children more space to themselves. When children want to work together on a project or work on each other's projects, they should be encouraged to do so. Activities that encourage collaboration include murals, large sculptures or weaving projects, body tracing, quilt making, and sidewalk painting.

What Do Children Do? So many materials! What do children do with them? They play. Art and play are indistinguishable, so children act on materials. They splash and pour, blow, bounce, spin, sort, squeeze, rub, stick, scrape, scratch, sand, cut, tear, drill, mix, crush, cover, drape, hang, polish, and fix (Szekely, 1991). As they perform these actions, they might explore and experiment, or they might make paintings, printings, sculptures, collages, wall hangings, woven cloth, sketches, and maps.

What Do Teachers Do? Teachers support and facilitate children's artistic expression in many active and playful ways. Here are some examples.

1. Teachers set a playful mood by exploring and experimenting with tools and materials and by showing they enjoy the process.

2. Teachers carefully observe the play patterns of children. They practice the art of "with-itness" and look for teachable moments. They support children by modeling new techniques for using tools and materials only when the children need the technique to gain greater control over the tools or materials. Teachers do not impose new techniques on children who are happy with the way things are going.

3. Teachers know when to add an element of surprise, puzzlement, or cognitive dissonance to an activity. They might bring out a new tool or change the texture or consistency of material such as paint or Play-Doh. Teachers find the right time to pose problems that facilitate children's thinking and lead them to hypothesize solutions.

4. Teachers move art outside whenever possible. They set up tables and easels under the eaves of the building. They take children for collection walks. They find trees for children to sit under while they draw. They point out interesting cracks in the sidewalk to use in a crayon rub.

5. Teachers utilize the power of suggestion to generate new ways of thinking among children who seem to be stuck. They pose open-ended questions such as, "What would happen if . . . ?" "What else could you do?" and "What do you need?"

6. Teachers are responsive to children's language. They listen attentively and encourage children to talk about their ideas, experiences, and feelings.

7. Teachers know the children in their classroom well and have realistic expectations for them. They share theses expectations with other significant adults. Teachers know when to challenge children in order to push them forward and when to back away and allow children to practice or perfect newly found abilities.

8. Teachers display children's art all around the room, the school, the neighborhood, and the community. They handle the art carefully and always ask the artist's permission. Children who want their work displayed have it displayed. Teachers do not spend budgeted funds for commercial bulletin board material or room decorations because they appreciate the art that is already in their room. They know that they can enlist willing artists to create any needed decorations.

9. Teachers entice reluctant artists by finding just the right project, material, or tool for them. They never force a child to participate in every activity but find the child's interests and talents and create bridges between those talents and art. Some children are storytellers and story writers. They may need to illustrate their books. Some children enjoy block building. They might need to draw blueprints for their next building.

10. Teachers find ways to connect art to all curricular areas and especially to the themes being studied and the projects that are underway in class. They may enlist the help of parents, older children, or senior citizen volunteers to help children carry out their projects.

11. Teachers know and respect the cultures and cultural preferences of the families of the children in their classes. They appreciate individual children's style regarding interactions and art. They understand that some families want to send children to school in their best clothes and become distressed if children get them dirty. Teachers encourage these children to wear smocks or aprons and do not insist that they get involved in messy activities. Table 8.7 suggests the essential elements of an art center.

TABLE 8.7 Art Center

Space Requirements
Large floor area near sink
Linoleum or plastic-covered floor
Storage shelves for art supplies
Cabinets for storage
Display area

Basic Materials
Easels
Tables for sculpture, drawing, printing, etc.
Drying rack or line
Art supplies (paper, paint, brushes, scissors,
    markers, glue, glue sticks, Play-Doh, cutters,
    collage materials, sponges)

Safety Considerations
Wet floors

Examples of Basic Learning Opportunities
Language and concept development (color, texture, tone,
    shade, dimension, size, space relationships, etc.)
Respect for space and efforts of others
Develop small muscle strength and coordination
Develop hand–eye coordination
Designing and carrying though ideas
Experimenting with tools
Observing changes (color, texture, wetness, etc.)
Caring for materials and tools
Expression of ideas through symbols

Examples of Extensions
Literacy
- develop and write stories about art work
- include books about artists and illustrators in center
- symbolic representations
- illustrating own stories

Numeracy
- measuring and use of precision in art design
- matching prints
- counting repetitions in art work
- developing a relationship between spaces in
  printing designs

Including Children with Special Needs

Art allows children with special needs a freedom of expression that may not be found in most other play activities. Through art, children can learn and explore in a less structured way than with toys and games. Children with special needs may not have had as many opportunities to explore and play with art materials as other children their age. Therefore, it is important to protect their time and make art experiences a priority for them. It is important to select activities that match the ability level and interests of each child and to offer assistance only when it is needed. Here are some suggestions for including children with special needs in art activities.

Children with Visual Impairments
- Use a variety of modeling materials and add different textures to paint so that children have a variety of tactile experiences.
- Make textured boundaries for work areas. Use masking tape, sandpaper or place mats to help children define their work space.
- Provide painting or coloring paper that has a high contrast, either in color or texture, to the surface of the table or easel used for painting.
- Talk to the children about what you or others are doing with art materials.
- Describe the colors, shapes, and sizes of the materials the children are using.
- Display the children's art in a place where they can find it easily and point it out to others.

Children with Hearing Impairments
- Use facial expressions to convey your pleasure when looking at children's creative work.
- Use sign language to converse with the children about their work.

- Get the children's attention and use sign language, visual, and physical cues to support their activities. For example, if they are out of paint, point to where more is stored.
- Allow children adequate time and opportunity to respond to questions or directions.

Children with Language or Communication Delays

- Encourage children to make puppets and they may then be encouraged to make the puppets speak.
- Blow painting or straw painting will give the children experiences using different muscles in their mouths.
- Encourage the children to identify the elements they are using: line, color, shape, mass, etc.
- Encourage the children to ask for the materials they need to complete their art work.
- Encourage children to talk about their experiences and feelings.

Children with Physical Disabilities

- Let the children hold modeling materials. If they are unable to do more than touch or hold the material, play with them, using their imagination. Ask questions such as, "Should we roll it or punch it?" and "Should we make a pancake?" If the children cannot respond, tell them what you are doing with the material and how it feels.
- Vary the moisture content in clay or Play-Doh to meet the strength and motor needs of the children. Encourage them to use tools and utensils as well as their hands while playing with the material.
- Adapt painting activities to fit the children's ability. For example, a child with no manual dexterity may be able to "toe paint" if assisted.
- Secure paper to the table with tape to help children gain control over their materials while they are painting, drawing or coloring.
- Felt-tip pens may be easier for children to use because they do not require as much pressure to make nice impressions.
- Provide extra large paper or have the children paint large objects such as boxes. This can become a group project.
- Provide scissors that have been adapted to fit the needs of the children.

Children with Learning Difficulties

- Allow adequate time and opportunity for children to respond to questions or directions.
- Have safety scissors available for the children to use.
- Post any guidelines for behavior, adding illustrations and the word *No* or an X through the picture. Also, post pictures of activities the children can do. You might even use their own pictures.

Children with Attention Disorders

- Provide activities and materials that allow the children to be expansive and use a large amount of space.
- Model use of material to help children release energy and emotion.

Children with Socioemotional Difficulties

- Encourage children to draw, color, or paint their feelings and then talk about their work.
- Modeling material will help children release energy and emotion.

(Cook, Tessier, & Armbruster, 1987; Deiner, 1983; Fewell & Kaminski, 1988; Morris & Schultz, 1989; Wesley, 1992).

Responding to Children's Art

The manner in which a teacher responds to a child's artistic endeavors will have a powerful effect on that child's self-confidence and future creative expression (Seefeldt, 1987). Teachers do not always need to talk to children about their art, but if they do, they should phrase their comments carefully. Teachers can respond to the art activities of individual children in verbal and nonverbal ways. Here are some examples of both.

1. Help children collect their art and make important decisions about whether a particular piece will be sent home with the child right away; be displayed in the community, school, or classroom; or become a part of the child's developmental portfolio.

2. Sit or stand near children as they engage in art and let your expression show that you enjoy watching them create.

3. When children are deep in concentration, avoid distracting them with questions, comments, suggestions, hints, advice, or praise.

4. Refrain from asking children what their painting, picture, or sculpture is. Not every piece of art is representational or has a meaning that can be expressed verbally. It is important that children learn this.

5. Let art speak for itself and let children initiate discussions about their art work.

6. When children initiate discussions about their work, help them reflect on the way they used different elements of art in their work. You can demonstrate your own perception of the way children used elements; for example, "There is nice balance in the way you used dark and light shades in your painting" and "This line is very busy! Isn't it?"

7. Make sure any appreciative comments do not distract children from the inner satisfaction they feel from their work. Avoid praise that is overgeneralized, empty, or gushy; for example, "That is the most beautiful picture I have ever seen!" Children see through this kind of praise, especially when they hear it often said to others.

8. When children invite your comments, respond sincerely. Again, talk about the elements the children used in their work or what you noticed about the effort they put into their work; for example, "The colors you used are so bright and lively, and I noticed you spent a lot of time getting just the right shade!"

9. Children sometimes ask you to tell them what they have drawn or painted. They are really not trying to trick you but have somewhere gotten the idea that every painting or drawing has to represent something. You could respond by saying, "You know, not every piece of art represents something. Sometimes art represents objects, people, or places the artist has seen or has dreamed about. Sometimes art represents feelings, and sometimes art is just art." You may not need to say anything else because the child may go away satisfied, even relieved. Or you might want to follow with, "Tell me about your drawing?" or " Tell me how you decided to use these colors?"

(Schirrmacher, 1986; Trawick-Smith, 1994).

Developing Advocacy Skills

Children's play with art and music is vital to their total development and therefore is an important issue to discuss with parents and administrators, especially when they have doubts about the value of these activities. However, some discussions become one-sided and defensive. When this happens, neither party gains a complete understanding of the issue, and both lose the opportunity to understand the differing perspectives and reach an amicable compromise. Strong advocates develop strong communication skills and the ability to formulate appropriate compromises.

Let us look at a specific example taken from *Early Childhood Training: Diversity* (Magna Systems, 1996). A young mother angrily approaches a preschool teacher with concern about all the time her child is spending "messing around" with Play-Doh and paint. The teacher immediately jumps in and defends the art curriculum by giving a theoretical explanation of the relationship between art and learning. When the teacher is finished, the young mother simply leaves, even more angry and frustrated. The teacher is also upset and feels that her hard work is not appreciated. In this example, the parent was never truly heard. The teacher assumed that the parent did not understand the value of art and play and therefore proceeded to try to convince the mother of its importance. Actually, the parent was concerned about the condition of the child's clothes and the statement it seemed to make about her parenting skills. This is a classic example of miscommunication: The first person begins to express an idea, opinion, or feeling; the other person, listens only briefly, makes assumptions regarding the perspective of the first, and reacts in a defensive manner.

If this mother had the opportunity to explain her concern thoroughly, she would have told the teacher that she was a single parent with little money and did not have easy access to a washer and dryer. Therefore, she could not keep her daughter's clothes clean. Furthermore, in her culture, keeping your children neat and clean was a sign of a good mother. Every day,

when she picked up her daughter from school, there were paint stains and blobs of dry Play-Doh stuck to her clothing. On days when the mother had to stop at the grocery store before going home, she would be embarrassed about the child's appearance as well as worried about getting her clothes clean and ready for the next day of school.

Good listening and communication require time, patience, and empathy. If the teacher had taken the parent aside, maybe to a quiet and comfortable place and even offered her a glass of water, the environment would have been more conducive to positive communication. The teacher could have focused on the mother and listened quietly and carefully. She could have asked the mother open-ended questions that would help her clarify her feelings and thoughts. Once the teacher saw clearly that the issue was not about art but about mess, she would have been able to offer useful suggestions that would lead to a compromise or solution that would satisfy everyone: the mother, the child, and the teacher. Perhaps the teacher could become more aware of when the child begins to play in the art area and make sure she wears a smock. When teachers take the time and expend the energy to truly listen to the concerns and perspectives of others, they find opportunities to make small compromises. Thus, they will be able to successfully advocate for children's right to play. Table 8.8 provides suggestions of activities that will help you refine your advocacy skills.

TABLE 8.8 Advocacy Activities: Informing and Involving Families and Administrators

	Listen and Seek Compromise	
Becoming Aware	*Furthering Your Understanding*	*Taking Action*
1. Visit several kindergarten classrooms. Observe how music and art are incorporated into daily activities. Compare what you observe with what you read in this chapter.	1. Read several early childhood journal articles concerning music and art in the classroom. Begin a file of possible art and music activities.	1. Develop a web of musical possibilities to accompany a theme study or project.
2. Repeat the above observation in a preschool or child care center. What differences do you find?	2. Visit an art museum and take a guided tour of the current exhibit. Develop a better understanding of the elements of art.	2. Volunteer in a classroom and assist in the art or music center.
3. Repeat observation in primary classrooms. Again compare the differences. Do you believe that any group you visited is missing valuable experiences? If so, why do you think this is happening?	3. Attend a concert where the musical genre is not familiar to you. What do you notice about the audience? About the musicians? Write about your experience.	3. Write a letter to parents explaining the difference between art, crafts, and artlike activities. 4. Volunteer in a classroom and assist a child with special needs in the art or music center. 5. Plan and present an appropriate music presentation for young children.
4. Interview a music or art specialist, or observe a specialist at work in a classroom. How is art or music different when presented by a specialist?	4. Observe children in a classroom art center or music center. Keep an anecdotal record of all their activities. Analyze your notes and list all the learning possibilities that took place in that center. 5. Review early childhood journals and collect art, craft, or artlike activities. Distinguish between the three.	6. Volunteer in a classroom and prepare a display of children's art work. 7. Make a poster depicting the elements of art and donate this to an early childhood classroom.

Summary

In early childhood classrooms, creativity and creative expression are not limited to one part of the curriculum or one area of the classroom but are expressed continually through the playful exploration of objects, language, and ideas in a risk-taking environment. In a psychologically safe, or risk-taking environment, children will feel free to invent, experiment, pretend, and explore ideas, symbols, and objects. Children in risk-taking environments do not feel pressured to conform to the ideas of others but can work and play without the risk of being wrong. Their ideas are accepted, valued, and supported by the adults in the environment. The foundation of a risk-taking environment lies in adults' interactions with children at work and play.

REVISITING FIRST IMPRESSIONS

Review your own list of creative endeavors. What insight do you have concerning how your own creativity was (or was not) nurtured and supported when you were a young child?

QUESTIONS FOR DISCUSSION

1. What is meant by the concept *risk-taking environment*? Describe ways teachers develop a risk-taking atmosphere.

2. Discuss how you would facilitate singing among preschool children, kindergarten children, and school-age children.

3. Your principal has asked you to have your class present three songs at the next Parent-Teacher Association meeting. Describe how you will respond to this request.

SUGGESTED READINGS

Hendrick, J. (Ed.). (1997). *First steps toward teaching the Reggio way.* Upper Saddle River, NJ: Merrill.
Isenberg, J., & Jalongo, M. (1997). *Creative expression and play in early childhood* (2nd ed.). Upper Saddle River, NJ: Prentice-Hall.
Schirrmacher, R. (1998). *Art and creative development for young children* (3rd ed.). Boston: Delmar.
Mayesky, M. (1998). *Creative activities for young children* (6th ed.). Boston: Delmar.

9 Fostering Language and Literacy through Playful Learning and Playful Teaching

Prereading Guide

First Impressions. Think back to your own introduction to reading and writing. At what ages do you recall beginning to read and write? How do you think young children begin learning to read and write? In your journal, describe how you believe young children develop literacy.

Revisit
Using a Learning Center System to Provide Opportunities for Playful Learning (Chapter 4)
Portfolio Assessment (Chapter 6)

Stories from the Field

Ms. Madden, a kindergarten teacher, is a firm believer in developmentally appropriate practice, and feels strongly that play should be a primary part of any instructional setting for young children. Yet her beliefs are sorely tested from time to time as she encounters parents, administrators, and even first-grade teachers who are concerned that her play-based classroom will not adequately prepare children for "real academic challenges," especially in the area of literacy. She explains:

> I know that the children in my classroom are learning! Even though I don't drill children on alphabet letters and phonic elements, I see them using letters and attending to sounds all the time. When a group of children were in a dramatic play center I had set up as a veterinary office, one of them gave me a receipt after taking care of my dog. I looked at the receipt and said, "I don't see here what you treated my dog for." So he took back the receipt and wrote, "RBES VXEN"—rabies vaccine! That's when I know that the minilessons we do on phonic elements are being used.
>
> Some of my colleagues seem to think that the only "real" reading and writing learning that occurs is in connection with their planned skills lessons and the basal reader and workbook activities that the children do. They don't really see the language and literacy skills children use as they play as being important

to their literacy development. I'm not saying that I don't teach strategy lessons, or that the children don't have access to workbook activities to practice what they've learned, but I see them making much more meaningful use of reading and writing strategies when they play and when they engage in projects.

Right now, the children are completing a project about construction. Two months ago, construction began on an empty lot across the street from our schoolyard. Every day, the children stood by the fence watching as dump trucks filled the lot, then bulldozers evened the fill, pile drivers laid pilings, and a cement truck poured the foundation for a new house. Their interest was sustained as the house began to be framed. They were fascinated and had all kinds of questions about the construction—what each of the machines did, how they worked, how the operator knew how deep to drive the pilings, how the crew knew where to leave spaces for doors and windows—on and on!

Out of that interest, a project was born. The children helped me write a class letter to the contractor asking if we could tour the house as it was being built. After our visit, they drew pictures and labeled pictures about their visit to make a book for our classroom library about construction. Many of the children used their own emerging phonics skills to sound out words. With my help, they each wrote notes to send to the contractor and the construction crew (along with a copy of our book) thanking them for letting us visit. They spent lots of time poring over books about construction equipment from our library, often marking pages that they wanted their friends to be sure to look at. As I listened to them sharing these books, and helped them think about what they wanted to write, I knew that they were beginning to read and write in ways that illustrate the emergent literacy anyone should expect to see from five- and six-year-olds.

While I'm sure that the children get a lot of information about reading and writing from lessons I do to help them develop literacy skills and knowledge, I believe it is their use of those skills for meaningful purposes that fosters their dispositions to use print for their own purposes. While they were immersed in their projects, the block center and the outdoor play spaces became construction zones. The children wrote warning signs, they made construction plans, and they drew up receipts for lumber and roofing tiles—you name it! It's clear that they don't just want to learn *about* reading and writing; they want to *use* their literacy knowledge all the time.

Developing Language and Literacy through Play: Revisiting Cognitive Theory

Ms. Madden's comments about how her colleagues view her approach to literacy suggest that she is encountering the dichotomous views of play discussed in Chapter 1. The teachers who criticize the time she allows for play seem to believe that learning time and play time are entirely separate and have no common goals. The critics of her program apparently fail to recognize that play can offer children opportunities to make meaningful use of language and literacy knowledge and skills. They are overlooking the unifying quality of play that enables it to unite and integrate the socioemotional, motor, and cognitive aspects of learning and development (Nachmanovitch, 1990; Van Hoorn, Nourot, Scales, & Alward, 1993).

Yet cognitive theorists have demonstrated conclusively that as children play they are significantly engaged in sophisticated cognitive learning. Piaget's (1962) cognitive-developmental perspective posits that children actively create knowledge as they play by practicing what they know and by testing new ideas and behaviors. Vygotsky's (1978) socio-cultural theory further suggests that play promotes language development and consequently the development of thought itself. As children experiment with meanings and objects, they incorporate language and symbols into their play. Thus, one of the greatest benefits of play is its contribution to children's language development, which is a critical component of their literacy learning.

Language and Literacy Connections

Although many view literacy learning as the mastery of discrete elements of written language such as letter names, phonic elements, and sight words, literacy researchers widely accept that literacy learning is actually *language* learning. (Goodman, 1980, 1986; Harste, Woodward & Burke, 1984; Snow, 1983, 1991). Literacy theorists maintain that oral language development is critical to literacy development because learning to read and write—to use written language—is simply an extension of oral language learning.

Language Learning

There is no need for children to learn discrete aspects of oral language in a predetermined sequence. Language theorists point out that children learn language quite naturally if they are immersed in a *language-rich environment.* When children are surrounded by language, they naturally learn its critical aspects—its sound system, the rules that govern it, its meanings, and its usage.

The key to a language-rich environment, in addition to surrounding children with language, is *language interaction.* For language to develop, children must be surrounded by it and *encouraged to use it.* They must have good language models so that they can internalize all aspects of the language they hear. Most important, they must be given the opportunity to experiment with language and test out their hypotheses about how language works. Children learn to communicate orally by listening to language, by imitating the language models around them, and by experimenting and playing with language as they infer the rules that govern it (Halliday, 1975).

That children do infer how language works can be seen in the following typical exchange between a three-year-old and her preschool teacher when her blocks were knocked down.

EMILY: Blocks!

TEACHER: Oh, your blocks fell down!

EMILY: Blocks falled down.

If oral language were purely a result of imitation, Emily would not have substituted the word "falled" for her teacher's word "fell." She did so because her experience with language suggested to her that the way to indicate past tense is to add a /d/ or /t/ sound at the ends of words. Although nobody had taught this three-year-old the syntactic rules governing past versus present tense, she had correctly extracted them from the language around her. Given many more language interactions like the one described above, Emily is just as likely to infer that there are exceptions to the past-tense rule; "fell" will naturally replace "falled" as she continues to refine her understanding of how language works.

Learning Language through Play

Classroom opportunities for play are ideally suited to facilitating interactions that will contribute to children's language learning (Levy, Wolfgang & Koorland, 1992; Morrow & Rand, 1991; Neuman & Roskos, 1992; Vukelich, 1990, 1991, 1994). The more children interact with each other, the more they talk. Dramatic play, in particular, requires children to talk with each other. They must use language to establish a common theme for their pretend scenarios, and they regularly describe what they are doing and what different props represent in order to extend the drama. Because so much of dramatic play is pretend, language is the only way a theme can be shared. Notice the manner in which talk facilitates the dramatic play of two four-year-olds in a housekeeping center.

EDWARD: I'm the daddy now. I have to fix breakfast for you. You're the little girl.

KEESHA: I'm not the little girl. I'm the wife.

EDWARD: But daddies don't fix breakfast for wifes.

KEESHA: My daddy fixes breakfast for everybody. I'm going to be the mommy. Do you want me to cook the breakfast?

EDWARD: I'll cook the breakfast for everybody. That place can be for our little girl. (He sets out three empty dishes, and pretends to spoon food into them.) Here's some eggs for you and some for Megan (the imaginary little girl).

KEESHA: Megan's crying. She doesn't like eggs. I'll fix her some pancakes.

In this scenario, the two children used language to establish the roles they were playing, to discuss the expected behavior for the roles, and to describe their actions and those of an imaginary participant. This pretend play episode could not have been sustained and mutually enjoyed by the two children had they not used language. What should be clear is that the more opportunities children have to engage in free-flowing play interactions with each other, the more incentive they will have to use their developing language.

Although much of the literature on children's language learning addresses its occurrence in the context of dramatic play, as seen in the preceding episode, language is also facilitated as children engage in other types of play. Children's *functional* or *practice play* offers many opportunities for engagement with language. One teacher, observing two-year-old Max repeatedly filling a cup with sand and then pouring it out, commented to him as he played, "You're filling it up and dumping it out. Fill it up, dump it out. Fill it up, dump it out." The child quickly began to chant, "Fill up, dump out," as he continued scooping and pouring. A few days later, the teacher introduced the concept of *empty* as Max engaged in similar play. As he poured out the sand, she remarked, "Oh, now your cup is empty!" Max looked in his cup and repeated, "Empty." Within the next few days, she heard Max using the word *empty* repeatedly in the sandbox. In this way, the language to describe his practice play was supplied, and he quite naturally began to use it on his own, illustrating how play can extend and expand children's semantic development.

Children's *constructive play* also provides teachers with opportunities to extend and support children's language. Young children playing in a block center are quite likely to describe to other children or to the teacher what they are building. Sometimes a simple statement demonstrating the teacher's interest in a construction is all that is needed to elicit verbalization from its builder. A simple, "Look how tall that is! I like the way you're building that," will often elicit a long description of what is being built and how it will be used. At other times, the teacher may need to be more direct, saying, "That looks really interesting. Can you tell me about it?" These language opportunities are as important for the three-year-old building with large waffle blocks as they are for the second grader shaping a papier-mâché model of a beehive in conjunction with a science exploration of bees.

Games with rules are especially conducive to language use for children who are experienced enough to play them. Every game with rules requires children to come to a shared understanding of how the game will be played. Often significant negotiation among players is needed when children have differing interpretations of particular rules; this negotiation always entails discussion and explanation of points of view. More language may be used when differences cannot be resolved, and the children turn to an adult referee.

Thus, most play experiences encourage language use and development. The effectiveness of play experiences for developing language may be weakened, however, if children are not allowed to adequately sustain individual play episodes. As noted in Chapter 4, children's language and learning is optimized when play episodes are allowed to continue for a minimum of twenty to thirty minutes. This length of time is particularly necessary for children to develop the elaborate scripts that invite intentional use of language and literacy (Christie, Johnsen, & Peckover, 1988). When children are allowed only brief play periods or are hurried from one center to another, they lose valuable opportunities to develop strong oral language skills. A schedule that ensures that children can engage in lengthy play sessions is necessary to adequately facilitate language development.

Literacy Development

Just as children naturally learn oral language—receptively as they come to recognize and understand what people say to them, and expressively as they attempt to verbalize their own ideas—they also learn to understand and use written language. They learn by observing the writing around them, hypothesizing about how it is used, and attempting to use it themselves (Anbar, 1986; Bissex, 1980; Ehri & Sweet, 1991; Galda, Cullinan, & Strickland, 1997; Snow, 1991; and Sulzby & Teale, 1991).

Those who believe in this natural acquisition of written language knowledge have used the term *emergent literacy* (Clay, 1966; Teale & Sulzby, 1986) to describe the process. Emergent literacy theorists emphasize that children's knowledge and use of written language emerges over time, much like their knowledge and use of oral language, as children are immersed in *print-rich environments* and encouraged to explore the ways written symbols can be used. They naturally construct their own models of how written language works. These models incorporate their evolving beliefs about the forms of written language, the meanings that it has, the connections between its meanings and form, and the functions it serves (McGee & Richgels, 1996).

Given sufficient exposure to print, children gradually begin to recognize many aspects of its *form.* While playing with cookbooks in a housekeeping center, they may notice that print appears as squiggly lines across a page. As they experiment with print then, their own "writing"—of recipes, menus for family meals, and grocery lists in the pretend kitchen— takes the form of linear scribbles. Soon, they discover that those lines are actually composed of individual symbols. At that point, their own writing begins to include discrete symbols that may or may not be actual alphabet letters. As their attention to print increases, children finally begin to use the real alphabet almost exclusively.

At the same time children are learning about the forms that writing takes, they are also growing in understanding of *meanings* attached to written language and the *functions* that print serves. When children are first exposed to picture books, for example, they are likely to believe that the pictures tell the story. They may not even notice the print on the page. As they gain experience with books, particularly as they notice that adults do attend to the print, children come to recognize that the written words on the page also hold meaning. Further recognition of print in their environments leads children to understand that, in addition to telling stories in books, written language serves a variety of functions, such as reminding adults what to buy at the grocery, telling them what ingredients to put into a cake mix, and communicating with family and friends who live far away. Their pretend play will begin to incorporate writing to serve many of these same purposes.

As they simultaneously develop knowledge about the forms, meanings, and functions of written language, children also grapple with learning the connections between meaning and form. To achieve conventional literacy, children must understand how meaning is connected to various forms of writing. In a pretend shoe store, they begin to use different forms of writing for shoe styles, colors, and sizes, recognizing that letters are needed for the first two, whereas numbers must be used for the last. They also move from early beliefs that words are composed of random letters to an understanding that letters are most often chosen to represent the sounds heard in words. Like other aspects of literacy, these *meaning–form links* are best learned through exploration and discovery, as children attempt to use print for their own purposes. Table 9.1 offers examples of the knowledge in each of these areas that children typically develop at different ages.

Learning Literacy through Play

A playful classroom offers many opportunities for children to discover all of these aspects of literacy. The key is to plant opportunities for literacy exploration throughout the classroom while infusing the curriculum with routines that foster attention to language, both oral and written (Christie, 1991). This does not mean trying to teach new concepts about language by filling the day with worksheets that focus children on discrete aspects such as form. Although worksheets may have a limited place in the literacy curriculum—for example, by offering a choice for practicing skills that have already been introduced—they are rarely effective for younger children who are just being exposed to new concepts and may even displace children's time and attention to more authentic exploration of language. Instead, infusing the curriculum with routines that foster attention to language means encouraging children to bring active, authentic language use into their play and center activities, and into their structured explorations of themes and projects.

To effectively interweave literacy and language into children's play, teachers must be aware of the literacy goals that are appropriate for children at different ages. The International Reading Association and the National Association for the Education of Young Children have published a joint statement on early literacy learning and teaching that describes benchmarks for literacy achievement from prekindergarten through third grade (IRA/NAEYC, 1998). The National Committee on the Prevention of Reading Difficulties in Young Children has constructed a similar list of typical literacy accomplishments for children in kindergarten through

TABLE 9.1   Four Aspects of Written Language Knowledge

Meaning

Develops concepts about language (birth–3 years)

Knows book sharing routines (birth–3 years)

Knows that print conveys meaning (3–5 years)

Assigns meaning to environmental print (3–5 years)

Intends to communicate in writing (3–5 years)

Constructs meaning from text (3–5 years)

Understands specialized literary language (e.g., literary syntax, alliteration, and letter-writing conventions) (6–8 years)

Form

Recognizes the alphabet as a special set of written signs (birth–3 years)

Learns alphabet letter names and formations (3–5 years)

Learns letter features (3–5 years)

Uses variety of text features to construct different texts (3–5 years)

Develops concept of spoken and written words (6–8 years)

Develops concept of word boundaries (6–8 years)

Uses different strategies (e.g., copying, asking for spellings, dictating, and invented spelling) to construct text (6–8 years)

Meaning–Form Links

Makes symbols (birth–3 years)

Differentiates pictures from print (3–5 years)

Pays attention to print (3–5 years)

Matches segments of printed text with segments of spoken text (although not always accurately) (3–5 years)

Develops beginnings of phonological awareness (3–5 years)

Develops phonemic awareness (6–8 years)

Uses letter–sound relationships for emergent reading (6–8 years)

Function

Sees drawing and sharing books as pleasurable activities (birth–3 years)

Uses writing to label pictures (3–5 years)

Uses reading and writing in play (3–5 years)

Uses reading and writing to interact with others (3–5 years)

Uses writing to create imaginary story world (3–5 years)

Reads and writes to experiment with written language (6–8 years)

Understands that written language is precise (6–8 years)

Adapted from McGee and Richgels (1996).

third grade (Snow, Burns, & Griffin, 1998). Both groups caution that not all children can be expected to achieve these goals at the same time.

> A continuum of reading and writing development is useful for identifying challenging but achievable goals or benchmarks for children's literacy learning, remembering that individual variation is to be expected and supported. . . . Teachers must set developmentally appropriate literacy goals for young children and then adapt instructional strategies for children whose learning and development are advanced or lag behind those goals. (IRA/NAEYC, 1998, p. 39)

Knowledge of literacy goals for young children enables teachers to make informed choices about materials, activities, and play opportunities that are effective and appropriate for each child. Snow, Burns, and Griffin (1998) state that a goal for kindergarten children is "Retells, reenacts, or dramatizes stories or parts of stories" (p. 80). A teacher who knows this may decide to set up a flannel board with cutouts of three goats, an ogre, and a bridge for children's use after they have read "The Three Billy Goats Gruff" together. She may also choose to sit under the bridge on an outdoor play structure imitating an ogre as children trip-trap above her, until the children themselves assume all of the relevant roles. The language use and literary retellings that evolve from this play will be much more meaningful to children than retellings that are elicited during a question-and-answer period after the reading because they are self-motivated and therefore authentic.

Authentic uses of print can be readily observed across many areas of the classroom. When a housekeeping center is well stocked with memo pads, blank recipe cards, and telephone message pads, for example, children will naturally incorporate the writing and reading of notes, grocery lists, recipes, and phone messages into their pretend play. This is especially likely to happen if the teacher joins in children's play and demonstrates how they might incorporate reading and writing into it. As they play, children will experiment with various forms of writing and interact with each other regarding their knowledge of written language.

This is exactly what happened when one teacher pretended to write down a phone message for a child in the housekeeping area of her nursery school classroom. The following exchange took place between two four-year-olds when the teacher moved away from the telephone and Brandon picked it up:

> **BRANDON:**   (handing a note to Jessica) You got a phone call. Here's a message.
>
> **JESSICA:**   (scanning the note) But there's no phone number. How can I call?
>
> **BRANDON:**   (pointing to a string of random letters) Here's the phone number. That's what you call.
>
> **JESSICA:**   No. That's letters. A phone number has to have, uhm, like 1s, 2s, and 3s. Like this. (She quickly adds a string of five numbers.) This is the phone number. I'll call now. I think it's my little girl.

This brief interaction, woven seamlessly by the children themselves into an episode of pretend play, led to an exploration of the difference between numbers and letters and perhaps a new understanding on Brandon's part that numbers take a different form and serve a different function than letters. Both children experimented with written language to extend the oral language involved in taking and relaying phone messages. It is also likely that the inclusion of a memo pad near the telephone prompted the children to use it more consistently in their play, thus stimulating more oral and written language than might have been the case without that prop.

Incorporating appropriate writing materials into other centers stimulates similar explorations and interactions with both oral and written language. A dramatic play center serving as an airport, for example, can be equipped with ticket forms, luggage tags, a board on which to post departure and arrival times, and credit card receipts. The block center can be stocked with materials for sign-making and paper for drawing and labeling blueprints for buildings. A music area may have a music stand and sheet music with lyrics that the children can pretend to read, as well as blank notation paper that might encourage children to create their own sheet music. Regardless of the type of center, children can be encouraged to experiment with written language while they play through the careful selection of props that stimulate attention to print, and through teachers' demonstrations of how these props can be used (Morrow & Rand, 1991; Vukelich, 1991).

Literacy Centers

Although infusing play-based centers with opportunities for children to use writing stimulates literacy learning, children also need more direct opportunities to learn about written language.

Thus, every classroom should be equipped with literacy-related centers. These include both the library center and the writing center.

The Library Center

The library should be an especially inviting area of the classroom. Teachers need to select a variety of books likely to appeal to the diverse range of abilities and interests represented in the classroom. Teachers should interact with children in the library center to engage children in exploration of age-appropriate books that span many genres, encompassing everything from fairy tales to nonfiction. Although many teachers and parents believe that children are more interested in stories than informational books, an explosion of nonfiction picture books in recent years attests to the insatiable demand children have for books about things that interest them. In many classrooms, informational books are the ones children seek out most often. Teachers can encourage this interest by engaging children with informational books related to ongoing themes and projects.

In addition to ensuring children's access to books representing a wide variety of genres, teachers must also carefully screen books to be sure that the collection offers a fair representation of issues related to gender, race, and class. The collection should be multicultural, with titles representing the literature and characters of varied ethnic and cultural groups. Care should be taken to screen out those books that offer broadly stereotypical or offensive depictions of any ethnic group, either in the stories or their illustrations. A balance in the depiction of roles assumed by characters of each gender portrayed in stories should be sought. Table 9.2 includes an overview of a classroom library center.

TABLE 9.2 The Library Center

Space Requirements	**Examples of Basic Learning Opportunities**
Fairly confined area	Language and concept development
Bookshelves at children's level, including one that can display books flat with covers facing outward	Awareness of print in books
	Understanding of story structure
Small bins to hold books	Comprehension of stories
Comfortable seating—pillows, bean bag chairs, carpet squares, etc.	Identification with characters' feelings and actions
	Word recognition and identification
Basic Materials	**Examples of Extensions**
Age-appropriate books—concept books, wordless picture books, predictable books (with repetitive text or text that closely matches pictures), informational picture books, easy chapter books, etc.	Dramatic play
	■ reenacting stories
	■ books related to dramatic play center themes
Books that represent a variety of genres—fairy tales, folktales, nursery rhymes, nonfiction, songbooks, realistic fiction, etc.	Themes and Projects
	■ reference books and informational picture books
Storytelling props—flannel boards with cutouts of book characters, puppets, dress-up clothes, etc.	■ storybooks
Tape player with headphones and audiobooks	
CD-ROM interactive storybooks	

The Writing Center

In addition to providing a good library center, teachers should also include space and materials for children to experiment with writing. One way to do this is by providing a writing center in which children are allowed to play with writing. The youngest children often "write" using broad scribbles befitting their level of fine motor development and their definition of writing. For many young children, writing is defined as simply putting marks on paper (or any other appealing surface). Their scribbles are similar to an infant's babbling. Just as an infant babbles to experiment with the sounds he or she can make, taking pleasure in repetition as well as variety, so do novice writers delight in discovering the infinite combination of marks that can be made and find satisfaction in gaining sufficient control to deliberately repeat the same marks intentionally. Thus, for the youngest children, writing takes on characteristics of both exploratory and practice play (Bissex, 1980; Clay, 1975). A good writing area solicits and encourages this playful exploration and practice.

As children gain a more conventional sense of writing, their products begin to include letterlike forms and eventually real letters, either in invented spellings or conventionally spelled words. Teachers can structure activities in the center to facilitate more direct exploration of the alphabet that will bring about the use of letters. A display of the alphabet is especially helpful to those children who are ready to experiment with conventional print. Children will also experiment with the alphabet if stamps or stencils of letters are provided. Many children enjoy manipulating magnetic letters; after forming words that interest them, some children attempt to copy their words onto paper to preserve them (Casbergue, 1998; McGee & Richgels, 1996).

Teachers can encourage primary-grade children to use the writing center for more than simply experimenting with print. Children at this age are likely to seek out the materials in the center to facilitate the writing they want to produce to support their exploration of themes and their project work. In addition to the exploratory and practice play that preschool and kindergarten children engage in at the writing area, these children immerse themselves in construction—the creation of a piece of writing that will serve a specific and personal purpose (Calkins, 1994; Tompkins, 1997). Table 9.3 offers an overview of a typical writing center.

Technology to Support Reading and Writing

Both the library and writing centers can be enhanced by interweaving technology with more traditional materials. Following are some means of using technology to facilitate children's literacy development.

■ Provide audiotapes to accompany printed texts. Ideally, a listening area within the library center should be equipped with a tape player that can accommodate at least two sets of earphones so that children can listen to the same book together, taking turns following print and turning pages.

■ Provide CD-ROM interactive storybooks. Individual copies of interactive storybooks are readily available at book stores and computer software outlets. Some publishers have compiled sets of interactive CD-ROM books specifically for classroom use. These include Broderbund's *Living Books Framework,* Computer Curriculum Corporations's *Discover English*

TABLE 9.3   The Writing Center

Space Requirements
Area with tables for individual children and
    small groups
Set aside from noisy areas

Basic Materials
Paper of different textures and sizes
Variety of writing implements—pencils, pens,
    washable markers (thick and fine point),
    crayons, chalk, etc.
Eye-level display of alphabet
Letter stamps and stencils
Magnetic letters
Displays of project and theme related words
    (word wall)
Books related to themes and projects
Age-appropriate word processing program(s)

Examples of Basic Learning Opportunities
Concepts about print
Concepts about letter–sound connections
Functions of writing
Strategies for conveying meaning
Strategies for spelling
Ability to compose
Basic research skills (locating and organizing information)

Examples of Extensions
Dramatic Play
- making signs
- making props (menus, receipts, etc.)

Themes and Projects
- informational writing
- letters and thank you notes
- child-constructed books related to theme or project

Blocks
- labels for constructions
- signs for buildings and streets
- plans for construction

(PreKindergarten–Kindergarten) and *First Adventures* (grades 1–3), and Scholastic's *Wiggle-Works: Beginning Literacy System* (Tompkins, 1997).

- Use sets like those mentioned previously to allow children to create their own versions of storybooks. Programs such as *WiggleWorks* often include a feature that presents a series of pictures in a format similar to wordless picture books. Children are invited to supply the text for each picture. Experiences sharing wordless picture books with teachers and friends will lead quite naturally to children constructing their own picture books from these programs. The books children create can then be printed and added to the classroom library.

- Provide simple word processing programs to encourage children to write (Labbo, 1998). For the youngest children, typing may be random and no more than a simple playful exploration of how a keyboard works. Once children have experimented enough with writing to become more intentional in their efforts, they will attempt composition. In many respects, children's writing attempts reflect the level of writing they engage in with paper and pencil, although by the ages of six or seven, they may produce lengthier pieces with a word processor (Cochran-Smith, Kahn, & Paris, 1988; DeGroff, 1990).

Table 9.4 provides criteria that can be used to select interactive storybooks for young children. Table 9.5 provides guidelines for selecting age-appropriate word processing programs.

TABLE 9.4   Criteria for Selecting Interactive Storybooks

1. Select titles that are true replicas of original books widely recognized by children. The text should be unabridged, and all of the original illustrations should be included.

2. Some programs function like audiobooks, reading the text to the children as they follow along, and highlighting each word as it is read, thus helping children make a connection between the stories they are hearing and the print itself. Select these books based on the extent to which the highlighting is able to keep pace with a normal, fluent reading. Teachers should reject any CD-ROM book in which the oral reading is significantly slowed or otherwise unnatural.

3. Select interactive storybooks in light of the kinds of interactions with the book that are encouraged. The best interactive books encourage children to extend their experience of a story by exploring the *language* on each page, or by encouraging children to compose alternative texts to accompany the same or similar illustrations. Less useful interactions are those that focus children's attention on discrete aspects of illustrations (such as clicking the mouse on a picture hanging on the wall to make it fall down, and then clicking again to move it back into place) that are not at all relevant to the story itself. In some interactions, the activities in which children engage have little to do with reading, and in fact divert children's attention away from the language and print of the story.

TABLE 9.5   Guidelines for Selecting Word Processing Programs

1. Make sure that their features are easy to use. Large fonts should be available so that children can easily see what they have written and find portions of the text that they want to revise. These fonts will also help call children's attention to features of print.

2. Check to see that ancillary features are simple enough that children can use them independently once they have been taught basic procedures. Commands for printing, saving, and retrieving documents should be uncomplicated, preferably signaled with icons as well as words.

3. Examine the programs' spellchecking features. Although correct spelling should *not* be the goal of exploratory writing for preschool, kindergarten, or even some first-grade children, by second or third grade, many children will want to produce conventional spellings (IRA/NAEYC, 1998). Some spellchecking programs are much better at recognizing children's emergent spellings than are others. When deciding which word processing program to introduce to children, a teacher should first try typing in some common invented spellings to determine how they are handled by the spellchecking feature.

The following are examples of word processing programs that young children find especially appealing; each is intended for use by children from kindergarten through second or third grade.

Bank Street Prewriter
Scholastic
555 Broadway
New York, NY 10012

FirstWriter
Houghton Mifflin
One Beacon Street
Boston, MA 02108

Print Shop Deluxe
Broderbund Software
P.O. Box 6125
Novato, CA 94948

Children's Writing and Publishing Center
The Learning Company
6493 Kaiser Drive
Freemont, CA 94555

Magic Slate
Sunburst Communications
39 Washington Street
Pleasantville, NY 10570

Writing Center
The Learning Company
6493 Kaiser Drive
Freemont, CA 94555

The Teacher's Role in Maintaining an Emergent Literacy Perspective

As is true for all other areas of the curriculum, teachers and children are encouraged to approach language and literacy playfully. Children's language and literacy knowledge and skills, as well as their dispositions to use those skills develop best when the children interact with print and with each other, exploring, hypothesizing, and creating their own uses for written language. Children must be able to *play* with language. As discussed throughout this book, children's play can take the form of free play, guided play, or directed play, depending on the teacher's level of control or interaction with the children. Think back to Ms. Madden's description of the ways her children demonstrated literacy knowledge, skills, and dispositions while engaging in playful activities in her classroom. They readily used their emerging knowledge of written language to independently incorporate writing into their dramatic play, an example of literacy in the context of free play. They used both oral and written language to further their investigation of a project that grew out of their fascination with construction. When Ms. Madden provided materials in the library and writing centers that encouraged children to relate their independent reading and writing to project themes, they were engaged in guided play. As they collaborated—with each other and with Ms. Madden—to produce a book that became a valued addition to their classroom library, they were engaged in more directed playful activity. Because the children were engaged in language use for their own purposes, they were invited to construct their own knowledge about critical aspects of language.

Although children's approach to language used for play and project activities like those described by Ms. Madden is quite naturally constructivist, it is important to keep in mind that even directed activities in the literacy centers also need to reflect children's emerging understanding of how written language works. Teachers must not attempt to force children to interact with print in ways that are too cognitively advanced or far outside of the concepts about language that children have constructed based on their language experiences. For example, expecting that all children who visit the writing center will be able to trace lines of letters or produce conventionally written stories or even sentences that resemble those of adults is unreasonable and inappropriate, given the range of development typically seen in classrooms for young children and the goals that have been determined to be developmentally appropriate for individual young children (IRA/NAEYC, 1998). By the same criteria, it is equally unreasonable to expect all children to read books conventionally. For many children, the fun of books is in the pictures, in the sometimes boisterous sharing of stories with friends, and in the translation of stories into new spin-offs related with puppets or acted out in a dramatic play center.

A playful and developmentally appropriate approach to early language and literacy development requires that teachers follow the lead of the children they teach. A teacher who implements a constructivist approach to language and literacy will support children's efforts to use language in meaningful ways while keeping in mind the broad goals appropriate for children in different phases of their development and nudging children toward achieving those goals. The teacher's role must also include careful *planning* for language and literacy learning, actively *engaging* children in the use of oral and written language, and *accounting* for the language and literacy learning that occurs during classroom activities.

Planning for Children's Language and Literacy Learning

Planning a classroom environment that supports and extends children's language and literacy learning entails designing classroom centers, theme studies, and projects so that they incorporate both oral and written language. A significant part of teachers' planning is their careful selection of materials that optimize children's language and literacy learning. A variety of materials that can accommodate the disparate needs of all the children in the class will enable teachers to better support children's learning. Materials should be carefully chosen to ensure that all children will have opportunities to learn from their play. For language and literacy development, this means selecting books appropriate for independent use and shared exploration, and selecting materials for all centers that will encourage experimentation with oral and written language.

In a kindergarten classroom, for example, some children are likely to enjoy books, and indeed "read" them, by looking at pictures and naming the things they see on each page. They may not yet be aware of the connection between print and the concepts illustrated. Other children in the same classroom, however, understand the function print serves, and are well aware of its presence in books. Although they are likely to "read" the stories by using the pictures, they may also run their fingers underneath the print as they pretend to read like grown-ups. Some children may arrive for kindergarten ready to read conventionally—that is, by using strategies such as phonics and context to read the words printed on the page just as competent, independent adult readers do. Teachers at any level are likely to encounter a similar range in children's developmental approaches to reading.

To ensure that each of these groups of children is appropriately challenged, a teacher must select books that enable all children to find what best suits their needs. When Ms. Madden's children undertook their investigation of construction sites, she collected informational picture books about construction, construction equipment, and construction-related professions and placed them in the writing center to help children as they composed pages for their own book. Some were simple picture books, whereas others were structured more like encyclopedias for young children. The key to children's success with the books was Ms. Madden's awareness of what was right for each child based on that child's experience and development.

Engaging Children in Oral and Written Language

Once teachers have planned for classroom themes, projects, and centers and carefully selected appropriate materials, their role must become that of an active participant in children's language and literacy learning. Language and literacy occur, not as a result of solitary exploration of things in the classroom environment, but from the rich interactions that should infuse every part of the curriculum.

For this reason, it is imperative for teachers to foster a classroom culture that values and promotes the social construction of language and literacy knowledge. In such a classroom, children understand that their play with each other and with their teacher is important, and they expect that they will explore and learn together. If teachers provide time for play but remain outside of it, interacting with children only when they are engaged in more traditional academic pursuits, children will not view their own play as valuable. The best way for teachers to demonstrate and reinforce the ideas that play is important and that the social construction of knowledge is valued is to take an active role in it.

Teachers who wish to foster language and literacy knowledge, skills, and dispositions in young children move beyond planning and providing materials to facilitating this development by engaging children in language use and interacting with them in ways that scaffold their learning. *Scaffolding* refers to an adult's structuring of a task so that it is both challenging enough to prompt new learning and simple enough that a child can achieve success with adult assistance (Cazden, 1988). Scaffolding is a critically important aspect of the teacher's role in playfully engaging children in multiple uses of language (Snow, Burns, & Griffin, 1998). Teachers engage in scaffolding whenever they make decisions about what they will have children do based on the children's current capabilities and the capabilities required for successful completion of the task. In a classroom for young children, teachers scaffold children's learning by structuring their own interactions with children to provide just the right amount of assistance to reinforce and extend children's learning.

In terms of language and literacy development, teachers' assistance may take many forms. It can entail simply providing language to accompany play, encouraging verbalization and written language attempts, elaborating on those attempts, and structuring interactions with print.

Providing Language to Accompany Play.   Vygotsky theorizes that language is critical to *all* learning and that without language, there can be no thought (1962). Accordingly, children will not truly have a concept such as *empty,* for example, until they have the word *empty* at their disposal, no matter how much experience they have filling up and emptying out containers, as we saw Max doing earlier in this chapter.

Thus, as a teacher observes two preschoolers playing in a sandbox, she or he may comment, "You've filled that bucket all the way to the top. It's really full! And this one is only half full. Are you going to fill it up too? Or do you just need half a bucketful of sand?" This quick interaction serves to introduce or reinforce the concepts of *full* and *half* to the children. As they hear these terms used consistently over time in response to their play, they will quickly incorporate them into their own sandbox conversations, and will eventually expand the concepts of *full* and *half full* to other contexts. Then they will be well on their way to learning both the underlying concepts and the words to talk about those concepts. This learning will be solidified with repeated modeling and reinforcement of new language and concepts.

In a similar vein, a teacher who notices two children during free-play time in the writing center making signs to help locate a lost cat may comment on their efforts in ways that provide words for written language concepts. As they are writing, he or she may say, "I see you wrote 'LOST CAT' in really big capital letters. That will help people notice your sign. You may want to put spaces between the words 'black and white' so people can read it more easily." Repeated interactions of this kind supply new vocabulary and reinforce understanding of concepts such as capital letters, words, and spacing.

Encouraging Verbalization and Written Language Attempts.   Children are not simply receptors of teachers' language. As suggested by the sandbox example earlier, children's mastery of language is best facilitated when they use it themselves. Teachers can play a significant role in making sure that children's language and literacy develop by encouraging them to verbalize and to experiment with print. As they observe children playing quietly in the block area, for example, teachers can ask them to describe what they are doing. This is especially important for young children who may still be likely to engage in parallel play, not truly interacting with other children who are also playing in the same area.

Many children may benefit from regular encouragement to use language. One teacher in a nursery school classroom for four-year-olds regularly admonished her charges to "use words" to get what they wanted and to settle differences. When she noticed two children shoving each other out of the way as they tried to get tricycles onto the bike path in the playground, she asked them, "What's wrong here? Can you find a way to use words to settle this?" Later, when a child responded by pointing when asked what kind of markers he wanted to use, she encouraged him to "tell me with words" before handing him his selection.

Similarly, teachers can encourage children to use written language. When children draw and then describe their pictures, they can be encouraged to write labels for them. Older children can be encouraged to make use of environmental print or to listen for sounds in words when they ask how to spell words they want to use during their play.

Teachers can also encourage children to attempt to experiment with reading on their own. Placing a small bin of books near a dramatic play area with baby dolls and doll furniture will invite many children to "read" bedtime stories to their babies. Depending on the age and reading experience of the children, their reading may take the form of talking about pictures, making up their own versions of stories, reciting text from memory, or actually reading the print (Sulzby, 1985).

Independent reading attempts can also be prompted by leaving group-constructed language experience stories, familiar big books, and favorite poems or songs on chart paper in places that are easily accessible for children's use during their free-play time. When these materials are available, it is not at all unusual to see small groups of children gathered around them, often taking turns playing teacher and pointing to print while others read.

Elaborating on Children's Oral and Written Language Attempts.   Teachers can also assist children's language development by routinely elaborating on their verbalizations and attempts to use written language. In an interchange between Jonathan, age three, and his preschool teacher, the child opened a conversation with the simple lament, "Bubbles!" when his container was accidently knocked over. His teacher elaborated on that simple statement by acknowledging what the child said, and adding to it, saying, "Oh, your bubble soap spilled. Let's clean it up. We can get you some more bubble soap." Jonathan then held out his container and said, "Bubbles spilled. More bubbles." Thus, his teacher's elaboration prompted Jonathan to extend his own language and use words for two additional concepts—*spill* and *more*. Regular elaboration of this type will increase children's language learning and use by modeling more complex sentence structures and by providing additional vocabulary.

Teachers can also extend and elaborate children's written language. Young children may fill a page with print without actually intending for it to mean anything. When this happens, teachers can extend children's concept of the function of print by *ascribing intentionality* and asking them what they have written. Regular prompts to "Tell me what that says" solidify the concept that print carries meaning, and will result in children beginning to "romance" their writing by making up messages after the fact to accompany their writing (Gardner, 1980).

Children who are reading and writing more conventionally also benefit from teachers' efforts to extend their attempts. A good example is the response of one second-grade teacher who noticed that two children were spending a good portion of their time in the writing center drawing pictures of sea creatures and writing simple facts about the animals to accompany each picture. The class had just completed a theme study of oceans, and the teacher suggested to the two children that other students would probably be interested in what they were doing. "It would be great if you made these into a book so that everyone could share it," she told them. It had not occurred to the children to do so, and that idea quickly led them to create more pages, construct a table of contents, and check out information about bookbinding from the school library for guidance in finishing their own book.

Structuring Interactions with Print.   Another way a teacher can actively engage children in language use is by structuring their interactions with the print that is in the classroom. Simply offering concept books, for example, will not guarantee that children will begin to attend to print in meaningful ways. Teachers needs to share these books with individual children, pointing out the print and inviting them to try to guess what it says. Teachers should point out specific features of the print to some children, calling their attention to letter–sound connections, for instance, as they begin to attend to print. Thus, when a child guesses that the word printed beneath a picture of a gorilla says "monkey," the teacher can respond by saying, "That's a good guess. It looks like a monkey. But monkey starts with M and this is a G. Do you know a word for a kind of monkey that starts with G?" In this way, the child is drawn beyond his or her accustomed way of reading concept books. The teacher raises the stakes by encouraging him or her to begin attending to initial sounds in words to try reading words printed on the pages of the book. The teacher provides extensive support to ensure that the child can do so, and thus scaffolds his or her learning.

The same kind of interactions should regularly occur across all areas of the classroom. As a teacher notices children constructing a list of menu items available in their pretend restaurant, for example, she or he might playfully suggest to the children that a menu should include prices and quickly demonstrate how the symbols used for money are written, perhaps writing "50¢" or ".50" beside the item written as "PTATOA CHPS" on the children's menu, then leaving them to determine and write down prices for the remaining items. Later, she or he may place a calculator in the dramatic play area, and suggest to children that they might want to add up purchases and write out bills to hand to restaurant customers. Through repeated interactions like these, the teacher extends children's play to stretch their understanding of written symbols and encourage the use of more sophisticated language than they might have incorporated on their own.

Accounting for Children's Language and Literacy Learning

In addition to planning and engaging children in language use, the teacher's role in children's language and literacy development entails accounting for children's learning as it is demonstrated through their play and project and theme explorations. A variety of means for assessing children's development in the context of their playful learning was detailed in Chapter 6. With regard to language and literacy, teachers need to regularly document development in these areas as they observe it.

Many of the literacy interactions described throughout this chapter offer opportunities to document specific aspects of language or literacy learning. When one of Ms. Madden's children handed her a receipt for a "RBES VXEN" she had a chance to document his use of phonemic spelling, and may have chosen to include this writing sample in his portfolio. When Max began to mimic his teacher's use of the terms *fill up* and *dump out,* and later began to spontaneously use the word *empty,* his teacher was presented with an opportunity to write an anecdotal note to document this vocabulary and concept development. When Jessica and Brandon included discussion of the difference between numbers and letters in their dramatic play, their interaction could also be documented with anecdotal notes as important evidence of the current literacy knowledge of each child. This kind of documentation enables teachers to demonstrate to parents, other teachers, and administrators that children are meeting the language and literacy goals set for them, and this will make it much easier for teachers to justify their approaches in the face of criticism of their methods.

Using Transitions and Routines to Support Language and Literacy

In addition to fostering language and literacy through play, center activities, and theme studies and project work, teachers can enhance language and literacy by incorporating reading, writing, speaking, and listening into transition activities and other routines in the classroom. These include providing time for oral sharing, reading aloud to children, and providing a print-rich environment that invites routine use of print for authentic purposes.

Oral Sharing

One obvious means of fostering children's language development is to engage children in talk. For many teachers, oral sharing immediately calls to mind "Show and Tell." Certainly, having children bring in items that they want to show to their classmates can stimulate oral language. But this need not be the only sharing routine. Indeed, because it is rather formal and requires advance preparation on the part of the children, not all of them will readily participate.

A less formal means of engaging children in oral language is to invite them to participate in informal sharing sessions. As children gather together between activities, for example, they can be invited to take turns sharing what they have just finished doing in centers and then to specify their intentions for the next free-choice period. As each child shares, the teacher can extend the child's language by probing for more elaboration, offering more sophisticated vocabulary in restating what a child has said, or adding to the child's comments.

Read-Aloud Sessions

Listening to books read aloud is among the most significant experiences children can have in terms of their language and literacy development. Hearing the language of stories and informational books exposes children to written language structures that they are not likely to hear in normal conversational language. Furthermore, because young children can usually comprehend books read aloud at a much higher level than those they can read independently, reading aloud to children exposes them to more complex vocabulary and more difficult concepts than might be the case without such book exposure. Read-aloud routines offer so many benefits for language and literacy development that teachers should try to read to children whenever possible, taking advantage of both regularly scheduled read-aloud times and more spur-of-the-moment opportunities.

Using books to settle and focus children between activities is a good way to build more read-aloud time into the day. Listening to a good reading of an interesting book can be a soothing, yet mentally stimulating process. Read-alouds then become points of the day that help children make transitions between activities.

Print-Rich Environments

Providing a print-rich environment is another way teachers can make children's use of language and literacy skills a routine part of the day. For many teachers, the phrase *print-rich environment* conjures visions of classrooms plastered with print—labels for materials, furniture, even doors and windows. Although there may be some benefits to offering children these opportunities to connect printed words with the things they represent, overuse of this strategy reduces the print in classrooms to little more than visual noise.

A true print-rich environment is one that invites children to *use* environmental print in meaningful ways. Labels in an art center that indicate which bin is for scissors and which is for markers, for example, are meaningful because they serve a clear purpose that is easily understood by young children. This contrasts sharply with labels on windows and doors, which serve no discernible function.

Environmental print in classrooms for young children can take many forms beyond functional labels. One routine that invites children to attend to environmental print is the use of a daily sign-in sheet. Beginning as early as kindergarten, teachers can post a list of children's names inside the door with blank spaces for children to sign their names as they enter the room each morning. This routine encourages children to distinguish their own names from those of their classmates and provides them with an opportunity to experiment with writing their own names while observing how other children write theirs. Children's understanding of the functional use of print is reinforced when this list is used to determine attendance.

Another routine that encourages children to experiment with reading and writing is the establishment of a message board or mailbox system in the classroom. One way to do this is to attach envelopes with each child's name to a bulletin board or chalk ledge. These serve as mailboxes into which children can place messages for each other. Teachers can prompt children to make use of this system by periodically leaving messages for children and encouraging children to write notes to each other. When a kindergarten teacher overheard one child tell another, "Don't forget to ask your mom if you can come to my house after school tomorrow," she said, "Why don't you write a reminder for him and put it in his mailbox?"

Teachers may also develop useful environmental print with the children themselves. When a reminder about upcoming events is needed, for example, the teacher can solicit the children's help in composing a sign to be posted on the classroom door or a note to be sent home to parents. Or when activities such as cooking are planned, teachers and children can construct recipes on chart paper with children's names written beside the ingredients they have volunteered to bring in. This chart is first used as a reminder of what is to be brought to the classroom and then as a useful guide for the actual cooking.

There are many other ways teachers can provide meaningful environmental print and encourage children's use of it, including the use of simple written instructions for using centers and equipment in the classroom. The key to optimizing children's learning from environmental print is for teachers to look for opportunities to infuse a wide variety of classroom activities with meaningful uses of written language.

Including Children with Special Needs

As is the case for any area of the curriculum, teachers need to be sure that children with special needs can fully participate in activities that promote language and literacy. It is imperative that teachers find ways to ensure that children with special needs are as fully included in the same variety of language and literacy experiences as are other children.

The emergent, constructivist models for developing language and literacy presented in this chapter are inherently adaptable for children of varying cognitive capabilities. Because such approaches are designed to facilitate children's progression from current understanding of basic concepts about language, symbols, and the world around them, teachers can interact with each child in ways that will scaffold his or her learning.

Children with physical, socioemotional, or attention disorders, however, may need to have materials and activities adapted to allow full access and facilitate learning. The following suggestions are offered for including children with special needs in language and literacy activities. All of the adaptations described here enhance the learning of children with special needs, and add new dimensions to the learning of children with no special challenges. Equally important, they will demonstrate that all children are capable of learning and are valued.

Children with Physical Disabilities

- Be sure that all materials in the literacy center are fully accessible to a child who uses a wheelchair, walker, or other device to assist movement.
- Provide some manipulative materials that can be handled by children with limited use of their hands. This may mean using larger (or smaller) objects, considering the weight of objects and artifacts, and adding pegs or handles to manipulatives such as magnetic letters, alphabet blocks and stamps, and figures to be placed on a flannel board.
- Find ways to facilitate writing for children who have limited motor control. In some cases, specially adapted keyboards for word processing may help. Computer programs that convert speech into print may be necessary for other children. In the absence of such technology, provide a scribe to whom the children can dictate what they want to write.
- Use CD-ROM interactive storybooks to allow independent reading by a child who cannot turn pages.

Children with Visual Impairments

- Obtain as many large-print books as possible for the classroom library for children with limited vision. Provide plastic magnifying pages for these children to use with materials that are not available in large print.

- When reading aloud, describe the illustrations on each page at appropriate stopping points in the text.
- Although visually impaired children will benefit from all the same oral language inter-actions and storybook readings as other children, depending on the severity of their impairments, activities designed to call their attention to print may need to be struc-tured around learning Braille.
- Stock the library center with books that are printed in both standard English and Braille.
- Help visually impaired children pass their hands over the raised dots in Braille books as they follow a story.
- Include a Braille typewriter in the writing center for all children to experiment with.
- Provide a Braille keyboard attached to a computer with a voice synthesizer capable of reading back to children what they have written.
- Use alphabet blocks and magnetic letters embossed with Braille symbols in the manip-ulative and literacy centers.

Children with Hearing Impairments

- Get an interpreter to sign for children each time a book is read aloud.
- Help the children's hearing classmates learn how to communicate with them. It is critical that hearing-impaired children have opportunities to share in the language that accompanies play. The more hearing children can be encouraged to sign to deaf chil-dren while they are speaking, the more language growth will be experienced by all the children.
- Teach children always to face hearing impaired children when speaking to them.
- Provide both visual examples and written instructions for activities in the literacy cen-ter and other areas of the classroom.

Children with Learning Difficulties

- Allow adequate time for the children to respond to questions and make comments dur-ing read-aloud sessions.
- Schedule more frequent and regular sessions with the child for one-on-one reading with the teacher.
- Recognize and support the child's need to engage in repeated readings of favorite sto-rybooks. Do not discourage him or her even if he or she selects the same book day after day for free reading in the library center.

Children with Attention Disorders

- Keeping in mind that play episodes should last a minimum of twenty to thirty min-utes for enhanced language and literacy development, observe when the children begin to lose interest in an ongoing activity and briefly interact with them and the other children to try to draw their attention back to the shared play and keep them en-gaged longer.
- Allow the children to play in the library and writing areas for brief periods at a time while encouraging them to return to those areas frequently for shorter durations.
- Encourage the children to develop clear achievable goals to be accomplished in the writing area, and help them focus on those goals while they are there.

Children with Socioemotional Difficulties

■ Recognizing the critical importance of interactive play to language and literacy development, encourage the children to engage with other children in play, and help them enter established play groups.

■ Encourage the children to draw or write about their feelings in the writing area. Offer to talk about any of their writing that they wish to share.

(Cook, Tessier, & Armbruster, 1987; Fewell & Kaminski, 1988; Morris & Schultz, 1989; Schwartz & Heller-Miller, 1988; Wesley, 1992; Woolery & Wilbert, 1994).

Developing Advocacy Skills

Teachers like Ms. Madden, who value the learning that occurs as children play, can come under tremendous pressure to conform to more traditional academic approaches used by other teachers in their schools. As Ms. Madden discovered, this is especially true with respect to approaches to literacy learning and teaching.

Since the 1980s, a debate has raged regarding the best means to introduce young children to reading and writing. Those with differing viewpoints often felt the need to "conquer" opponents and bring them into compliance with the practices they favored.

In the case of the debate about reading instruction, opposing viewpoints regarding the best means of developing literacy knowledge, skills, and dispositions mainly centered on the importance placed on direct skills instruction versus more language-based immersion in print. Yet Bredekamp and Copple (1997) point out that such *either/or* thinking is often counterproductive; they suggest that teachers think in terms of *both/and*. Indeed, the IRA/NAEYC (1998) joint position statement on early literacy notes that research points to the conclusion that "learning to read and write is a complex, multifaceted process that requires a wide variety of instructional approaches" (p. 38). At the same time, the position statement clearly affirms that children must be viewed as active constructors of their own understanding, and must be allowed opportunities to use print for purposes that they find meaningful.

Teachers like some of Ms. Madden's colleagues, who may not share this view of children and the way they learn, continue to be uncomfortable with the idea that children can develop literacy by any means other than direct skills instruction. This discomfort is often manifested in the form of criticism of the amount of play some teachers allow in school. Their reasoning is that time spent at play is time lost for the instruction that children need to become good readers and writers.

Teachers who are less secure than Ms. Madden in their beliefs about language and literacy learning and the importance of play for children's development may let such criticism shake their convictions. Younger or newer teachers in particular are likely to have their confidence undermined by more experienced teachers who question their methods.

Teachers who want to be strong advocates for children and their right to play must choose not to worry about criticism. Instead, they must continue to do what they know is best for the children entrusted to them, especially when their practice is supported by research and the policies of the major professional associations in their fields. Table 9.6 offers advocacy activities that will help develop awareness of developmentally appropriate goals for young children's literacy development and criticisms and concerns teachers hear about their literacy instruction, and facilitate playful approaches to literacy.

TABLE 9.6   Advocacy Activities: Involving and Informing Families and Administrators

Don't Worry about Turf, Credit, or Critics—Keep Doing Your Work.

Becoming Aware	*Furthering Your Understanding*	*Taking Action*
1. Familiarize yourself with developmentally appropriate goals for young children's literacy learning.	1. Observe children while they are playing in centers and while they are engaged in projects. Make note of any evidence you see that demonstrates their achievement of literacy goals appropriate for children their ages.	1. Based on your observations of children at play and engaged in projects, as well as your observations of their use of environmental print, draft a written response to the concerns of the teachers you interviewed. Include in your response the evidence of learning you saw that might respond to their concerns.
2. Interview five different teachers in schools in your area about their views on literacy learning. Do they mention a role for play or project approaches? If not, ask how they feel about these approaches. Do you hear any criticism of play in their responses? What forms does the criticism take? What concerns do the teachers express?	2. Read the professional literature to find ideas for infusing literacy into children's play.	
3. Interview three parents of school-age children in your neighborhood about their children's literacy learning. How do they think children develop language and literacy? What do they think about playful approaches to literacy instruction in schools?	3. Visit a classroom that is identified by your instructor or by other professionals as print-rich. Note all of the environmental print in the room, and observe how children use this print. Also note any ways that the teacher encourages children's interaction with environmental print in the classroom.	2. Identify one of your own special interests (such as cooking, gardening, and making paper) that might also be of interest to young children. Volunteer to visit a classroom to lead children in an activity related to your interest, being sure to weave meaningful uses of print into your interaction with them.
4. With your instructor's help, identify a teacher who *does* include play in her or his classroom. Talk to this teacher to see if she or he faces criticism and how she or he handles it.		

Summary

This chapter opened with a discussion of the importance of language development to literacy learning, and presented theories of emergent literacy that recognize literacy learning as an extension of oral language learning. The manner in which teachers can facilitate both language and literacy through play was followed by an overview of library and writing centers as focal points for language and literacy learning in the classroom. Means of interweaving technology into center activities were described.

The teacher's role in maintaining a constructivist, emergent literacy perspective was described in terms of planning for children's language and literacy learning, engaging children with oral and written language, and accounting for children's language and literacy development. The use of transitions and routines to support language and literacy focused on oral sharing, read-aloud sessions, and print-rich environments. Specific suggestions for including children with special needs in these activities were given, followed by a discussion of ways teachers can develop advocacy skills that will help them to ignore criticism and keep doing what they know is best for children.

R E V I S I T I N G   F I R S T   I M P R E S S I O N S

Compare the early literacy experiences you recall from your own childhood to the way literacy development is described in this chapter. What new insights do you have regarding language and literacy learning? How have your beliefs changed about what teachers can do to facilitate language and literacy in the context of children's play as a result of your reading?

Q U E S T I O N S   F O R   D I S C U S S I O N

1. Identify two themes for a dramatic play center that could be established in a typical classroom for young children. Brainstorm as many materials as you can that could be woven into these centers to promote language and literacy learning.

2. Consider the following interaction Ms. Dwyer had with a first-grade student in the writing center in her classroom. How might Ms. Dwyer adapt the center and her interaction with the child to further encourage his literacy development?

    Adam was in the writing center when Ms. Dwyer stopped to see what he was doing. The school had recently installed a small pond in the garden outside the entrance to the school, and the children's interest in the pond had resulted in a study of aquatic plants. Adam had filled an entire page with blue for water, and was drawing in a variety of plants.
    Ms. Dwyer pointed to one of the plants and asked, "What kind of plant is that?"
    Adam replied, "It's just a plant. I don't remember what the different kinds look like. See, this is the leaves, and this is the flower, and these are the roots under the water."
    Ms. Dwyer replied, "That's a really nice picture. It looks like you know a lot about plants that grow in water. Are you going to write about your picture?"
    Adam shrugged as he kept on coloring. "Maybe," he responded.
    "Bring me your picture when you finish, and we can hang it up. It's very pretty."

S U G G E S T E D   R E A D I N G S

Christie, J. (Ed.). (1991). *Play and early literacy development*. Albany, NY: State University of New York Press.

Gunning, T. (1998). *Best books for beginning reading*. Boston: Allyn & Bacon.

McGee, L., & Richgels, D. (1996). *Literacy's beginnings: Supporting young readers and writers*. Boston: Allyn & Bacon.

Neuman, S., & Roskos, K. (1998). *Children achieving: Best practices in early literacy*. Newark, DE: International Reading Association.

10 Fostering Cognitive Competence through Playful Learning and Playful Teaching

Prereading Guide

First Impressions.   Think back to your own experiences in preschool, kindergarten, and primary grades. When do you recall first encountering mathematical and scientific concepts? How were they introduced? What kinds of activities did your teachers engage you in to help you learn these concepts? Describe your experiences in your journal.

Revisit

Logico-Mathematical Knowledge; Developing Cirricula That Foster Playful Learning (Chapter 3)

Using Anecdotal Notes (Chapter 6)

Stories from the Field

The following conversation took place among three first-grade teachers after an in-service session in which they were introduced to the new math and science textbook series that their school had adopted.

MS. SCHULTZ: I think the math series is going to be pretty good. The publishers seem to have done a good job including all of the concepts and cognitive processes recommended by the NCTM (National Council of Teachers of Mathematics) standards. If I follow the lessons as they are presented in this book, I can meet the standards much better than I could with the old texts. Those were terribly outdated.

MS. MORALES: The kids will really like these workbooks much better too. They're so bright and colorful—they almost look like pages from children's literature books. I also really like how colorful the sciences books are. Our old ones had mostly drawings for different concepts, but these are full of clear colorful photographs. These are much more appealing. I think the kids will really like them when we read them together.

MS. BLOUNT: I think these books are much better than what we've had, too. They look great. But I don't know. They showed us so many things to do to get through these series! I find myself wondering when I can fit it all in. I mean, just getting through the math book and all the workbook pages alone could take up all the time I have for math. The whole time the presenters were speaking, I was picturing kids sitting quietly following along with the problems I'm solving and then working by themselves to complete their own problems. The workbook pages are bright and appealing, but I wonder how meaningful they will be to my kids. If we spend all that time with this series, when will they get to actually do real math? I think my kids learn so much math when they have time to play in the centers I set up. When will they get to do this if I have to spend a lot of time with a math book?

MS. SCHULTZ: You know, I was thinking the same thing about the science book. It does offer some good ideas for fun experiments that the kids can do, but I'll have to be careful that my kids spend more time *doing* science than reading about it.

MS. MORALES: Now that you mention it, that could be a problem. We don't want to spend all of our time with the kids doing work from their textbooks. In math especially, I think kids really need to do real-life problem solving–solving problems that they care about, like figuring out how many packages of valentines they need to buy so they can give one to everybody in the class. Now that's meaningful math! I want children to learn to love to do math and science and to develop dispositions for thinking in logical, scientific ways. Nobody develops a disposition for problem solving, for example, by reading about it. They develop a disposition for problem solving by successfully solving problems!

MS. BLOUNT: The biggest problem that I have with basing my teaching on a series of textbooks is that doing so really interferes with the way I've integrated the curriculum in my classroom. We've all worked really hard the past few years designing our curriculum and providing learning centers and other play opportunities that address goals from across the curriculum. The children learn math while they solve problems in science, and they develop literacy skills as they read and write about what they are doing. I've gotten to the point where I almost don't think about math and science as separate subjects anymore. They're both about helping children to be good thinkers and problem-solvers. If I base my teaching on these books, it's too easy to slip into regarding math and science as unrelated areas. I've made a lot of progress toward integrating the curriculum in my classroom. I don't want to give that up just because we have some bright new science and math books.

MS. SCHULTZ: Yes, but the school system is spending an awful lot of money on these materials. I think we will face lots of pressure to use these books and finish all of the pages in the workbooks. I'm not sure we can resist and refuse to use books they've spent so much money on.

MS. BLOUNT: I'm not saying we should put them away on a shelf to collect dust. But we can use the books in ways that make sense for our curriculum. I'll probably keep doing what I'm doing now—lots of projects and theme units—and only use the books as a resource for the concepts we're studying. For example, I can use the chapter on insects in my first-grade science book as part of our theme unit on ants, probably midway through when kids are ready to think about how ants fit into the larger class of insects. I can use the math books and workbooks to reinforce concepts the kids are learning and to provide individual practice for children who need it. If I use the materials like that, each child can work on concepts that they are ready for, rather than everyone having to learn the same concepts at the same time. These new materials can be useful resources, as long as we fit them to our curriculum and protect our children's time for play and exploration.

Developing Cognitive Competence

Ms. Blount's ideas about math and science, especially her belief that these areas of the curriculum are both primarily about teaching children to think and to solve problems, are accurate in terms of the goals for young children in each of these disciplines. What she is referring to is the ideas that a major thrust of each curricular area is to develop *cognitive competence.* We use the term in this chapter to refer to children's ability to use a variety of processes involved in thinking and learning about new concepts.

Math and science are two areas of the early childhood curriculum that are critical to children's development of cognitive competence. Both focus on developing children's emerging development of both *physical knowledge* and *logico-mathematical knowledge* (Piaget, 1952, 1967).

As defined in Chapter 3, physical knowledge can be observed and derived from *acting on* objects, or physically handling and manipulating them. An infant may see ice cream, but only learns that it is very cold and sweet after his or her first taste of it. By the time he or she is a toddler, he or she has likely "acted on" ice cream even more, trying to keep it in a cone and licking it from the sides as it melts all over. As a result of acting on the ice cream—tasting a tiny spoonful, licking it, catching drips in his or her hands, and bathing the mess away from his or her arms and legs—he or she will gain a wealth of physical knowledge about it.

Logico-mathematical knowledge, on the other hand, requires moving beyond acting on single objects. As discussed in Chapter 3, Piaget (1952, 1967) defined *logico-mathematical learning* as the construction of mental relationships to represent categories and hierarchies of objects. This kind of knowledge comes about from observing and making relationships *between objects.* Although a child may know that ice cream is cold (physical knowledge), the notion that it is colder (and sweeter, and somewhat more solid) than a cup of milk is logico-mathematical knowledge. The comparison between ice cream and milk is something that cannot be observed *in* the ice cream or *in* the milk itself. The comparison is in the mind of the child and is created only through logical reasoning. Examples of other relationships that are included in logico-mathematical knowledge are *the same as, different from, equal to, similar, most,* and *least* (Williams & Kamii, 1986). Children's development of both physical and logico-mathematical knowledge is supported by their ability to recognize and understand *correspondences* and *transformations,* both of which are conceptual understandings that are critical to math and science learning.

Logico-mathematical knowledge depends on a child's ability to make correspondences between objects or events, that is, the ability to recognize how two objects or events are alike or different (Forman & Hill, 1984). Children establish correspondence when they recognize that two groups of five beans are equivalent and, later, when they come to understand that both can be represented by the number "5." They recognize correspondence when they see, for example, that three plants blooming in the garden are all gardenias because they look and smell the same, whereas two other plants are not gardenias because the leaves are larger, the flowers are different colors, and they have no fragrance.

The development of physical and logico-mathematical knowledge also depends on children's ability to recognize and understand transformations. A transformation is something that happens (either naturally or as a result of a child's or adult's action) to change something (Forman & Hill, 1984). A transformation occurs when a group of five blocks are combined with three blocks, resulting in a new group of eight blocks. A child who understands that a transformation has occurred realizes that, although the appearance of the blocks has changed (from two distinct groups to one larger group), the total quantity is still the same. The same conceptual understanding is evident when a child watches a chick emerge wet and featherless from an egg, then recognizes it as the same chick days later when it is covered with soft, dry down.

Children develop the ability to recognize correspondences and transformations as they mature and gain experience handling objects and observing and participating in events. This is because they learn to rely less on perceptual strategies (does it *look* like the same chick?) and more on logical, cognitive strategies (I know that babies and plants change as they get older. I guess that happened here too!) (Siegler, 1981; Siegler & Robinson, 1982). Children only gradually acquire the ability to reason inductively (from specific to general knowledge) and deductively (from general to specific) (Flavell, 1985). These cognitive processes have been shown to apply to all areas of cognitive development, from art and language to science and math (Case, 1992).

Much as children construct language and literacy concepts as they are immersed in language and experiment with its use, so too do they develop physical and logico-mathematical knowledge, including the ability to deal with correspondence and transformation. This knowledge cannot be taught directly; rather, children must construct their own concept of the relationships between objects through experience with real-life materials and situations (Kamii & DeClark, 1985; Kamii & Joseph, 1989).

Young children often gain this experience with real-life materials and situations as they play. Most experts on play agree that sensorimotor play facilitates a young child's cognitive development (Piaget, 1962; Smilansky, 1968; Sutton-Smith, 1986). Play with objects (blocks, pegs, toy cars, jacks, balls, etc.) often involves a four-step sequence—exploration, manipulation, practice, and repetition (Garvey, 1990). This repetitive play with objects facilitates the development of both physical and logico-mathematical knowledge (Piaget, 1969).

For this reason, Ms. Schultz, Ms. Morales, and Ms. Blount are right to be concerned about their school's adoption of materials for math and science instruction that might limit children's opportunities for real-life, hands on exploration of math and science concepts and might interfere with the continued development of an integrated curriculum. Clearly, children need opportunities to discover concepts for themselves through active play, alone and with each other. These teachers are justified in fiercely protecting their children's time for the play that will facilitate their development of both physical and logico-mathematical knowledge and their dispositions to use that knowledge.

Fostering Cognitive Competence

Professional organizations representing both math and science teachers and researchers have produced standards for effective teaching in their respective disciplines. Each set of standards emphasizes the importance of developing children's ability to engage in cognitive processes that are critical to understanding the world around them (NCTM, 1989; National Research Council, 1996). Many of the cognitive competencies outlined by each group overlap, although there are some differences. The goal of an integrated science and math curriculum should be to ensure that children have opportunities to engage in all kinds of thinking. Table 10.1 highlights the thinking processes embedded in both the science and mathematics national standards. These will be discussed in more detail in the following sections.

Processes Involved in Logico-Mathematical Thinking

Many people believe that children's competence with logico-mathematical thinking will automatically be developed if they are taught to count, to recognize written numerals, and to carry out simple arithmetic computations such as adding and subtracting. Although these are important competencies, particularly as children move into the middle primary grades, they do not adequately reflect the range of concepts and knowledge that children must develop. The National Council of Teachers of Mathematics (1989) outlined five strands of logico-mathematical knowledge that should be addressed to support children's cognitive competence.

One strand is *logical and mathematical reasoning.* This encompasses *sorting and classifying* information. As children mature, they will be required to use number as a category of classification. When a second grader must use a set of chips to compute 5 + 3, for example, he or she must put five chips in one pile, which is then classified as *five,* and three more chips into another pile, which is classified as *three.* He or she then may put the two sets of chips together, reclassifying them as one set of *eight.* Before he or she can carry out this computation successfully, however, the child must first develop basic understanding of the *concept* and *process* of sorting and classifying.

Another aspect of logical and mathematical reasoning is *seriation,* which entails putting series of objects in order. Anytime a child places objects in order, whether by arranging them

TABLE 10.1   Thinking Processes in Science and Math Standards

National Science Standards	National Math Standards
Observing—using senses to lean about the environment and things in it	Logico-mathematical reasoning—sorting, classifying, and seriating
Comparing—examining objects in terms of similarities and differences	Collecting and recording statistical information—gathering data to answer questions
Organizing—systematically compiling and ordering information	Measuring—determining length, distance, quantity, volume, and weight
Relating—relating ideas to test or explain phenomena	Recognizing geometric shapes—describing and analyzing the three-dimensional world
Inferring—predicting the meaning of information	Recognizing and creating patterns and functions—recognizing, describing, and extending patterns; representing mathematical relationships
Applying—using knowledge and skills to solve problems	
Communicating—naming, recording, and sharing information	

from smallest to largest, shortest to longest, or lightest to darkest color, she or he is engaged in seriation. The ability to recognize attributes such as size and color and then also discern relationships among objects that share attributes is a critical component of mathematical operations the children will carry out with numbers later in their schooling.

Statistics and probability is another strand of logico-mathematical knowledge to be developed. Even very young children can be led to construct knowledge of statistics when it is presented as comparing and analyzing information. A preschool teacher recognized her children's ability to recognize and use statistical information in the following exchange between two four-year-olds.

> **TAMEKA:** Yesterday everybody wanted to swing. Let's get outside first so we can get a swing today.
>
> **ROCHELLE:** But only two boys got bikes. There's lots of bikes. Let's go get those. We can have races.
>
> **TAMEKA:** And we can play car wash when we ride past the water table.

The same kind of comparison and analysis is evident when children realize that more classmates chose peanut butter and jelly than cheese sandwiches at snack time. These abilities are also apparent when children recognize that they have had more rainy days than sunny days in one week and complain that they have not had enough time to play outside. Children's learning from these observations will be stimulated even further if teachers help them to make simple graphs of this information. Competency in making note of information, quantifying it, and making comparisons are all important precursors to more abstract statistic and probability problems children will encounter in math courses when they are older.

Measurement is another strand of the NCTM model. Concepts such as shorter versus longer, lighter versus heavier, and smaller versus bigger are discovered with relative ease as children explore their world and talk about their observations. Measurement offers them a way to extend these basic observations and, eventually, to quantify the differences they notice. This does not mean that young children should be expected to use standard tools such as tape measures and rulers to derive measurements in terms of inches, feet, yards, or meters. They can develop the underlying concept of measurement by using lengths of string to measure height or girth or by pacing off an area to see how many steps big it is. Specific terms for their measurements can be added once they are comfortable with the concept of measuring.

Geometry is yet another strand of mathematics. It includes the study of shapes and forms as well as the relationships among them. The youngest learners attend to geometry when they begin to develop concepts of physical space and the placement of objects within it. As they gain experience, children increase their geometric understanding as they begin to differentiate between different shapes and learn to label shapes such as circles, squares, and triangles correctly. By manipulating objects of various shapes, such as blocks, Legos, and puzzle pieces, they begin to conceptualize complex notions such as volume and area.

Patterns and functions make up the final strand of the mathematical model defined by NCTM. Recognition of patterns is critically important to higher-level mathematical understanding and higher-order critical thinking in general. Pattern recognition helps children predict and estimate. When a four- or five-year-old notices that a pair of beads is strung with alternating red and blue beads, he or she is recognizing a pattern. This recognition will later lead the child to begin using similar patterns in his or her own constructions, and will form the basis for an understanding of more abstract patterns such as those formed by adding odd and even numbers.

Processes Involved in Scientific Thinking

Just as national standards have been developed for knowledge and skills in math, standards have been established that focus on the processes children should learn to use as they develop scientific awareness (California State Department of Education, 1984; National Research Council, 1996).

Observing is a critically important process in scientific learning, especially for young children. While adults tend to define observing as watching, in the science standards the term is meant to include any exploration using the senses to learn about characteristics of the environment. Children are engaged in observation when they look at, feel, taste, smell, and listen to different things in the environment. Engaging children in the construction of a home for hermit crabs, for example, can lead to observations related to earth science. When filling the bottom of an aquarium with marine sand, the teacher can encourage children to observe its texture and the size of the individual grains.

This type of active observation facilitates another process, namely, *comparing*. As children observe the marine sand, they may notice that it is coarser than the sand used for making pictures in the art center, and different from the sand mixed into the garden soil outside. Young children can be encouraged to make comparisons by measuring, counting, or otherwise quantifying objects they examine in terms of their similarities and differences. Their comparison of different sands can be extended if children are invited to examine and compare soils collected from different areas such as gardens, house plants, play yards, river banks, or swamps in order to observe different textures and compositions.

A related process is that of *organizing*. Children's learning about the world is enhanced when they learn to be systematic in their explorations. Thus, they should be encouraged to carefully compile, classify, and order information they collect from their observations and comparisons. Children may extend their observations about shadows and light, for example, by taking systematic observations of how light moves across the classroom over time and how quickly shadows move. Children can be encouraged to place masking tape around a few prominent shadows in the room, indicating the time of day on the tape. They can then return to the shadows every fifteen minutes or so and lay down new tape on which the new time is noted. With teachers' help, children can be invited to predict where the shadows will be by the end of the day, and can then gather to confirm their predictions before going home.

As can be seen in the previous example, organizing information is necessary to facilitate children's attempts at *relating* information gleaned from comparisons and observations to formulate and test hypotheses or to explain a particular phenomenon. Young children on the playground, for example, might observe dark clouds, hear a sudden clap of thunder, and almost immediately feel raindrops blowing into their faces. If they are able to relate those different observations, they may formulate the hypotheses that dark clouds are the reason for the rain.

That same experience may lead children to engage in another important process, that of *inferring*. Once they relate dark clouds to the rain that sends them indoors to play, they may infer that they will be able to go out again when the sun comes out—in adult terms, when the skies clear of dark clouds. Their prediction that the rain will stop when the clouds move away is an inference; further observation on the children's part is necessary to determine if it is accurate.

An additional process important to cognitive competence is *applying* information, knowledge, and skills to solve problems. Children who have determined, for example, that heavier toy cars roll faster down inclines than lighter cars may apply this knowledge to select those cars most likely to win in races against friends.

The final process outlined in the science standards is *communicating*. A major component of cognitive competence is the ability to communicate—orally, with pictures or other graphic representations, or in writing—new information to others. One way to encourage this type of communication is to provide informational picture books that model one way information can be communicated. If a teacher asks questions such as, "I wonder how a bird builds a nest like this one? How can we find out?" children may be prompted to use the books purposefully to collect, organize, and report the answers to their questions. Teachers can encourage children to explore the books by reading aloud suitable portions to the children and pointing out interesting pictures and illustrations for discussion.

Children will naturally use all of these processes, at least superficially, as they explore everything in the world around them. Preschool and kindergarten children will best develop skills of observing, comparing, and communicating, whereas children in primary grades can become more adept at organizing and relating information. Inferring and applying are processes that require a high level of abstract thinking, and will only begin to emerge with young children (Bredekamp & Rosegrant, 1995).

Developing Cognitive Competence through Play

Young children will naturally engage in each of the processes involved in mathematical and scientific thinking as they play. When they scoop shovels full of sand into dump trucks for transport in the sandbox, or when they fill buckets with water to pour into a hastily dug "pond" for their plastic animals, they make discoveries about volume and measurement and observe and compare the properties of sand and water. When they carefully select alternating long and short blocks to construct a fort, they experiment with patterns and geometric principles. When they evenly distribute a set of marbles among four players and begin playing, they exercise logico-mathematical thinking and experiment with movement and variables of friction, speed, distance, and angle as they aim and shoot at other players' marbles.

Children's cognitive competence can be facilitated as they engage in all types of play. *Constructive play* is quite conducive to developing this kind of knowledge. As children build structures with blocks, whether a two-year-old attempting to stack three blocks one atop the other or a seven-year-old building a complex castle complete with parapets, they use a variety of thinking processes. While deciding what kind of block they need next—square, round, heavier, lighter—they view the blocks in relation to each other, and solidify their understanding of those relationships. When children's constructions begin to include attempts to represent actual things in their environment, as when they make papier-mâché volcanoes or maps of their neighborhood, they attend to how their construction compares with what they wish to represent.

Functional, or *practice play* also offers opportunities to develop cognitive competence. This can be as obvious as a child practicing the formation of numbers over and over again on a large piece of paper at the writing table (which is play only if the *child* initiates this practice) or as subtle as a child jumping rope and counting over and over again how many times she or he can jump without missing—in the process practicing counting and one-to-one correspondence, as well as experimenting with principles of movement and patterns. Older children who practice shooting baskets or taking penalty kicks past a soccer goalie may begin to keep track not only of total number of successful shots, but also successful shots as a portion of the total shots attempted. Perhaps without even being aware of it, these children are beginning to use and understand the concept of percentage. As they play, they also experiment with relationships such as cause and effect as they notice that the force with which the ball is kicked is related to its speed and that the angle at which it is struck is related to its path to the goal.

Playing *games with rules* also enhances children's logico-mathematical learning. A five-year-old boy who regularly plays simple board games using dice to determine how many spaces to move forward illustrates this process. When he first begins using dice, he is likely to count the dots of the dice each time they are rolled, and then move his marker one space at a time until it is in the right position. With more experience, however, he will come to recognize dots in four corners of a die as *four* without having to count them. At that point, he will have internalized a new symbol for the number four. Even younger children who may use spinners rather than dice must recognize that the numeral three on the spinner represents three spaces on the board, and understand that the higher the number they spin, the more spaces they can move. Many other games with rules contribute to children's exploration with number concepts even more directly. Games such as Bingo require children to recognize numerals for the numbers they hear called out and realize when they have completed the required pattern to win, whether it is five in a row horizontally, vertically, or diagonally, or four corners and the middle space. Traditional games with rules, for example, Jacks and Dominoes, also entail significant counting, regrouping, adding, and subtracting and offer significant benefits to children's learning of mathematical concepts (Casbergue & Kieff, 1998).

Dramatic play is another type of play that provides ample opportunities for developing cognitive competence. Any time the dramatic play center is set up to represent some business—airport, shoe store, restaurant, post office, ice cream shop, bus terminal, hospital, and so on—there are opportunities for children to use numbers and number concepts in their play. They can establish prices and time schedules, write bills, collect play money in return for service, and give change to customers. If the dramatic play area is set up as a newsroom weather station, children can observe weather, use symbols to represent it, and practice communicating weather concepts to others.

Using Centers to Encourage Cognitive Competence

Although children do explore a variety of mathematical and scientific concepts as they play, their explorations can be further prompted by establishing centers that offer play opportunities focused on specific concepts. Manipulative and discovery centers are especially effective for promoting cognitive competence.

Both of these centers should take advantage of children's natural interest in the world around them. Center activities should

- encourage children's curiosity and interest in their environment
- prompt children to explore and investigate a wide range of materials and natural phenomena

- get children to use a wide range of thinking processes
- help children to acquire factual knowledge
- encourage children to develop dispositions for scientific and logico-mathematical thinking and exploration (Kilmer & Hoffman, 1995; National Research Council, 1996)

Teachers should also keep in mind that learning for young children occurs most readily in the context of things that are familiar to them. Often curricula are designed to help children learn about exotic places and unusual phenomenon. Katz (1998) suggests, however, that rather than attempting to make the exotic familiar, teachers of young children should work to make the commonplace and familiar exotic.

There are many common phenomena that can be made exotic for young children. For example, children in southern coastal states are likely to find ants and anthills commonplace. They know that when an anthill is disturbed, armies of ants swarm to the surface. They may also know from painful experience that it is not a good idea to stick around after kicking a hill built by red ants. Bringing an ant farm into a classroom discovery center, however, can serve to make what seems familiar incredibly exotic and intriguing. Once children's interest is piqued, they will generate all kinds of questions about ants that can lead to careful observation, comparison, experimentation, and inferring. They may want to know why some ants bite and others do not. They may try to find out how anthills are constructed. They may want to know what the different chambers they observe in an ant colony are for. They may want to know what ants eat. What was once familiar quickly becomes intriguing and worthy of extensive investigation and may prompt the start of a new project that incorporates these insights.

Phenomena as common as shadows moving across the classroom or weeds sprouting up in a flower garden have great potential for sparking children's interest. As they are prompted to question these things in new ways—wondering how shadows are formed, why they move, and how quickly they move, or where weeds come from and what distinguishes weeds from desirable flowers—they will explore and experiment to find answers. When the commonplace is seen in a new light, children will be naturally drawn into the kind of theme studies and projects described in Chapter 3.

Manipulative Centers

A manipulative center is an area of the classroom designed to encourage children's physical manipulation of objects and learning through exploration, both of which are important to physical and logico-mathematical learning (Williams & Kamii, 1986). There are many types of materials that are appropriate for use in manipulative centers, although they are most often used to support mathematical learning. The materials to be included in a manipulative center designed to foster mathematical thinking will vary with the range of ages and experiences of the children.

Regardless of the materials, the math curriculum for young children should include activities designed to invite children to solve problems and playfully explore mathematical concepts. Just as children are encouraged to experiment freely with oral language and print (see Chapter 9), they should be given the freedom to play with various manipulatives in ways that make sense to them by choosing to use them to experiment for their own purposes. Table 10.2 offers an overview of basic processes, materials, and activities that are appropriate for inclusion in a manipulative center for young children.

TABLE 10.2   Manipulative Center Processes, Materials, and Activities

Process	Materials	Activities
Logico-mathematical thinking	Buttons, miniature animals, blocks, pictures, number tiles, objects with incremental differences (in size, color, weight)	Sorting; classifying; placing objects in series based on increments in size, color, weight, etc.
Collecting/recording statistical information	Stacking blocks, tiles, paper strips, graph paper	Polling classmates on "favorites" (pets, toys, foods); voting for choices (snacks, playground games or equipment) by stacking tiles; coloring in squares to create graph of results
Measuring	Lengths of yarn, tape measures, rulers, meter sticks, scales, balances, sand and water with scoops and containers of varying size	Tracing feet and comparing sizes; using yarn to measure height and gluing to poster to represent class; making predictions of how many scoops (cups, spoons) will fill a container; weighing and comparing large and small objects in the classroom
Recognizing/exploring geometry	Buttons, blocks, other objects of different shapes, pattern blocks, attribute blocks, geoboards	Sorting objects according to shape; observing and drawing/tracing examples of shapes in the classroom; recording shapes created on geoboards or used with attribute or pattern blocks
Recognizing/creating patterns/functions	Attribute blocks, pattern blocks, stamps and ink pads, paper to fold and cut, beads to string, geoboards	Finding and recording naturally occurring patterns in the classroom; creating/ reproducing patterns with pattern blocks, attribute blocks, or beads; folding and cutting paper—predicting and observing resulting patterns

Discovery Centers

One excellent way of organizing opportunities for scientific exploration in early childhood classrooms is to establish discovery centers. These are areas of the classroom where materials that encourage exploration of the environment are made available, and specific activities using those materials are suggested. Discovery centers can also become the place where many projects begin and are carried out. Materials in a discovery center will change frequently, depending on the classroom curriculum and the children's interests.

When discovery centers are intended to fit the science curriculum, care should be taken to ensure that life sciences, physical science, and earth science are equitably represented over time. In addition, the activities suggested should be varied to engage children in many of the thinking processes that have been outlined in national science standards (National Research Council, 1996). Table 10.3 provides an overview of materials and activities that can be included to facilitate children's exploration of concepts related to all three areas of science.

TABLE 10.3   **Discovery Center Materials and Activities**

Science Areas	Materials	Activities/Processes
Life Sciences	living creatures (fish, snakes, birds, guinea pigs, hermit crabs, insects); animal artifacts (nests, hives, feathers, bones, eggs); plants, seeds, leaves, flowers; magnifying glasses, microscopes	*observe* and chart creatures' behaviors; *compare* observed behaviors and characteristics; *classify* animals, plants, seeds, etc.; *relate* animals' characteristics to their habitats; *infer* what animals need to survive in the wild, how they live, how parts of plants function; *communicate* knowledge orally, with pictures or in writing
Earth Sciences	instruments for recording weather information (indoor/outdoor thermometers, rain gauges, barometers); materials for representing weather conditions (flannel cutouts of clouds, sun, raindrops, lightning bolts, snowflakes); audiotapes of weather sounds; materials for exploring landforms (sand, gravel, rocks, soils, models of mountains, swamps, prairies, volcanoes)	*observe* and *compare* daily weather patterns and changes, properties of soils found in different areas, landforms in geographic region; *classify* types of rocks and shells; *relate* weather patterns to seasons, composition of soil to environments; *infer* weather conditions from appearance of sky; *apply* knowledge about weather to decisions about outdoor wear; *communicate* through charts, graphs, and reports
Physical Sciences	materials to explore movement (pull or push toys, balls and small cars with inclines, pendulum apparatus); materials to explore properties of solids and liquids (sand and water tables, modeling clay, putty); materials to explore how things work (small machines and appliances to take apart, pulleys, levers, gears, woodworking and construction materials)	*observe* movement (of objects down inclines, water through sand, pendulums, shadows, functioning machine parts); *compare* and *predict* how movement varies with speed, weight, and friction, how shadows shorten and lengthen during the day; *classify* substances as solid, liquid, or semi-solid; *relate* substance properties to environmental conditions

Using Technology to Support Cognitive Competence

Young children will most easily develop cognitive competence as they manipulate objects in their environment and incorporate basic cognitive processes into their play and other daily routines. Technology can, however, offer a wonderful supplement to this hands-on learning.

Calculators are one form of technology that should be readily available, even for preschoolers' use. Oversized calculators with large number keys will prompt three- and four-year-olds to experiment with typing in numbers and using function keys. Although most will neither comprehend the quantity represented by an eight-digit number nor understand the functions carried out by particular keys, their interest in numbers will be piqued. Many kindergarten and first-grade children will be able to begin making simple calculations that are necessary to support their play, as is the case when they decide to "ring up a bill" for purchases made in a classroom pet shop. Children in primary grades are generally quite competent with calculator use; many will be ready to turn to calculators to help them solve complex problems that are meaningful to them, for example, how many of the thirty oatmeal cookies on a tray each of the fifteen children in the class may have at snack time.

Computers also present opportunities to weave technology into children's learning. Many CD-ROM games focus children's attention on mathematical and scientific concepts and allow them to engage in meaningful practice with math- and science-related skills. When choosing programs for young children, teachers need to be sure that the tasks are appropriate for children's ages and experiences and that they are engaging. Some programs are little more than electronic worksheets designed to provide drill and practice with numbers and computations. Such programs are of little benefit and tie up a valuable and often limited classroom resource that can be put to much more productive use. Other programs incorporate mathematical and scientific concepts into games that are naturally appealing to young children. Look for games that engage children in a variety of activities that require them to recognize, sort, classify, and predict as well as to carry out simple computations as a natural part of the game. Programs such as *Number Munchers* (1996), *Sesame Street Numbers* (1994), and *Early Math* (1993) have won acclaim from parents and educators for encouraging children to experiment with number concepts in ways they enjoy. Other popular programs offer simulations that encourage children to create virtual environments to sustain life; they allow children to see the effects of different environmental conditions as they manipulate temperatures, amounts of rainfall, and other variables. Although these simulations are generally too difficult for preschool, kindergarten, and most first-grade children, older students may enjoy playing and solving problems together.

Finally, teachers should not overlook the Internet as a source of vast quantities of information. Even though independent net surfing is generally not advisable for young children, teachers can log onto interesting websites related to projects or themes and allow children to explore those sites, or they can download information—including pictures and films—into electronic folders that children can easily access when they are seeking information or wish to explore a particular topic.

Maintaining a Constructivist Approach

Each of the types of materials and activities recommended here for inclusion in manipulative and discovery centers has great potential for enabling children to develop cognitive competence. It is important to remember, however, that this will best be accomplished as children use the materials playfully in personally meaningful ways. Teachers should not imply to children that there is only one correct way to use the materials. Rather, activities should be structured to facilitate children's exploration so that they can construct their own understanding of concepts and processes. Kamii and DeVries (1978) offered four criteria for facilitating young children's construction of knowledge. Applying these criteria to center activities will maximize children's abilities to observe the effects of their actions on the objects they manipulate and thus help them to construct knowledge.

The first criterion is that children must be able to produce effects *based on their own actions*. Watching their teacher weigh and measure two objects to determine which is heavier, for example, will not help the children understand concepts related to weight as well as if they do the measuring and weighing themselves.

Second, the children must be able to *vary their own actions*. If children are shown one pattern (e.g., alternating red and blue beads on a string) and asked to reproduce it on their own, they will learn to construct that pattern. If they are allowed to vary their actions so that they can create any pattern they want, however, they are more likely to learn to understand the concept of patterns in general and be able to apply this knowledge to other situations. If they are provided with an incline ramp that is set at one height, and given one set of identical toys to roll down it, they are able only to repeat the same action over and over. Having the opportunity to vary the height (and weight and size) of objects to be rolled down the ramp enables children to learn underlying principles about the physics of motion.

The third criterion is that the *reaction of objects* that are manipulated *must be observable*. Having children look at pictures in a math workbook showing how two cups equal one pint will not be nearly as effective as giving them the opportunity to use containers of different sizes to scoop water into a pint-sized container and record their findings. As children engage in science explorations, the results of many of their actions occur too quickly for them to see or are not visible at all. For example, children rolling small cars down a ramp trying to make them land in a particular place at the bottom will need to vary their placement of cars at the top of the ramp and the angle at which they launch them. But the paths the cars take and the effect of the children's actions on the paths are not readily visible because the actions happen so quickly. Teachers can remedy this by providing a shallow pan of powdered chalk or tempera paint for the children to place the cars in before they roll them. Then, the cars will leave visible tracks that indicate their paths (Chaillé & Britain, 1997).

The final criterion for maintaining a constructivist approach is that the *reaction of objects that are manipulated must be immediate*. Many of the materials suggested here for inclusion in manipulative and discovery centers meet this criteria. When a child changes the placement of rubber bands on a geoboard, for example, the effect on the patterns and geometric shapes created is immediate. When a child chooses to select different pattern blocks than those included in a model pattern, it is immediately evident that his or her placement of new blocks leads to a different pattern.

By making sure that math and science activities designed for young children meet these four criteria, teachers can increase the likelihood that the youngsters' interest will be sustained and that their attention will be focused on concepts that are meaningful and interesting. Moreover, a playful approach to centers, one that allows children the freedom to choose when and how they will use materials and suggested activities, places a premium on the process of exploring math and science concepts rather than on any resulting products. Such an approach ensures that children will play and experiment with the materials provided and will gain all of the benefits that can be derived from playful learning.

The Teacher's Role

As in other areas of the curriculum, teachers play a pivotal role in fostering children's cognitive competence. Again, their efforts should be directed to planning for children's learning, engaging children in meaningful interactions that enhance their development, and assessing the extent of that development.

Planning. As teachers plan for constructivist activities to foster children's cognitive competence, they must be aware of the extent to which they balance free play, guided play, and directed play. Teachers' planning decisions about when to engage children in each type of play should be based in large part on the objectives for different activities.

Free play is especially conducive to open exploration of math and science concepts and processes. During free play, children will readily engage in observation and, perhaps, comparison. They might not so naturally begin to sort and classify, however, thus suggesting that teachers may need to provide guided play activities (perhaps in centers) that will prompt children to use these processes. At other times, teachers may have specific objectives planned for children, and will need to engage them in highly directed activities to meet those objectives.

Engagement. Simply planning activities for children and providing materials for their free, guided, and directed play will not automatically bring about cognitive competence. As we have maintained about every other area of development, teachers need to be actively engaged with children to scaffold their learning. In terms of developing cognitive competence in young children, this engagement takes many forms.

One way teachers can further children's cognitive competence is to *ask constructivist questions* that lead children to construct or reconstruct ideas. When a teacher brings pets into the classroom, for example, he or she can ask questions such as, "How can we find out how often we need to fill the hamster's water?" This will encourage children to observe the animal's habits and anticipate its needs. When a collection of seashells is placed in a discovery center, the teacher might ask, "What types of sea creatures might use these different kinds of shells for their homes?" thus prompting speculation about the characteristics of the shells and their possible functions in relation to the needs of different animals. As children examine different soils as part of an exploration of earth science, they might be asked questions such as, "How is this swamp mud different from the soil we used to plant our garden? Let's look at each one. What do you find in the swamp mud that isn't in the garden soil?" Questions like these may nudge children to observe more carefully, record their observations, and engage in comparison, classification, and prediction.

Teachers may also enhance children's cognitive competence by *calling their attention to properties* of objects or processes in the environment and *providing vocabulary* to represent those properties. In the interaction that follows, note how the teacher supplies the geometric terms for block shapes with which the children are familiar.

TEACHER: I noticed that some of you were having trouble finding the kind of blocks you needed when you were building yesterday. That's because most of the blocks were all mixed up on the shelves. Maybe it would help if we put the blocks in order when we pick them up today. I've cut out some cardboard shapes that match the shapes of the blocks. Let's put these on the shelves to show what kind of blocks go in each place. Can someone show me what kind of blocks go with this small square?

ANDREW: These square kind.

TEACHER: Yes. Let's put those right here. Let's find all the square blocks and put them on this shelf.

LUCY: Does this one go? It's like a square.

TEACHER: No, that one's a rectangle like this. (She holds up the cardboard rectangle.) It's longer than a square. Let's put the rectangle blocks next to the squares on the shelf. (This process continues until children have identified and sorted the square, rectangle, triangle, circle, and half-circle blocks.)

Also notice how the kindergarten teacher in the example that follows playfully introduces the concepts of light, lighter, and lightest in circle time, then suggests that children experiment with them some more in centers.

TEACHER: Look at this turtle shell I brought in to put on our discovery table today. It's from a box turtle. You all know how heavy our turtle is when we pick him up, but this shell is really light. That's because it doesn't have a turtle in it. I'm going to pass it around so everyone can see how light it is.

JACOBY: It's much lighter than I thought it would be.

MARISSA: It's not heavy at all!

ANTONIO: It's light like a sheet of paper.

TEACHER: Do you think it's that light? Why don't you get a sheet of paper from the art table, and we'll see which one is lighter? (Antonio brings a piece of paper back to the circle. The teacher holds one item in each hand to feel their weight.) Even though the turtle shell is pretty light, I think the paper is even lighter. I wonder if the paper is the lightest thing in the room. Can anybody think of something else that might be even lighter than the paper?

BETH: I think a feather is lighter. Can I get one from the discovery table?

TEACHER: Good idea, Beth. Let's see, is the feather lighter than the paper? Let's pass them around so everyone can decide. (The children take turns, and finally agree that the feather is lighter than the art paper.) So, if we put them in order from light to lightest, we should put the turtle shell first, then the paper, then the feather—light, lighter, lightest. In the math center today, you'll find a whole collection of things like buttons, and pebbles, and strings. They're all pretty light. You may want to see if you can find things that you can put in order from light to lightest. You can glue them onto strips of paper in order, so everyone can see what you found.

Finally, teachers can interact with children to encourage cognitive competence by *prompting them to make predictions and offer explanations.* When children have completed a sorting activity, for example, they should be encouraged to explain their classification criteria, as the following exchange illustrates.

TEACHER: Maylie, I see that you divided the animal pictures into two groups. Can you tell me how you decided which animals to put in each group?

MAYLIE: This group has animals that can be pets. This group is just wild animals. They can't be pets. Like you can't keep a lion for a pet.

LIONEL: I did it another way. I made one group with animals that have fur. See? Dogs, cats, bears, and a wolf. My other group is animals without fur, like the alligator and the dolphin.

TEACHER: So there are different ways the animals can be grouped. Those are two good ones. Can you think of any others?

This process is further illustrated by the following interchange between a teacher and two of her first-grade students a few days after they had planted beans in clear plastic cups. Note how she prompted Luis to explain his belief that his plant is growing without

roots, and encouraged both children to determine a way to figure out if his bean had indeed sprouted roots.

ABBY: Look! Mine has white strings hanging from the bean.

TEACHER: Those are the roots. The bean is sprouting roots so it can get food from the soil.

LUIS: Mine doesn't have roots. It's growing from the top instead. See? I have a green piece coming up!

TEACHER: All plants have to have roots before they sprout through the soil. Why do you think yours doesn't have roots?

LUIS: I can't see any. (He looks carefully around all sides of his cup.)

ABBY: My bean is right up against the side of my cup. I can't see your bean. Maybe it has roots, but we just can't see them 'cause they're in the middle of your cup.

TEACHER: How could we find out if Luis has roots growing from his seed?

LUIS: Could we dig it up and look?

TEACHER: Sure. That's a good idea. Then we can plant it again so it can keep on growing.

Teachers can also encourage children in a playful approach to prediction (and statistics and probability) by helping children to collect and graph data about their favorite toys and activities. One preschool teacher sets aside every Friday as the day for children to bring in their favorite item from a category—for example, stuffed animals, shoes, or toys—to school. When children come into the classroom, they go to the manipulative center and either place their object into a group with others like it or start a new group if theirs is the first of its kind. With stuffed animals, for example, groups of five bears, eight dogs, two monkeys, a pig, and an iguana might be organized. Before the collection is quantified, the teacher asks the children to observe and predict which group has the most animals, which one, the least, and so on. The teacher then engages the children in stacking blocks to represent each group of animals to determine which groups are the largest and the smallest. Sometimes these sets of blocks are laid end to end on a large sheet of chart paper and traced to form a simple bar graph. Materials are left in the manipulative center for children to construct and trace their own bar graphs to take home with them and explain to their families.

Engaging children in activities of this kind will help them to recognize that data can be collected, recorded, quantified, represented graphically, and even used to make generalized statements such as, "Our class's favorite stuffed animals are bears and dogs." Additionally, children can participate and accept information about statistics and probability that makes sense according to their varied levels of experience or conceptual development. Some children will use these activities to strengthen their understanding of counting and one-to-one correspondence. Other children who have already mastered those concepts might focus more on the way the graphic representation—the bars in the bar graph—depicts quantities that are in turn represented by numbers. Still others may be most intrigued by the process of making generalized statements based on the information displayed.

Assessing Development.   As is true for all other areas of development, teachers need to observe, document, organize, and share information about children's developing cognitive competence. The kinds of activities and interactions described in this chapter lend themselves especially well to using anecdotal notes to document progress. A full explanation of how to write and analyze anecdotal notes was given in Chapter 6. Here, we offer a brief example of the ways anecdotal notes can be used to assess development of cognitive competence.

One teacher has provided geoboards for children to use if they choose during their free-play time. She observes that two children, Miguel and Frank, go to the center four times in two days to play with the geoboards. As she observes the two boys at play, she sees that they are experimenting with creating four-sided figures. As she listens to their talk while they play, she hears a lot of discussion about why the four-sided shapes each has made look different. Finally, Frank counts the pegs on two sides of his shape and realizes that he has stretched his rubber bands one space more than Miguel. He quickly adjusts his rubber bands so that his shape is identical to Miguel's.

This play interaction between two children provided a wealth of information about each child's cognitive competencies and dispositions for logico-mathematical thinking. It is clear that Frank and Miguel have a strong disposition toward engaging in mathematical thought and problem solving. It is also evident that the children are interested in exploring geometric shapes. As he compared his geoboard shape to Miguel's, Frank demonstrated that he could observe (his shape and Miguel's), compare (how his shape was different), infer (that using two extra pegs caused his shape to look different), and apply that knowledge to solve his problem (creating a shape that looked like Miguel's).

All of this could be documented in an anecdotal note for each child. Then, the teacher will have taken one step toward meeting her responsibility for assessing children's development of cognitive competence.

Including Children with Special Needs

Given the importance of object manipulation and play to children's development of physical and logico-mathematical knowledge, it is clear that every effort must be made to include all children in free play, centers, and project activities, regardless of their special needs. There are many adaptations of materials and activities suggested here that will serve to include children with special needs.

Children with Physical Disabilities
- Be sure that all materials in manipulative and discovery centers are fully accessible to a child who uses a wheelchair, walker, or other device to assist movement.
- Include artifacts that can be lifted by children with limited use of their hands, or hold the object for them to feel and handle with assistance.
- Attach pegs or handles to puzzle pieces, pattern and attribute blocks, and other math manipulatives so that they can be picked up and handled by children with limited use of hands.
- Construct larger homemade geoboards and provide elastic strips to aid children who may not have the fine motor ability to handle smaller boards and rubber bands.

Children with Visual Impairments
- Provide materials in the manipulative center that can be sorted by touch according to texture or size. Do the same for materials used for constructing patterns or attribute series.
- Give detailed verbal descriptions of artifacts in the discovery center while the children handle them.
- Create audiotapes of instructions for different centers to supplement any written instructions.

Children with Hearing Impairments
- Interact with the children using sign language to provide vocabulary to accompany concepts the child is exploring.
- Provide written as well as oral instructions for all center and project activities.

Children with Learning Disabilities
- Allow adequate time for the children to contribute to discussions and formulate statements of agreement or disagreement with peers' observations.
- Recognize that the children may need more time to grasp the concepts that you have as a goal for specific activities.
- Allow for repeated use of the same manipulatives as long as the children's interest is sustained.

Children with Attention Disorders
- Observe the children for signs of rapidly waning attention, and interact with them to encourage continued sustained engagement in play activities.
- Allow the children to bring math manipulatives, science artifacts, or other objects to a quiet place with fewer distractions than the center itself if their attention is easily drawn away from center activities.

(Cook, Tessier, & Armbruster, 1987; Fewell & Kaminski, 1988; Morris & Schultz, 1989; Wesley, 1992).

Developing Advocacy Skills

Teachers who advocate for appropriate playful learning opportunities for children are often frustrated to find that even when others understand their positions and agree with them, they hesitate to take action to bring about change that can enhance children's learning. Such opponents do not overtly reject the idea of acting on behalf of children, they simply respond to most ideas with, "Yes, but . . ." and offer reasons the change will not work for them. This is especially likely to be the case when teachers or administrators are asked to view children's instruction in critical areas such as math and science from a different, more integrated and play-oriented perspective.

Think back to the discussion among Ms. Blount, Ms. Morales, and Ms. Schultz that opened this chapter. With the adoption of new textbooks for math and science and general faculty excitement about the new materials, they may well find themselves in the position of having to advocate for their children's right to continued engagement in playful learning of these subjects. As they do so, "Yes, but . . ." responses are quite likely. Even Ms. Schultz responded with, "Yes, but . . ." when Ms. Blount suggested that they should continue to implement their integrated, play-based curriculum, offering the belief that they might not be able to do so because the books were so expensive that they would have to be used.

Typical responses to their efforts to move forward with a play-based, integrated curriculum might include statements such as, "Yes, but these books are designed around the math and science standards for learning in those areas. Why shouldn't we use them?" or, "Yes, but the math workbooks are really fun to do. And the children can always play when they finish the lessons." Good advocates for children's right to play will have to meet these "Yes, but . . ." responses head on.

Doing so requires significant research and preparation. First, teachers proposing a change in approach must anticipate as many of the potential "Yes, buts . . ." as possible. To do so, they have to listen to the concerns parents, administrators, and other teachers have about children's learning, whether those concerns are related to learning through play or reflect more generalized worry about particular aspects of the curriculum they feel children aren't mastering.

Then, those advocating for children's right to play have to arm themselves with information about ways to address those concerns and allay others' fears about play in the classroom. This means gathering evidence from the professional literature that supports play as a significant means of learning. It is also necessary to collect evidence of children's learning from teachers' experimentation with new approaches. Finally, advocates have to be prepared to take action themselves, even if it is on a limited trial basis, and then be willing to invite others in to see the results of their innovation and learn firsthand that children really will develop cognitive competence using a new, more playful approach. Table 10.4 includes a variety of activities that will help you to advocate for new approaches to teaching.

TABLE 10.4   Advocacy Activities: Informing and Involving Families and Administrators

Don't Take "but" for an Answer

Becoming Aware	*Furthering Your Understanding*	*Taking Action*
1. Familiarize yourself with standards for math (NCTM, 1989) and science (National Research Council, 1996).	1. Focus your attention on one type of center described in this chapter. Find journal articles that discuss how to enhance children's math and science learning in this center.	1. Using what you learned from the professional literature, design at least one center that will allow children to playfully explore math and science concepts.
2. Observe children playing in the manipulative and discovery centers as outlined in this chapter. Note any specific math or science knowledge they gain or discoveries they make as they interact in the center.	2. Explore the professional literature and talk to early intervention teachers to determine how the center you select can be adapted to accommodate the particular special-needs children in a regular classroom.	2. Draft a newsletter that you might use to help parents, teachers, or administrators understand how play promotes children's math and science learning, and why you intend to devote significant time to play.
3. Talk to parents of young children in your area. What concerns do they have related to children's math and science learning?	3. Interview parents representing a variety of cultural groups in your area to find out what they believe is most important for their children to learn in the areas of science and math. What goals do they have for their children in these content areas?	3. Volunteer to help a classroom teacher set up a manipulative or discovery center. Offer to help collect materials that fit the classroom curriculum.
4. Honestly assess whether you share any of those concerns. Are there other concerns that make you hesitant to establish play centers as a significant aspect of your math and science instructional program? List all of these concerns.		4. Think of five familiar phenomena that could be made exotic for children's exploration. Brainstorm discovery center activities that will help extend children's interest in these phenomena.
5. Read your local newspaper with a focus on articles related to education. Is there any sentiment expressed regarding the time children have for play?		

Summary

In this chapter, we have identified cognitive competence as an important area of children's development. Cognitive competence was defined as children's ability to use a variety of processes involved in thinking and learning about new concepts. The concepts of physical knowledge, logico-mathematical knowledge, correspondence, and transformation were all described as important components of cognitive competence. In addition, processes identified in national standards for math and science learning as being critical to learning in those areas were discussed.

The manner in which children develop cognitive competence through play was described. In addition, it was suggested that both manipulative and discovery centers offer additional opportunities for engaging children in activities with materials that will foster the development of cognitive competence. Criteria for maintaining a constructive approach to math and science learning were given, and the teacher's role in promoting cognitive competence in a constructivist classroom was explored. Specific suggestions for including children with special needs were also provided.

R E V I S I T I N G   F I R S T   I M P R E S S I O N S

Compare your own science and math experiences as you described them before beginning this chapter to the types of experiences suggested here. In what ways was your learning similar or different? What new insights do you have about how children develop cognitive competence in these areas?

Q U E S T I O N S   F O R   D I S C U S S I O N

1. Consider the following play scenario. What math and science knowledge is this child using or developing as he plays? How might the teacher interact with him to facilitate his learning?

   Four-year-old Miguel is playing in the block center. He begins by stacking four square blocks one atop the other. He adds a rectangular block by standing it upright and then decides to make his stack taller by adding more square blocks. Despite repeated attempts, he is unable to balance the square blocks on top of the narrow end of the rectangle. He removes the rectangle, and places two cylindrical blocks on top of the squares, then four more squares, and, finally, two more cylinders.
   "Look at my tower. Squares, then circles, then squares, then circles," he says. "I'm going to build another one just like it."
   He then builds an identical tower, except that he miscounts and places five, rather than four, square blocks between the two sets of cylinders. When the second tower is finished, he notices that it is slightly taller than the first.
   "Squares, circles, squares, circles . . . it's the same," he says, puzzled.
   Then he begins counting each set of blocks. At that point, he realizes that he has put too many square blocks in the middle of the second tower. He removes the top of the tower, takes away a square block, then rebuilds so that the two towers are identical. Satisfied, he walks around both towers, measuring how high they come on his body. He then asks his friend to come over so they can see "how high the blocks are on you."

2. A kindergarten teacher notices a group of her students intently examining a spider web that stretches between two posts on the fence of their play yard. As she joins them, they all speak at once, pointing out different features of the web and asking questions about how it was built and why spiders build webs. If you were that teacher, how might you capitalize on the children's interest in something as commonplace as spider webs in order to expand their learning? What kinds of theme study or project might they undertake to answer their questions? What kinds of activities (including free play, manipulative center, and discovery center) could be designed to further their learning?

3. Examine the following activity in light of the four criteria for a constructivist approach presented in this chapter. To what extent does the activity meet (or fail to meet) each of the criteria?

A second-grade teacher shows an animated video that illustrates electrical currents and how electricity travels through wires to work various household appliances. After children watch the video and talk about it with the teacher, she introduces them to a battery apparatus that will be available in a discovery center. It consists of a board with a battery on one end and a light bulb on the other. When the ends of a wire are touched to the battery, the light bulb is illuminated. The children are encouraged to try lighting the bulb themselves when they visit the center.

SUGGESTED READINGS

Blackwood, D., & Bird, M. (1993). *Science workshop: A whole language approach.* Portsmouth, NH: Heinemann.

Chaillé, C., & Britain, L. (1997). *The young child as scientist: A constructivist approach to early childhood science education.* New York: Longman.

McCracken, J. (1987). *More than 1,2,3—The real basics of mathematics.* Washington, DC: National Association for the Education of Young Children.

REFERENCES

Aaronson, S. (1988). Safe, fun playgrounds. *Exchange,* 35–40.

Anbar, A. (1986). Reading acquisition of preschool children without systematic instruction. *Early Childhood Research Quarterly, 1,* 69–83.

Anderson, R. F. (1980). Using guided fantasy with children. *Elementary School Guidance and Counseling, 15* (1), 226–234.

Bandura, A. (1977). *Social learning theory.* Englewood Cliffs, NJ: Prentice-Hall.

Bauer, K. L., & Dettore, E. (1997). Superhero play: What's a teacher to do? *Early Childhood Education Journal,* 25(1) 17–21.

Bayless, K. M., & Ramsey, M. E. (1991). *Music: A way of life for young children* (4th ed.). Columbus, OH: Merrill.

Beaty, J. J. (1992). *Skills for preschool teachers* (4th ed.). New York: Merrill.

Bergen, D. (1988). *Play as medium for learning and development.* Portsmouth, NH: Heinemann.

Berk, L. (1994). Vygotsky's theory: The importance of makebelieve play. *Young Children, 50*(1), 30–39.

Berk, L., & Winsler, A. (1995). *Scaffolding children's learning: Vygotsky and early childhood education.* Washington, DC: National Association for the Education of Young Children.

Bissex, G. (1980). *GNYS AT WRK: A child learns to write and read.* Cambridge, MA: Harvard University Press.

Blank, H. K. (1997). Advocacy leadership. In S. Kagan & B. Bowman (Eds.), *Leadership in early care and education* (pp. 39–47). Washington, DC: National Association for the Education of Young Children.

Blurton-Jones, N. (1976). Rough and tumble play among nursery school children. In J. Bruner, A. Jolly, & K. Sylva (Eds.), *Play: Its role on development and evolution* (pp. 352–363). New York: Basic Books.

Bolton, G. (1985). Changes in thinking about drama in the classroom. *Theory into practice, 24*(3), 151–157.

Bredekamp, S., & Copple, C., (1997). *Developmentally appropriate practice in early childhood programs* (Rev. ed.). Washington, DC: National Association for the Education of Young Children.

Bredekamp, S., & Rosegrant, T. (1995). *Reaching potentials: Transforming early childhood curriculum and assessment* (Vol. 2). Washington, DC: National Association for the Education of Young Children.

Brewer, J. A. (1998). *Early childhood education: Preschool through primary grades* (3rd ed.). Boston: Allyn & Bacon.

Brewer, J. A., & Kieff, J. (1997). Fostering mutual respect for play at home and school. *Childhood Education,* 73(2), 92–96.

Bronfenbrenner, U. (1979). *The ecology of human development: Experiments by nature and design.* Cambridge, MA: Harvard University Press.

Brunner, J. S. (1966). *Toward a theory of instruction.* Cambridge, MA: Harvard University Press.

Brunner, J. S. (1986). *Actual minds, possible worlds.* Cambridge, MA: Harvard University Press.

California State Department of Education. (1984). *Science Frameworks Addendum.* Sacramento, CA: Author.

Calkins, S. D. (1994). Origins and outcomes of individual differences in emotion regulation. In N. A. Fox (Ed.), The development of emotion regulation: Biological and behavioral considerations (pp. 53–72). *Monographs of the Society for Research in Child Development, 59*(2–3, Serial No. 240).

Cantor, N. (1990). From thought to behavior: "Having" and "doing" in the study of personality and cognition. *American Psychologist, 45*(6), 735–750.

Carlsson-Paige, N., & Levin, D. E. (1990). Who's calling the shots? How to respond effectively to children's fascination with war play and war toys. Philadelphia: New Society.

Casbergue, R. (1998). How do we foster young children's writing development? In S. Neuman & K. Roskos (Eds.), *Children achieving: Best practices in early literacy* (pp. 198–222). Newark, DE: International Reading Association.

Casbergue, R., & Kieff, J. (1998). "Marbles anyone? The role of traditional games in elementary classrooms." *Childhood Education,* 74(3), 143–147.

Case, R. (1992). *The mind's staircase: Exploring the conceptual underpinnings of children's thought and knowledge.* Hillsdale, NJ: Erlbaum.

Cazden, C. (1988). *Classroom discourse.* Portsmouth, NH: Heinemann.

Chaillé, C., & Britain, L. (1997). *The young child as scientist: A constructivist approach to early childhood science teaching.* New York: Longman.

Charles, C. M., & Barr, K. B. (1989). *Building classroom discipline* (3rd ed.). New York: Longman.

Checkley, K. (1997). The first seven . . . and the eighth: A conversation with Howard Gardner. *Educational Leadership, 55*(1), 8–13.

Cherow-O'Leary, R. (1997). Healthy beginnings. *Early Childhood Today, 11,* 42–49.

Children's nutrition and learning (1994). Champaign, IL: ERIC Clearinghouse for Elementary and Early Childhood Education.

Christie, J. F. (Ed.). (1991). *Play and early literacy development.* Albany, NY: State University of New York Press.

Christie, J. F., Johnsen, E., & Peckover, R. (1988). The effects of play period duration on children's play patterns. *Journal of Research in Childhood Education, 3,* 123–131.

Christie, J. F., & Wardle, F. R. (1992). How much time is needed for play? *Young Children, 47*(3), 28–32.

Chugani, H. T. (1997). Neuroimaging of developmental non-linearity and developmental pathologies. In R. W. Thatcher, G. R. Lyon, J. Rumsey, & N. Krasnegor (Eds.), *Developmental neuroimaging: Mapping the development of brain and behavior* (pp. 38–64). San Diego, CA: Academic Press.

Church, E. (1997). Look at my body. *Early Childhood Today, 11,* 36–37.

Clay, M. (1966). *Emergent reading behavior.* Unpublished doctoral dissertation, University of Auckland, New Zealand.

Clay, M. (1975). *What did I write?* Portsmouth, NH: Heinemann.

Clemens, S. G. (1991). Art in the classroom: Making every day special. *Young Children, 46,* 4–11.

Clements, D. H. (1987). Longitudinal study on the effect of Logo programing on cognitive abilities and achievement. *Journal of Educational Computing Research, 3*(1), 77–98.

Cochran-Smith, M., Kahn, J., & Paris, C. (1988). When word processors come into the classroom. In J. L. Hoot & S. B. Silvern (Eds.), *Writing with computers in the early grades* (pp. 43–74). New York: Teachers College Press.

Cook, R. E., Tessier, A., & Armbruster, V. B. (1987). *Adapting early childhood curricula for children with special needs.* Columbus, OH: Merrill.

Corsaro, W. (1985). *Friendship and peer culture in the early years.* Norwood, NJ: Ablex.

Csikszentmihalyi, M., (1979). The concept of flow. In B. Sutton-Smith (Ed.), *Play and learning* (pp. 257–274). New York: Gardner.

Csikszentmihalyi, M. (1988). Introduction. In M. Csikszentmihalyi & I. S. Csikszentmihalyi (Eds.), *Optimal experience: Psychological studies in flow consciousness* (pp. 3–14). New York: Cambridge University Press.

Csikszentmihalyi, M. (1993). *The evolving self: A psychology for the third millennium.* New York: Harper-Collins.

Cunningham, C., Jones, M., & Taylor, N. (1994). The child-friendly neighborhood: Some questions and tentative answers from Australian research. *International Play Journal, 2*(2), 79–95.

Curry, N. (1977). Considerations of current basic issues on play. In N. Curry (Ed.), *Play: The child strives for self-realization* (pp. 51–61). Washington, DC: National Association for the Education of Young Children.

Davidson, J., & Wright, J. L. (1994). The potential of the microcomputer in the early childhood classroom. In J. Wright & D. D. Shade (Eds.), *Young children: Active learners in a technological age* (pp. 77–89). Washington, DC: National Association for the Education of Young Children.

DeBono, E. (1992). *Teach your child how to think.* New York: Viking,

DeGroff, L. (1990). Is there a place for computers in whole language classrooms? *The Reading Teacher, 43,* 568–572.

Deiner, P. (1983). *Resources for teaching young children with special needs.* New York: Harcourt Brace Javanovitch.

Delpit, L. (1988). The silenced dialogue: Power and pedagogy in educating other people's children. *Harvard Educational Review, 58,* 79–95.

DeMille, R. (1955). *Put your mother on the ceiling.* New York: Viking.

DeVries, R., & Kohlberg, L. (1987). *Constructivist early education: Overview and comparison with other programs.* Washington, DC: National Association for the Education of Young Children.

Dewey, J. (1916). *Democracy and education.* New York: Macmillan.

Dewey, J., (1933). *How we think.* Boston: Heath.

DiPietro, J. (1981). Rough and tumble play: A function of gender. *Developmental Psychology, 17,* 50–58.

Discovery English (Pre-K) [Computer software]. (1996). Sunnydale, CA: Computer Curriculum Corporation.

Donaldson, M. (1978). *Children's minds.* Glasgow, Scotland: William Collins Sons.

Donoghue, M. (1990). *The child and the English language arts* (5th ed.). Dubuque, IA: W. C. Brown.

Dunn, J. (1988). *The beginnings of social understanding.* Cambridge, MA: Harvard University Press.

Early math [Computer software]. (1995). Bellevue, WA: Bright Star Technologies.

Edelman, M. W. (1997). Introduction: Standing strong and together for our children. In Children's Defense Fund, *The State of America's Children, Yearbook 1997* (pp. ix–xxiii). Washington, DC: Children's Defense Fund.

Edelsky, C., Altwerger, B., & Flores, B. (1991). *Whole language: What's the difference?* Portsmouth, NH: Heinemann.

Edwards, C. E. (1990). *Affective development and creative arts: A process approach to early childhood education.* Columbus, OH: Merrill.

Edwards, C., Gandini, L., & Forman, G. (Eds.). (1993). *The hundred languages of children.* Norwood, NJ: Ablex.

Ehri, L., & Sweet, J. (1991). Finger point reading of memorized text: What enables beginners to process the print? *Reading Research Quarterly, 26,* 442–462.

Elkind, D. (1987). *Miseducation: Preschoolers at risk.* New York: Alfred A. Knopf.

Engle, S. (1995). *The stories children tell: Making sense of the narratives of childhood.* New York: Freeman.

Erickson, K. L. (1988). Building castles in the classroom. *Language Arts, 65*(1), 14–19.

Erikson, E. (1963). *Childhood and society* (2nd ed.). New York: Norton.

Farrell, C. (1991). *Storytelling: A guide for teachers.* New York: Scholastics.

Fein, G., (1981). Pretend play in childhood: An integrative review. *Child Development, 52,* 1095–1118.

Fein, G., & Stork, L. (1981). Sociodramatic play: Social class effects in integrated preschool classrooms. *Journal of Applied Developmental Psychology, 2,* 267–279.

Fewell, R. R., & Kaminski, R. (1988). Play skills development and instruction for young children with handicaps. In S. L. Odom & M. B. Karnes (Eds.), *Early intervention for children and infants with handicaps.* (pp. 145–158). Baltimore: Paul H. Brooks.

First adventures [Computer software] (1996). Sunnydale, CA: Computer Curriculum Corporation.

Flack, M. (1932). *Ask Mr. Bear.* New York: Macmillan.

Flavell, J. (1985). *Cognitive development* (2nd ed.). Englewood Cliffs, NJ: Prentice-Hall.

Forman, G. E., & Hill, F. (1984). *Constructive play: Applying Piaget in the preschool* (Rev. ed.). Menlo Park, CA: Addison-Wesley.

Fox, M. (1987). *Teaching drama to young children.* Portsmouth, NH: Heineman.

Fraiberg, S. (1959). *The magic years: Understanding and handling the problems of early childhood.* New York: Scribners.

Freud, S. (1958). *On creativity and the unconscious.* (I. F. Grant Doff, Trans.). New York: Harper & Row. (Original work published 1928)

Fromberg, D. P. (1992). A review of research on play. In C. Seefeldt (Ed.), *The early childhood curriculum: A review of current research* (2nd ed.) (pp. 42–84). New York: Teachers College Press.

Fromberg, D. (1998). Play issues in early childhood education. In C. Seefeldt & A. Galper (Eds.), *Continuing issues in early childhood education* (2nd ed.) (pp. 190–212). Columbus, OH: Merrill.

Frost, J., & Wortham, S. (1988). The evolution of American playgrounds, *Young Children, 43,* 19–28.

Gag, W. (1928). *Millions and millions of cats.* New York: Coward McCann.

Galda, L., Cullinan, B., & Strickland, D. (1997). *Language, literacy, and the child* (2nd ed.). Fort Worth, TX: Harcourt.

Gandini, L. (1997). Foundations of the Reggio Emilia approach. In J. Hendrick (Ed.), *First steps toward teaching the Reggio way* (pp. 14–25). Upper Saddle River, NJ: Merrill.

Gardner, H. (1980). *Artful scribbles.* New York: Basic Books.

Gardner, H. (1983). *Frames of mind: The theory of multiple intelligence.* New York: Basic Books.

Gardner, H. (1993). *Multiple intelligence: The theory in practice.* New York: Basic Books.

Garvey, C. (1990). *Play.* Cambridge, MA: Harvard University Press.

Goodman, Y. (1980). The roots of literacy. In M. Douglass (Ed.), *Claremont reading conference, 44th Yearbook* (pp. 1–32). Claremont, CA: Claremont Graduate School.

Goodman, Y. (1986). Children coming to know literacy. In W. Teale & E. Sulzby (Eds.), *Emergent literacy: Writing and reading* (pp. 1–14). Norwood, NJ: Ablex.

Gottfried, A. E. (1985). Academic intrinsic motivation in elementary and junior high school students. *Journal of Educational Psychology, 77,* 631–645.

Greenberg, J. (1995). Making friends with the Power Rangers. *Young Children, 50*(5), 60–61.

Grineski, S. (1988). Teaching and learning in physical education for young children. *Journal of Physical Education, Recreation and Dance, 59,* 91–94.

Griffing, P. (1980). The relationship between socioeconomic status and sociodramatic play among black kindergarten children. *Genetic Psychology Monographs, 101,* 3–34.

Groos, K. (1901). *The play of man.* New York: Appleton.

Gunnar, M. R. (1996). *Quality of care and the buffering of stress psychology: Its potential in protecting the developing human brain.* Minneapolis, MN: University of Minnesota Institute of Child Development.

Halliday, J., & McNaughton, S. (1982). Sex differences in play at kindergarten. *New Zealand Journal of Educational Studies, 17,* 161–170.

Halliday, M. A. (1975). *Learning how to mean: Explorations in the functions of language.* London: Edward Arnold.

Harste, J. C., Woodward, V. A., & Burke, C. L. (1984). *Language stories and literacy lessons.* Portsmouth, NH: Heinemann.

Harter, S. (1983). Developmental perspectives on self-esteem. In E. M. Hetherington (Ed.), *Handbook of child psychology: Vol. 4. Socialization, personality, and social development* (pp. 275–386). New York: Wiley.

Haugland, S. W., & Shade, D. D. (1990). *Developmental evaluations of software for young children: 1990 edition.* New York: Delamar.

Helm, J. H., Beneke, S., & Steinheimer, K. (1998). *Windows on learning: Documenting young children's work.* New York: Teachers College Press.

Hendrick, J. (1992). *The whole child* (5th ed.). Upper Saddle River, NJ: Merrill.

Hendrick, J. (Ed.). (1997). *First steps toward teaching the Reggio way.* Upper Saddle River, NJ: Merrill.

Hendrick, J. (1998). *Total learning: Developmental curriculum for the young child* (5th ed.). Upper Saddle River, NJ: Merrill.

Hennings, D. G. (1990). *Communication in action. Teaching the language arts* (4th ed.). Boston: Houghton Mifflin.

Hereford, N. (1997). Mission: Good nutrition. *Early Childhood Today, 11,* 52–55.

Hills, T. (1993). Assessment in context: Teachers and children at work. *Young Children, 48,* 20–28.

Holden, C. (1987). Creativity and the troubled mind. *Psychology Today, 21*(4), 9–10.

Hostetler, L. (1981). Child advocacy: Your professional responsibility? *Young Children, 36,* 3–8.

Howes, C. (1992). *The collaborative construction of pretend.* Albany, NY: State University of New York Press.

Huck, C. S., Hepler, S., & Hickman, J. (1987). *Children's literature in the elementary school.* New York: Holt, Rinehart & Winston.

Hughes, F. P. (1999). *Children, play, and development* (3rd ed.). Boston: Allyn & Bacon.

Hutchins, P. (1986). *The doorbell rang.* New York: Scholastics.

IRA/NAEYC. (1998). Learning to read and write: Developmentally appropriate practice for children: A joint position statement of the International Reading Association and the National Association for the Education of Young Children. Adopted 1998. *Young Children, 53,* 30–46.

Isbell, R. (1995). *The complete learning center book.* Beltsville, MD: Gryphon House.

Isenberg, J. P., & Jalongo, M. R. (1997). *Creative expression and play in early childhood* (2nd ed.). Upper Saddle River, NJ: Merrill.

Jensen, M. (1986). *Preparing early childhood teachers to become advocates: A new challenge for teacher education.* Paper presented at the conference of the National Association for the Education of Young Children, Washington, DC. (ERIC Document Reproduction Service No. ED 275–456)

Jibson, J. (1991). Developmentally appropriate practice: Culture, curriculum, connections. *Early Education and Development, 2,* 120–136.

Johnson, J., & Ershler, J. (1981). Developmental trends in preschool play as a function of classroom program and child gender. *Child Development, 52,* 995–1004.

Jones, E. (1986). *Teaching adults.* Washington, DC: National Association for the Education of Young Children.

Jones, E., & Nimmo, J. (1994). *Emergent curriculum.* Washington, DC: National Association for the Education of Young Children.

Kamii, C. (1982). *Number in preschool and kindergarten.* Washington, DC: National Association for the Education of Young Children.

Kamii, C., & DeClark, G. (1985). *Young children reinvent arithmetic: Implications of Piaget's theory.* New York: Teachers College Press.

Kamii, C., & DeVries, R. (1978). *Physical knowledge in preschool education.* Englewood Cliffs, NJ: Prentice-Hall.

Kamii, C., & Joseph, L. (1989). *Young children continue to reinvent arithmetic—second grade: Implications of Piaget's theory.* New York: Teachers College Press.

Katz, L. G. (1985). Dispositions in early childhood education. *ERIC/EECE Bulletin, 18* (2).

Katz, L. G. (1988). What should young children be doing? *American Educator* (Summer), 28–33, 44–45.

Katz, L. G. (1993). What can we learn from Reggio Emilia? In C. Edwards, L. Gandini, & G. Forman (Eds.), *The hundred languages of children* (pp. 19–37). Norwood, NJ: Ablex.

Katz, L. G. (1998). The project approach. *Early Childhood Today, 12*(6), 43–44.

Katz, L. G. & Chard, S. (1989). *Engaging children's minds: The project approach.* Norwood, NJ: Ablex.

Kavenaugh, R. D., & Engle, S. (1998). The development of pretense and narrative in early childhood. In O. N. Saracho & B. Spodek (Eds.), *Multiple perspectives on play in early childhood education* (pp. 80–99). New York: State University of New York Press.

Kieff, J., (1994). Early childhood education in the McAllen Independent School District: A Contracted Study. McAllen, TX: McAllen Independent School District. (ERIC Document Reproduction Service No. ED 371 876)

Kieff, J., & Wellhousen, K. (in press) Planning family involvement in early childhood programs. *Young Children.*

Kilmer, S., & Hoffman, H. (1995). Transforming science curriculum. In S. Bredekamp & T. Rosegrant (Eds.), *Reaching potentials: Transforming early childhood curriculum and assessment* (pp. 43–63). Washington, DC: National Association for the Education of Young Children.

Kostelnik, M. J., Whiren, A. P., & Stein, L. C. (1986). Living with he-man: Managing superhero fantasy play. *Young Children, 41*, 3–9.

Kotch, J., & Shackelford, J. (1989). *The nutritional status of low-income preschool children in the United States: A review of literature.* Washington, DC: Food Research and Action Center.

Krasnor, L., & Pepler, D. (1980). The study of children's play: Some suggested future directions. In K. H. Rubin (Ed.), *Children's play: New directions for child development* (pp. 85–94). San Francisco: Jossey-Bass.

Krauss, R. (1945). *The carrot seed.* New York: HarperCollins.

Labbo, L. (1998). What's the role of computer-related technology in early literacy? In S. Neuman & K. Roskos (Eds.), *Children achieving: Best practices in early literacy* (pp. 180–197). Newark, DE: International Reading Association.

Lakin, M. B. (1996). The meaning of play: Perspectives for Pacific Oaks College. In A. Phillips (Ed.), *Topics in early childhood education: Playing for keeps* (pp. 33–45). St. Paul, MN: Redleaf Press.

Levy, J. (1978). *Play behavior.* New York: Wiley.

Levy, A., Wolfgang, C., & Koorland, M. (1992). Sociodramatic play as a method for enhancing the language performance of kindergarten age students. *Early Childhood Research Quarterly, 7*(2), 245–62.

Linder, T. (1990). *Transdisciplinary play-based assessment.* Baltimore: Paul H. Brookes.

Living books framework [Computer software]. (1996). Novato, CA: Bröderbund.

Lombardi, J. (1986). Public policy report. Training for public policy and advocacy: An emerging topic in teacher education. *Young Children, 41*, 65–69.

Lowenthal, B. (1996). Teaching social skills to preschoolers with special needs. *Childhood Education, 72*, 137–140.

Lucky, S. (1990). Music-movement-make-believe: The link between creativity and thinking skills. Paper presented at 41st annual conference of Southern Association of Children Under Six, Dallas, TX.

Magna Systems. (1996). *Video modules on diversity.* Barrington, IL: Author.

Markus, H., & Nurius, P. (1986). Possible selves. *American Psychologist, 41*, 65–69.

Marshall, H. (1989). The development of self-concept, *Young Children, 44*, 44–51.

Mayesky, M. (1998). *Creative activities for young children* (6th ed.). New York: Delmar.

McCaslin, N. (1996). *Creative drama in the classroom and beyond* (6th ed). White Plains, NY: Longman.

McDonald, D. T. (1979). *Music in our lives: The early years.* Washington, DC: National Association for the Education of Young Children.

McDonald, D. T., & Simons, G. M. (1989). *Musical growth and development: Birth through six.* New York: Schirmer.

McGee, L., & Richgels, D. (1996). *Literacy's beginnings: Supporting young readers and writers.* Boston: Allyn & Bacon.

McLoyd, V. (1982). Social class differences in sociodramatic play: A critical review. *Developmental Review, 2*, 1–30.

Meier, T. (1996). "They can't even play right." Cultural myopia in the analysis of play—Cultural perspectives on human development. In A. Phillips (Ed.), *Topics in early childhood education: Playing for keeps* (pp. 99–115). St. Paul, MN: Redleaf Press.

Melton, G. (1983). *Child advocacy: Psychological issues and interventions.* New York: Plenum Press.

Monighan-Nourot, P. (1997). Playing with play in four dimensions. In J. Isenberg & M. Jalongo (Eds.), *Major trends and issues in early childhood education: Challenges, controversies, and insights* (pp. 123–148). New York: Teachers College Press.

Morris, L. R., & Schulz, L., (1989). *Creative play activities for children with disabilities.* Champaign, IL: Human Kinetics.

Morris, P. (1991). *Heading for a health crisis: Eating patterns of America's school children.* Washington, DC: Public Voice for Food and Health Policy.

Morrow, L., & Rand, M. (1991). Promoting literacy during play by designing early childhood classroom environments. *The Reading Teacher, 44*, 396–402.

Nachmanovitch, S. (1990). *Free play: The power of improvisation in life and the arts.* New York: Putnam.

National Council of Teachers of Mathematics (NCTM). (1989). *Curriculum and evaluation standards for school mathematics.* Washington, DC: Author.

National Research Council (NRC). (1996). *National science education standards.* Washington, DC: National Academy Press.

Nelson, K. (1986). *Event knowledge.* Hillsdale, NJ: Erlbaum.

Neuman, S., & Roskos, K. (1992). Literacy objects as cultural tools: Effects of children's literacy behaviors in play. *Reading Research Quarterly, 27*, 203–225.

Number munchers [Computer software]. (1997) Cambridge, MA: The Learning Co.

Ogbu, J. (1981). Origins of human competence: A cultural-ecological perspective. *Child Development, 52*, 413–429.

Oremland, J. (1997). *The use of music in early childhood classrooms.* Unpublished class assignment. University of New Orleans.

Oremland, J. (1998). *Weather: A web of musical ideas.* Unpublished class project. University of New Orleans.

Paley, V. G. (1981). *Wally's stories*. Cambridge, MA: Harvard University Press.

Paley, V. G. (1992). *You can't say you can't play*. Cambridge, MA: Harvard University Press.

Papert, S. (1980). *Mindstorms: Children, computers and powerful ideas*. New York: Basic Books.

Parnes, S. J. (1967). *Creative behavior guidebook*. New York: Scribner's.

Parten, M. B. (1932). Social participation among preschool children. *Journal of Abnormal and Social Psychology, 27,* 243–269.

Patrick, G. T. W. (1916). *The psychology of relaxation*. Boston: Houghton Mifflin.

Paulson, F., Paulson, P., & Meyer, A. (1991). What makes a portfolio a portfolio? *Educational Leadership, 48,* 60–63.

Pellegrini, A. (1984). The effects of exploration and play on young children's associative fluency: A review and extension of training studies. In T. D. Yawkey & A. D. Pellegrini (Eds.), *Child's play: Developmental and applied* (pp. 237–253). Hillsdale, NJ: Erlbaum.

Pellegrini, A. (1992). Kindergarten children's social-cognitive status as a predictor of first grade success. *Early Childhood Research Quarterly, 7,* 564–577.

Pelligrini, A. (1996). *Observing children in their natural worlds: A primer in observational methods*. Hillsdale, NJ: Erlbaum.

Pellegrini, A. (1998). Play and the assessment of young children. In O. Saracho and B. Spodek (Eds.), *Multiple perspectives on play in early childhood education* (pp. 220–239). Albany, NY: State University of New York Press.

Pellegrini, A., & Boyd, B. (1993). The role of play in early childhood education: Issues in definition and function. In B. Spodek (Ed.), *Handbook of research on the education of young children* (pp. 105–121). New York: Macmillan.

Pellegrini, A., & Perlmutter, J. (1989). Classroom contextual effects on children's play. *Developmental Psychology, 25,* 289–296.

Peller, L. (1971). Models of children's play. In R. Herron & B. Sutton-Smith (Eds.), *Child's play* (pp. 110–125). New York: Wiley.

Phillips, A. L., (Ed.). (1996). *Topics in early childhood education: Playing for keeps*. St. Paul, MN: Redleaf Press.

Piaget, J. (1952). *The origins of intelligence in children*. New York: International University Press.

Piaget, J. (1962). *Play, dreams and imitation in childhood*. New York: Norton.

Piaget, J. (1967). *Biology and knowledge*. Chicago: University of Chicago Press.

Piaget, J. (1969). *Six psychological studies*. New York: Norton.

Piaget, J., & Inhelder, B. (1969). *The psychology of the child*. New York: Basic Books.

Pintrich, P. R., & Schunk, D. H. (1996). *Motivation in education: Theory, research, and application*. Englewood Cliffs, NJ: Prentice-Hall.

Powlishta, K., Serbin, L., & Moller, L. (1993). The stability of individual differences in gender typing: Implications for understanding gender segregation. *Sex Roles, 28*(11–12), 723–737.

Pulaski, M. A. (1976). Play symbolism in cognitive development. In C. Schaefer (Ed.), *Therapeutic use of child's play* (pp. 27–42). New York: Aronson.

Raines, S. R., & Isbell, R. (1994). *Stories*. Albany, NY: Delmar.

Read, K. (1980). *The nursery school: Human relations and learning*. Philadelphia: W. B. Saunders.

Reicks, M., Randall, J., & Haynes, B. (1994). Factors affecting consumption of fruits and vegetables by low-income families. *Journal of American Dietetic Association, 94,* 1309–1311.

Reifel, S., & Yeatman, J. (1993). From category to context: Reconsidering classroom play. *Early Childhood Research Quarterly, 8*(1), 347–367.

Rhodes, L., & Nathenson-Mejia, S. (1992). Anecdotal records: A powerful tool for ongoing literacy assessment. *The Reading Teacher, 45,* 502–509.

Robertson, C. (1998). *Safety, nutrition, and health in early childhood education*. Albany, NY: Delmar.

Rogoff, B. (1990). *Apprenticeships in thinking: Cognitive development in social context*. Oxford, England: Oxford University Press.

Rogoff, B., Gauvain, M., & Ellis, S. (1990). Development viewed in cultural context. In P. Light, S. Sheldon, & M. Woodhead (Eds.), *Learning to think* (pp. 292–339). London: Routledge.

Rogoff, B., Mistry, J., Goncu, A., & Mosier, C. (1993). "Guided participation in cultural activities by toddlers and caregivers." *Monographs of the Society for Research in Child Development, 58*(8, Serial No. 236).

Roig, P. (1997). *The fireboat project*. Unpublished course project. University of New Orleans.

Roopnarine, J., Johnson, J., & Hooper, F. (1994). *Children's play in diverse cultures*. Albany, NY: State University of New York Press.

Rowe, D. (1997). The literate potentials of book related dramatic play. *Reading Research Quarterly, 33,* 10–35.

Rubin, K., Fein, G., & Vandenberg, B. (1983). Play. In E. M. Hetherington (Ed.), *Handbook of child psychology: Volume 4. Socialization, personality, and social development* (pp. 698–774). New York: Wiley.

Rubin, K., Maioni, T., & Hornung, M. (1976). Free play behaviors in middle- and lower-class preschoolers:

Parten and Piaget revisited. *Child Development, 47,* 414–419.

Rubright, L. (1996). *Beyond the beanstalk: Interdisciplinary learning through story telling.* Portsmouth, NH: Heinemann.

Saltz, E., & Brodie, J. (1982). Pretend play training in childhood: A review and critique. In D. J. Peppler & K. H. Rubin (Eds.), *The play of children: Current theory and research* (pp. 231–264). Basel, Switzerland: Karger AG.

Saltz, E., & Johnson, J. (1977). Training disadvantaged preschoolers on various fantasy activities: Effects on cognitive language functioning and impulse control. *Child development, 48,* 367–380.

Saul, J. (1993). Ready, set, let's go! Using field trips in your curriculum. *Day Care and Early Education, 21* (1), 27–29.

Schirrmacher, R. (1986). Talking with young children about their art. *Young Children 41,* 3–7.

Schlank, C. H., & Metzger, B. (1997). *Together and equal: Fostering cooperative play and promoting gender equity in early childhood programs.* Boston: Allyn & Bacon.

Schwartz, S., & Heller-Miller, J. (1988). *The language of toys: Teaching communication skills to special needs children.* Bethesda, MD: Woodbine House.

Seefeldt, C. (1984). Physical fitness in preschool and elementary school-aged children, *Journal of Physical Education, Recreation, and Dance, 55,* 33–37.

Seefeldt, C. (1987). Art. In C. Seefeldt (Ed.), *The early childhood curriculum: A review of current research* (pp. 183–211). New York: Teachers College Press.

Seefeldt, C., & Barbour, N. (1990). *Early childhood education: An introduction.* Columbus, OH: Merrill.

Sesame Street number [Computer software]. (1994). San Mateo, CA: Electronic Arts.

Shaftel, F. R., & Shaftel, G. (1983). *Role playing in the curriculum* (2nd ed.). Englewood Cliffs, NJ: Prentice-Hall.

Shalala, D. (1997). Donna Shalala on young children's health. *Scholastic Early Childhood Today, 11,* 39–41.

Shore, R. (1997). *Rethinking the brain.* New York: Families and Work Institute.

Siegler, R. (1981). Developmental sequences within and between concepts. *Monographs of the Society for Research in Child Development, 46,* (Serial No. 189).

Siegler, R., & Robinson, M. (1982). The development of numerical understandings. In H. W. Reese & L. P. Lipsitt (Eds.), *Advances in child development and behavior* (pp. 213–241). New York: Academic Press.

Skinner, B. F. (1953). *Science and human behavior.* New York: McMillan.

Skinner, B. F. (1957). *Verbal behaviorism.* New York: Appleton-Century Crafts.

Skinner, B. F. (1974). *About behaviorism.* New York: Knopf.

Skrupskelis, A. (1990). Going places with young children. *Dimensions of Early Childhood, 18*(3), 3–6.

Slobodkina, E. (1941). *Caps for sale.* New York: Scott.

Smilansky, S. (1968). *The effects of sociodramatic play on disadvantaged preschool children.* New York: Wiley.

Smilansky, S., & Shefatya, L. (1990). *Facilitating play: A medium for promoting cognitive, socio-emotional, and academic development in young children.* Gaithersburg, MD: Psychosocial and Educational Publications.

Smith, A. & Inder, P. (1983). Social interactions in same- and cross-gender preschool groups: A participative observation study. *Educational psychology, 13*(1), 29–42.

Snow, C. (1983). Literacy and language: Relationships during the preschool years. *Harvard Educational Review, 53,* 165–189.

Snow, C. (1991). The theoretical basis for relationships between language and literacy in development. *Journal of Research in Childhood Education, 6,* 5–10.

Snow, C., Burns, M. S., & Griffin, P. (Eds.). (1998). *Preventing reading difficulties in young children.* Washington, DC: National Academy Press.

Spodek, B. (1985). *Teaching in the early years* (3rd ed.). Englewood Cliffs, NJ: Prentice-Hall.

Sulzby, E. (1985). Children's emergent reading of favorite storybooks: A developmental study. *Reading Research Quarterly, 20,* 458–481.

Sulzby, E., & Teale, W. (1991). Emergent literacy. In R. Barr, M. Kamil, P. Mosenthal & P. Pearson (Eds.), *Handbook on reading research, Vol. 2* (pp. 727–757). New York: Longman.

Sutton-Smith, B. (1971). The playful modes of knowing. In N. Curry & S. Arnaud (Coordinators). *Play: The child strives toward self-realization* (pp. 13–24). Conference Proceedings: Washington, DC: National Association for the Education of Young Children.

Sutton-Smith, B. (1986). The spirit of play. In G. Fein, M. Rivkin (Eds.), *The young child at play: Reviews of research, Vol. 4* (pp. 3–13). Washington, DC: National Association for the Education of Young Children.

Sutton-Smith, B. (1988). The struggle between sacred play and festive play. In D. Bergen (Ed.), *Play as a medium for learning and development* (pp. 158–184). Portsmouth NH: Heinemann.

Sutton-Smith, B., & Heath, S. (1981). Paradigms of pretense. *The Quarterly Newsletter of the Laboratory of Comparative Human Cognition.* San Diego: University of California.

Szekely, G. (1991). *From art to play.* Portsmouth NH: Heinemann.

Taylor, S., & Morris, V. (1996). Outdoor play in early childhood education settings: Is it safe and healthy for children? *Early Childhood Education Journal, 23,* 153–158.

Teale, W., & Sulzby, E. (1986). *Emergent literacy: Writing and reading.* Norwood, NJ: Ablex.

Thorndike, R., & Hagen, E. (1997). *Measurement and evaluation in psychology and education.* New York: Wiley.

Tizard, B., & Hughes, M. (1976). *Young children learning.* Cambridge, MA: Harvard University Press.

Tobin, J., Wu, D., & Davidson, D. (1989). *Preschool in three cultures: Japan, China, and the United States.* New Haven, CT: Yale University Press.

Tompkins, G. (1997). *Literacy for the 21st century: A balanced approach.* Upper Saddle River, NJ: Prentice-Hall.

Tompkins, G. E., & Hoskisson, K. (1995). *Language arts: Content and teaching strategies* (3rd ed.). Columbus, OH: Merrill.

Torrance, E. P. (1962). *Guiding creative talent.* Englewood Cliffs, NJ: Prentice-Hall.

Torrance, E. P. (1963). *Creativity.* Washington, DC: National Education Association.

Trawick-Smith, J. (1994). *Interaction in the classroom: Facilitating play in the early years.* Columbus, OH: Merrill.

Udwin, O., & Shmukler, D. (1981). The influence of socio-cultural, economic, and home background factors on children's ability to engage in imaginative play. *Developmental Psychology, 17,* 66–72.

Van Hoorn, J., Nourot, P., Scales, B., & Alward, K. (1993). *Play at the center of the curriculum.* New York: Macmillan.

Vukelich, C. (1990). Where's the paper? Literacy during dramatic play. *Childhood Education, 66,* 205–209.

Vukelich, C. (1991). Materials and modeling: Promoting literacy during play. In J. F. Christie (Ed.), *Play and early literacy development* (pp. 215–231). Albany, NY: State University of New York Press.

Vukelich, C. (1994). Effects of play interventions on young children's reading of environmental print. *Early Childhood Research Quarterly, 9,* 153–170.

Vygotsky, L. (1962). *Thought and language.* Cambridge, MA: MIT Press.

Vygotsky, L. (1978). *Mind in society: Development of higher psychological processes.* Cambridge, MA: Harvard University Press.

Weaver, C., Chaston, J., & Peterson, S. (1993). *Theme exploration: A voyage of discovery.* Richmond Hill, Ontario: Scholastic.

Weaver, C. (1994). *Reading process and practice: From sociopsycholinguistics to whole language.* Portsmouth, NH: Heinemann.

Weikart, P. S. (1982). *Teaching movement and dance* (2nd ed.). Ypsilanti, MI: High Scope Press.

Wells. G. (1988, April). *Developing literate minds.* Paper presented at annual meeting of the American Educational Research Association, New Orleans, LA.

Wesley, P. (1992). *Mainstreaming young children: A training series for child care providers.* Chapel Hill, NC: University of North Carolina, Frank Porter Graham Child Development Center.

Whitebrook, M., & Almy, M. (1986). NAEYC's commitment to good schools for young children: Then and now, a developmental crisis at 60? *Young Children, 41,* 37–40.

Wide, T. (1998). *Reflections on authentic assessment for young children.* Unpublished course project. University of New Orleans.

WiggleWorks [Computer software]. (1994). Jefferson City, MO: Scholastic.

Williams, C., & Kamii, C. (1986). How do children learn by handling objects? *Young Children, 42*(1) 23–26.

Wolery, M., & Wilbert, J. (Eds.). (1994). *Including children with special needs in early childhood programs.* Washington, DC: National Association for the Education of Young Children.

Wolf, J. (1994). Singing with children is a cinch! *Young Children, 49,* 20–25.

Woodward, C. (1985). Guidelines for facilitating sociodramatic play. In J. Frost & S. Sunderlin (Eds.), *When children play* (pp. 291–295). Wheaton, MD: Association for Childhood Education International.

Wright, J. L., & Samaras, A. (1986). Play worlds and microworlds. In P. Campbell & G. Fein (Eds.), *Young Children and microcomputers* (pp. 24–38). Englewood Cliffs, NJ: Prentice-Hall.

Zigler, E., & Finn-Stevenson, M. (1987). *Children: Developmental and Social Issues.* Lexington, MA: Heath.

INDEX